Christian Criticisms, Islamic Proofs

Christian Criticisms, Islamic Proofs

Rashīd Riḍā's Modernist Defense of Islam

Simon A. Wood

ONEWORLD

A Oneworld Book

Published by Oneworld Publications 2008

Reprinted 2010
This paperback edition first published 2012

A CIP record for this title is available
from the British Library

ISBN 978–1–85168–671–1

Typeset by Jayvee, Trivandrum, India
Cover design by Liz Powell
Printed and bound in Great Britain by CPI Antony Rowe

Oneworld Publications
185 Banbury Road
Oxford
OX2 7AR
England

For

Professor Frederick Lloyd Whitfeld Wood (1903–1989)

Contents

Preface x
Acknowledgements xi
Note on Transliteration xii
Introduction xiii

1. Muslim Interpretations of Christianity 1
The Qur'anic Foundation 1
The Medieval Period 6
The Modern Period 12

2. Muḥammad Rashīd Riḍā and his Environment 17
The Impact of Colonialism and Muslim Responses 17
A Sketch of Rashīd Riḍā's Life and Works 23

3. Riḍā's View of Christianity in *The Criticisms of the Christians and the Proofs of Islam* 30
Calling to the Good: Islamic Daʿwah and the Religion of the Other 33
Missionary Criticisms 35
Responding to Criticisms: Dialogue or Polemics? 37
The Religion of Innate Disposition (*dīn al-fiṭrah*) 39
Christian Scripture and Doctrine 40

4. Rashīd Riḍā and the Origins of Islamic Fundamentalism 48

Non-Equivalence between English and Arabic Terminology 51
Uṣūl al-Dīn 53
The Fundamentals of Fundamentalism 54
Resistance to Rationalism 55
Literalism or Scripturalist Fundamentalism 56
The Uncreated Qur'an 58
Prophetic Tradition 59
The Consensus of the Companions (*ijmāʿ al-ṣaḥābah*) 60
The Enclave Culture 62

5. A Translation of the Criticisms of the Christians and the Proofs of Islam 65

Preliminary Note on Translation Theory 65
Title Page and Preface 67
Article One: On the Need to Respond and Clarify the Muslim View of the Torah and Gospel 71
Article Two: Historical Doubts about Judaism and Christianity; Comparison of the Three Prophets 77
Article Three: Comparison between Islam and Christianity in Terms of the Three Goals of Religion 86
Article Four: On Judaism and Christianity Being Derived from Paganism 93
Article Five: In Response to the Book *Researches of the Mujtahids*' Qur'anic Evidence for the Veracity of the Torah and Gospel 99
Article Six: On the Verses on the Character of the Torah and Gospel 103
Article Seven: On Responding to the Periodical *Bashā'ir al Salām* (*The Glad Tidings of Peace*); Comparison between Jews and Muslims; Muḥammad's Superiority over Moses and the Rest of the Prophets 109
The First Part: The Blessed Family Tree 109
That Periodical's Second Part: On Ishmael 114
The Third Part: New Testament Authors and the Call to Religion 114

Article Eight: On the Books of the New Testament 117
Article Nine: Also on the Books of the Two Testaments 124
Article Ten: The Sinlessness of the Prophets and Salvation 131
Article Eleven: The Muslim View of Fear and Hope; Defamation of the Companions and Successors on the Basis of this View 135
Article Twelve: Muslim Faith and Practice 139
Article Thirteen: *The Glad Tidings of Peace*'s Absurd Treatment of Islam and the *Jāhiliyyah* 144
Article Fourteen: Response to the Periodical *Al-Jāmi'ah*'s Attacks on Islam 153
Causes or God Almighty's Ways in Creation (and Imam al-Ghazālī's Proof of them) 156
Reconciling this with what Al-Ghazālī States in *The Incoherence of the Philosophers* 161
Agreement of Al-Ghazālī's Two Statements with Bacon's Teaching 166
Article Fifteen: Response to *Al-Jāmi'ah*'s Denial that Islam is the Religion of Reason 169
Contradictions between Rational Evidence and Transmitted Evidence 171
Doubts about the Issue 173
The Development of Religions and their Culmination in Islam 183
The Similarity of Religious Education and Education in Schools 188
Article Sixteen: Civil and Religious Authority – In Response to *Al-Jāmi'ah*'s Denial of Civil Authority and the Shari'ah in Islam 189
A Testimony on the Subject from *al-Manār*'s First Year 193
Summary of the Evidence for Denying Religious Authority in Islam 195
The Shari'ah and the Religion in Islam 198
The Doubts of the Instiller of Doubts 200
Religious and National Unity 204

Bibliography 209
Index 217

Preface

Muḥammad Rashīd Riḍā (1865–1935) was one of the foremost Muslim authors of the late nineteenth and early twentieth centuries. He played a major role in the propagation of a modernist interpretation of Islam; his work has an abiding influence. Between 1901 and 1903, Riḍā wrote a series of sixteen articles on Muslim–Christian relations, published in his journal *Al-Manār al-Islāmī* (The Islamic Lighthouse). The articles were prompted by the activities and publications of Christian missionaries in Egypt and the wider Muslim world. Riḍā felt that missionary criticisms of Islam were leading some Muslims to entertain doubts about the basis of their own religion. As required by the dictates of Islamic law, Riḍā felt impelled to address these criticisms and uphold the integrity of his religion. In so doing, he presented a modernist defense of Islam.

In 1905, Riḍā published the articles in a book, *Shubuhāt al-Naṣārā wa Ḥujaj al-Islām* (The Criticisms of the Christians and the Proofs of Islam). Second and third editions were published after Riḍā's death, in 1947 and 1956. In general, this work has received less scholarly attention than many of Riḍā's other works. As far as works on religion are concerned, *Shubuhāt* has been overshadowed by *Al-Waḥy al-Muḥammadī* (The Muhammadan Revelation, 1934), which has been translated into numerous languages; into English twice. To my knowledge, *Shubuhāt* has yet to be translated into English or analyzed in full; in this translation and analysis, I am attempting to rectify this situation

Chapters One through Four provide a background for the translation, setting the work in its historic and thematic context. A brief note on translation theory follows. The rest of the book is a complete English translation of Riḍā's book. Footnotes provide factual details and information on technical terms, and draw attention to significant themes in the text.

Acknowledgements

Special thanks to are due to Mahmoud Ayoub, Khalid Blankinship, Angie Kenna, Hew McLeod, and Jane Smith. I am especially grateful to professors Ayoub and Blankinship for the time they devoted to reviewing the manuscript. Finally, thanks to my parents.

Note on Transliteration

Arabic transliteration generally follows the Library of Congress system. *'Ayn* is rendered (ʻ) and thus distinguished from *hamzah* (ʼ). The two-letter combination *yāʼ-tāʼ marbūṭah* is rendered "*iyyah*," not "*īyah*," hence "*jāhiliyyah*." *Tāʼ marbūṭah* is rendered as "h" unless it appears in the first word in a genitive construct, in which case it is rendered "t." Arabic and other foreign words are italicized, with diacritical marks included for Arabic words. Exceptions are made for all Arabic words that have been incorporated into standard modern English. Examples of such words include "Islam" (instead of *Islām*), "Shiʻah" (instead of *Shīʻah*), Sufi (instead of *Ṣūfī*), "hadith" (instead of *ḥadīth*) and "ulama" (instead of *ʻulamāʼ*).

Introduction

This book is a translation and analysis of Muḥammad Rashīd Riḍā's *The Criticisms of the Christians and the Proofs of Islam* (1905), a collection of sixteen articles originally serialized in the journal, *Al-Manār al-Islāmī*, between 1901 and 1903 in response to a variety of Christian missionary publications on Christianity and Islam. These include Niqūlā Ghibrīl's book *The Researches of the Mujtahids* (1901), the Protestant missionary magazines *The Glad Tidings of Peace* and *The Standard of Zion*, and the humanist journal *Al-Jāmi'ah*, published by Faraḥ Anṭūn.

Riḍā is among the most influential Muslim thinkers of the modern period. Yet, with the significant exception of his late work *Al-Waḥy al-Muḥammadī* (The Muhammadan Revelation), his writings on religious reform are unavailable in English. I hope this translation and analysis will make a contribution to our understanding of Riḍā's thought.

Riḍā addresses a wide variety of topics in these articles, including scripture and exegesis, doctrine, historical themes, philosophical discussions, and the nature of religious authority. I have not attempted to analyze comprehensively all these topics in the introductory chapters or footnotes to the translation. Rather, I have chosen to focus on two specific themes: Muslim–Christian relations and Islamic fundamentalism. At the present time, both topics are highly relevant to wider issues of the role of religion in the public and private domains. I hope this translation and analysis will make a useful contribution to the discourse.

Chapter One provides a thematic context, setting Riḍā's work against the background of classical and modern Muslim discourse on Christianity. Chapter Two provides a historical context, examining the emergence of the major trends in modern Islam and the labels that scholars have used to label them – notably traditionalist, secularist, modernist, and fundamentalist – and suggests a framework within which Riḍā's work may be analyzed. It also provides a brief summary of Riḍā's life and major publications. Chapter Three analyzes Riḍā's interpretation of Islam and Christianity in the articles, as he responds to the claims of his missionary opponents, addressing both his general posture towards Muslim–Christian relations and his treatment of specific issues. These include Islamic daʿwah, the notion of an innate "religion of natural disposition," and Christian scripture and doctrine. Chapter Four critiques and rejects the claim that Riḍā articulated a "fundamentalist" interpretation of Islam; I advance the different claim that Riḍā was a modernist.

The translation is preceded by a note on translation theory. Although brief, this is important, as it explains my approach to translation, which is quantitatively the greater part of this book.

In the footnotes, I have attempted to add the factual information and commentary necessary to explain the articles in terms of the stated thematic focus.

I based my translation on the second edition of Riḍā's book. Page numbers of the Arabic text are shown in the translation in square brackets. The pagination differs from the first edition, although the text does not.

1

Muslim Interpretations of Christianity

The Qur'anic Foundation

Any discussion of Muslim attitudes towards Christianity and Christians must begin with the Qur'an, the foundation of the Islamic faith. The Qur'anic attitude towards Christians is ambivalent: they are both praised and condemned; religious pluralism is endorsed yet Islam is claimed to supersede all previous religions. There is no attempt to synthesize these inconsistencies or produce a comprehensive definition of the Christian religion.[1] Rather, as for certain other topics (notably the status of women), the Qur'an reflects a tension between an "ideal Christianity," which is praised, and the Christianity encountered by Muḥammad and his followers in seventh-century Arabia, which gets a mixed reception. This was an environment in which issues were addressed in response to particular

1. For Qur'anic praise of Christians, see especially 2:62; 3:55; 3:199; 5:66, 69, 82–83; 28:52–55; 57:27. For a detailed discussion of these verses and their treatment in Muslim exegesis, see Jane McAuliffe, *Qur'anic Christians: An Analysis of Classical and Modern Exegesis* (Cambridge: Cambridge University Press, 1991). On 2:62 in Muslim exegesis, see Mahmoud Ayoub, *The Qur'an and its Interpreters Vol. 1.* (Albany: State University of New York Press, 1984), 108–112. On 3:55 and 3:199, see Ayoub, *The Qur'an and its Interpreters Vol. 2.* (Albany: State University of New York Press, 1992), 169–83; 414–15. Prominent examples of Qur'anic criticism of Christians include 5:14–15, 66, 72–73; 9:28–35.

situations. As those situations changed, so the Qur'an's attitude changed. Hence Qur'anic criticism of Christians is more prominent in later, Medinian, than early, Meccan, chapters.

The Qur'anic embrace of diversity is upheld most forcefully in verse forty-eight of chapter five, which reads in part:

> For each [people] We have appointed a divine law (*shir'ah*) and a traced-out way (*minhāj*). Had Allah willed He could have made you one community but that He may try you by that which He hath given you (He hath made you as ye are). So vie one with another in good works.[2]

Thus diversity is both providential and a sign of mercy. But is this is a specifically *religious* diversity? In this verse, the Qur'an comments that each community has its own divinely revealed law or *shir'ah*, a word that might also be suggestive of "divinely revealed religion." The verse is preceded by references to Jews and Christians, hence interpreting the diversity referred to as that distinguishing Jews, Christians, and Muslims appears reasonable and suggests a Qur'anic precedent for religious diversity. Elsewhere, the Qur'an specifically approves of a diversity of "languages," "colors," "nations," and "tribes."[3] However, I must add an important qualification; the Qur'an does not use the word *dīn*, the normal word for "religion," in such a connection.

We should also note that the Qur'an does not regard all other religions as equal. Religions that have revealed scriptures are distinguished from those that do not, as seen in the Qur'anic formulation "People of the Book," which occurs fifty-four times and is reserved for Jews, Christians, and Sabeans.[4] More importantly, from the Qur'anic perspective,

2. Unless stated otherwise, all Qur'anic citations are from Mohammed M. Pickthall, *The Meaning of the Glorious Qur'an* (Elmhurst, NY: Tahrike Tarsile Qur'an, Inc., 1999). In *Shubuhāt*, Riḍā quotes the beginning of this verse which reads: "And unto thee have We revealed the Scripture with the truth, confirming whatever Scripture was before it, and a watcher over it" (5:48). Article One (*Shubuhāt*, 4).
3. On diversity of languages and colors as providential, see 30:22; on diversity of nations and tribes, see 49:13.
4. The term "People of the Book" might also apply to Zoroastrians, although the classical exegetical tradition lacks this incorporation. In recent times the term has

monotheism is distinguished from polytheism, or the association of God with another – *shirk* – the dominant religion in pre-Islamic Arabia. While monotheism may be regarded favorably, the Qur'an emphatically denies the legitimacy of polytheism, considering it an unforgivable sin; repeatedly emphasizing the painful doom that awaits the polytheist.

This must be an exception to the argument for tolerance. It is notable that where the Qur'an criticizes Christians, it does so by conflating their religious practices with those of the pagan Arabs. Christians are chastised for "disbelief" (*kufr*), "association" (*shirk*) and other transgressions including deviation and blasphemy.[5] However, the Qur'an maintains a subtle distinction: the terms for "disbelievers" (*kāfirūn, kuffār*) and "associators" (*mushrikūn*), while common, generally apply to polytheists, not Christians. From the perspective of Christian orthodoxy Arabia, and Arabic Christianity, was very much on the margins of the civilized world. The paradoxical Christological formulation adopted by the councils of Nicaea (325) and Chalcedon (451), and enforced in Rome and Byzantium, probably differed from that of Arabian Christians. It is also possible that some Monophysite and Nestorian Christians may have fled to Arabia to escape Byzantine persecution. Qur'anic Christianity, then, was not "normative," a point some Orientalist scholars interpreted as reflective of Muḥammad's deficiencies in understanding Christian doctrine. It has also been suggested that the Qur'anic Christology is Docetic, based on the text's assertion "They slew him not nor crucified him *but it was made to appear to them*" (4:157).[6] Significantly, as Zebiri notes, the Qur'an appears to understand the Trinity as a doctrine of tritheism – the three being Jesus, Mary and God – as opposed to the normal Christian understanding of it as three manifestations subsisting in a single essence.[7]

been extended to Hindus and Buddhists. In his *tafsīr*, Riḍā extends the term to Zoroastrians, Hindus, Buddhists, Confucians, and practitioners of Shinto. Riḍā, *Tafsīr al-Manār* (Cairo: Dar al-Manār, 1953), vi, 187–88. (Hereafter *Tafsīr*.)

5. See, for example, 3:110; 5:66; 5:72–73.
6. Trans. Khalid Blankinship (adapted from Pickthall).
7. See 5:116. Kate Zebiri, *Muslims and Christians Face to Face* (Oxford: Oneworld, 1997).

While the form of Christianity to which Muḥammad was exposed and the Qur'anic attitude towards it have been somewhat controversial, it is clear that, in the Qur'anic world-view, these issues fall within the discussion of the nature of prophecy, a major theme of the text. The Qur'an's distinctive style – highly oracular and lacking any chronological or historical detail in its treatment of the topic – belies the Orientalist claim of dependence on Biblical texts. The Qur'an claims no originality for its message, but merely claims to confirm the messages of previous prophets that had become corrupted at the hands of their followers. It unites human prophecy – "We make no distinction between any of them" (2:285; 3:84) – and asserts that each prophet essentially brought the same message: a call to submit (*aslama*) to divine oneness. Thus, the Qur'an is able to describe Abraham (3:67), Jesus, and his disciples as "muslims," that is, those who had submitted to the divine will. The Qur'anic vision reflects a tension between the primordial and evolutionary aspects of all human religions.[8] With regard to primordial religion, the Qur'an stresses that all true religion is essentially *islam*, the lower case denoting the verbal noun with the generic meaning of "submitting." With regard to evolutionary religion, it stresses that the *islam* of all previous religions culminates in *Islam*, the historical religion founded by Muḥammad and one particular form of "submitting:" the concrete *Islam* is the most perfect form of the generic *islam*. Qur'an 5:3 reads: "This day I have perfected your religion for you . . . and have chosen for you as religion *Islam*."

This tension leads to the ambivalent treatment of Christians, an ambivalence the Qur'an candidly acknowledges: "they are not all alike" (3:113). The Qur'an never makes a definite statement, but prefaces its references to Christians – positive and negative alike – with comments such as "some of them" (2:146), "most of them" (3:110), "among them are those" (3:78), and "among them a portion" (3:113). Viewed positively, Qur'anic Christians exemplify *islam*, submission to God, piety and avoidance of evil. They bow down during the night in humble prayer and submission (3:113), and weep upon hearing scripture recited. Negative

8. Compare the Qur'anic reference to the primordial origin of all revelation, the "hidden book" (56:78) or "well-guarded tablet" (85:22).

references to Christians are linked by the recurrent theme of excess or exaggeration (4:171; 5:77): Christians take priests as lords (9:31), just as Jews take rabbis.

The Qur'an considers the doctrines of the Trinity and divine incarnation particularly egregious examples of excess (4:171; 5:17, 72, 73, 116, 117). Jesus, named twenty-five times, is called "the messiah" (*al-masīḥ*) eleven times. However the Qur'an offers no explanation of this title's meaning (and Jesus never refers to himself as the messiah). It is simply used as a name. The Qur'an emphasizes that "the Messiah is only a messenger" (4:171; 5:75). Significantly, this is the same description used for Muḥammad: "Muḥammad is only a messenger" (3:144). The connection between the two is emphasized by Jesus' foretelling of the coming of "the praised one" (61:6). The Qur'an stresses the same points with regard to the miracles – evidences – of Jesus: he performs miracles only "by God's leave" (3:49). As in the Qur'anic treatment of the birth of Jesus (interestingly, the teachings of Jesus are hardly discussed), his humanity is emphasized. It is in elevating Jesus to divine status that Christians are guilty of a grave sin.

The Qur'anic attitude towards Jewish and Christian scripture is also ambivalent. The text refers to the leaves of Abraham (87:19), the Psalms of David (4:163), and on numerous occasions to the Torah of Moses and Gospel of Jesus, but it is unclear exactly what they are. Christians are chastised for corrupting, suppressing, and misinterpreting their scriptures, for leading Muslims astray, and for not accepting the prophecy of Muḥammad when, according to the Qur'an, their own scriptures clearly dictate that they should. Similar accusations are made against Jews with regard to the Torah. It seems plain that the Qur'anic definitions of "Torah" and "Gospel" differ greatly from those of Jewish and Christian tradition. In the Qur'anic view they were originally pure, divine revelations which were distorted by human beings (2:75, 79; 3:78; 4:46; 5:13–15, 41). On the other hand, the Qur'an pointedly refers Jews and Christians back to their own scriptures – "let the people of the Gospel judge by the Gospel" (5:47) – which, logically, would indicate that an at least partially-sound Torah and Gospel must be available to Jews and Christians.

The problems inherent in the Qur'anic tension between praise and condemnation of Christians and between dismissal and partial validation of Christian scripture lack a clear solution, but raise enticing questions: can "good Christians" be identified and distinguished from their corrupt co-religionists? If there is an uncorrupted Torah or Gospel, where is it and where are Christians to find it? The Qur'an does not attempt to resolve these tensions or answer these questions but presents its audience with alternative paradigms that may be developed: the universalistic and accommodationist on the one hand and the supersessionist or rejectionist on the other.

The Medieval Period

Medieval Muslim interpretations of Christianity refer to a vast array of materials, including collections of prophetic tradition or hadith, Qur'anic exegesis (*tafsīr*), and historical and apologetic works. Accordingly, I shall address only the most prominent themes and salient features of this literature in this summary (specifically Shiʿi works will not be discussed).[9]

Turning to the hadith, the secondary Islamic scripture, perhaps the most immediately notable feature of the treatment of Christians and Christianity therein is that it is not a matter of primary concern. The nine major collections, the most significant of which are those of al-Bukhārī (died 870) and Muslim (died 875), do not include separate sections on Jesus, Christianity or Christians; instead, various traditions are scattered throughout books and chapters organized under different topic headings.[10] The numerous traditions of Jesus' appearance, behavior, and teaching do not address the Christian religion itself, but recast the Christian Christ in Islamic terms. This is seen especially

9. On Shiʿi interpretations of Jesus and Christianity, see Mahmoud Ayoub, "Towards an Islamic Christology: an Image of Jesus in Early Shiʿi Literature," *The Muslim World* 66 (1976): 163–88.

10. The nine collections are those of al-Bukhārī, Muslim, Abū Dawūd, al-Tirmidhī, al-Nasāʾī, Ibn Mājah, al-Dārimī, Mālik, and Aḥmad ibn Ḥanbal. Unless stated otherwise, all references to the hadith are from the *Ḥarf* Hadith Encyclopedia CD, Version 3.

in relation to the "descent" of Jesus, which is distinctly seen in terms of Muslim belief.[11]

In a recent study of approximately five hundred traditions concerning Christians, Marston Speight corroborates the prevailing view that the hadith reflects a general mistrust of Christians. However, he notes that the collections are not without statements that show "touches of human warmth" towards Christians. A notable example is the prophet's affirmation of affinity between the monotheistic religions, "all prophets are brothers; their mothers are different, but their religion is one."[12] None the less, negative sentiments predominate. These include declarations of Christian errors, unfavorable comparisons between Christians and Muslims, eschatological judgments, and strictures against Christians. In relation to Christianity, the hadith is more concerned with community than with religion. They give voice to Muslim religious identity relative to non-Muslims more than they engage questions of non-Muslim religious doctrine.[13] Theologically, the hadith diverges from the Qur'an in being

11. On traditions on Jesus, see F. Peter Ford's introduction to his translation of ʿAbbās Maḥmūd al-ʿAqqād's *The Genius of Christ* (Binghamton, N.Y.: Global Publications: Institute of Global Cultural Studies (IGCS), Binghamton University; Provo, Utah: Center for the Preservation of Ancient Religious Texts, Brigham Young University, 2001), 5–9.
12. Marston Speight, "Christians in the Ḥadīth Literature," in *Islamic Interpretations of Christianity*, edited by Lloyd Ridgeon (New York: St Martin's Press, 2001), 32. The tradition in full reads:

    Abū Hurayrah, may Allah be pleased with him, reported: I heard Allah's Messenger (may peace be upon him) as saying: I am most akin to the son of Mary among the whole of mankind and the Prophets are brothers of different mothers, (but of one religion) and no Prophet was raised between me and him (Prophet Jesus).

    Among the nine collections, it is found in those of al-Bukhārī (Prophets, 48), Muslim (Virtues, 4360), Abū Dawūd (Sunnah, 4055), and in several places in Ibn Ḥanbal.
13. The following tradition is emblematic of the concern with identity: "Abū Hurayrah, may Allah be pleased with him, reported: Allah's Messenger (may peace be upon him) said: The Jews and the Christians do not dye (their hair), so do the opposite." It is included in all the major collections, except those of al-Dārimī and Mālik.

more unambiguously exclusivistic, laying the foundation for a religious separation between Muslims and Christians.[14]

While the enormous diversity of other medieval materials makes generalization difficult, a notable difference from the Qur'anic foundation emerges. Whereas the Qur'an offers both universalist and supersessionist paradigms, post-Qur'anic tradition, following the hadith, is generally supersessionist, downplaying or entirely ignoring Qur'anic universalism.[15] In legal, exegetical, and apologetic discourse, there is an emphasis on definition, which involves a shift away from a vision of religious pluralism towards one of binary opposition. The privileged status indicated by the expressions "people of the book" and "people of the pact (*dhimmah*)"[16] loses its distinction as Christians dissolve into the generalized categories of "unbelievers" (*kuffār*) and "associators" (*mushrikūn*).[17] Christianity becomes but one form of unbelief or paganism.

The turn from Qur'anic pluralism is clearly apparent in classical exegesis, of which Muḥammad ibn Jarīr al-Ṭabarī (died 923), Abū Qāsim al-Zamaksharī (died 1144), Fakhr al-Dīn al-Rāzī (died 1209) and 'Imād al-Dīn ibn Kathīr (died 1373) are pre-eminent representatives.[18] Qur'anic phrases explicitly or implicitly praising Christians are down-played,

14. Speight, 48–49. Speight deems the hadith's concern with Muslim religious identity to be reflective of the dominant community's relationship to its Christian minority population in the eighth and ninth centuries. He does not address the question of how such a sociological interpretation might be reconciled (or not) with the traditional Muslim view of the hadith's general integrity, and its relationship with the prophetic sunnah, as upheld by hadith criticism.
15. The relationship between the Qur'anic ambivalence towards Christianity and the more uniform and negative portrayal of Christians that emerges in the post-Qur'anic tradition parallels the Qur'anic ambivalence towards equality of the sexes and its subsequent denial in jurisprudence. See Leila Ahmad's *Women and Gender in Islam* (New Haven: Yale University Press, 1992).
16. This term refers to the protected but secondary legal status of Jews and Christians living under Muslim rule. Although it has a Qur'anic basis – the word "*dhimmah*" occurs twice in the text (9:8, 10) – it is not, strictly speaking, Qur'anic.
17. Jane McAuliffe, "Legal Exegesis: Christians as a Case Study," in *Islamic Interpretations of Christianity*, 71.
18. See Ayoub, *The Qur'an and its Interpreters*, I, 3–5.

if not passed over, by these exegetes, although they show little reticence in elaborating Qur'anic condemnation of Christians. Al-Ṭabarī and others, foreshadowing 'Abduh and Riḍā, interpreted Qur'anic references to Jesus as the "son of God" metaphorically while chastising Christians for their overly literal understanding. As Mahmoud Ayoub has noted, the Qur'anic use of the terms *ibn* (son) and *walad* (son) presented a difficult challenge, less easily reconciled with the Islamic doctrine of divine transcendence. Qur'anic references to the power of Jesus "to create" (3:49; 5:110) – Jesus apart, the Qur'an uses the positive sense of the verb *khalaqa* (he created) only of God – were down-played as exegetes sought to limit the creative aspect of this verb.[19] Overall, we can note a general exegetical shift away from accommodationism and pluralism.

Classical historical and apologetic works cover a vast corpus of materials and articulate a range of views of Christianity, from the accommodationist to the unabashedly rejectionist and polemical. While rejectionist views predominate, there are some significant examples of accommodationist views. Perhaps the most explicit is found in the works of the Isma'ili missionary Nāṣir Khusraw (died around 1075), who argued for Biblical authenticity and its identity with the Qur'an.[20] More commonly, however, Muslims argued for the invalidity of Christianity, generally stressing its corrupt character and/or its irrationality.

A prominent critique of Christian corruption is found in *Al-Radd 'alā al-Naṣārā* (Response to the Christians) by 'Amr al-Jāḥiẓ (died 869), which launches a scathing attack on Christianity and the Bible.[21] The works of 'Alī ibn Aḥmad ibn Ḥazm (died 1064), a Ẓāhirī scholar from Islamic Spain, possibly represent the peak of Muslim hostility towards Christianity. The

19. Ayoub, "Jesus the Son of God: A Study of the Terms *Ibn* and *Walad* in the Qur'an and Tafsīr Tradition," in *Christian–Muslim Encounters*, eds Yvonne Haddad and Wadi Zaidan Haddad (Gainsville, FL: University of Florida Press, 1995), 66–78.
20. Malise Ruthven, "Introduction" to *Islamic Interpretations of Christianity*, xi. Khusraw also took an accomodationist approach towards Hinduism and its scriptures.
21. Hugh Goddard, *Muslim Perceptions of Christianity*, (London: Grey Seal, 1996), 32–33.

first section of his *Kitāb al-Faṣl fī al-Milal wa al-Aḥwā' wa al-Niḥal* (The Book on the Religious Communities and Sects) is entitled *Iẓhār Tabdīl al-Yahūd wa al-Naṣārā* (Demonstration of Jewish and Christian Corruptions) and meticulously mines the Bible for internal contradictions and inconsistencies. As with Ibn Ḥazm's literalistic interpretation of the Qur'an, few followed him to this level of anti-Christian enmity.[22]

The works of Taqī al-Dīn ibn Taymiyyah (died 1328) were more influential. Although some scholars have observed that Ibn Taymiyyah adopted a more moderate tone than his Andalusian predecessor, he was, none the less, harshly critical of Christianity. Malise Ruthven deems him to be the preeminent classical representative of Muslim rejectionism, and places him at the opposite end of the spectrum from Nāṣir Khusraw.[23] Ibn Taymiyyah's *Kitāb Iqtiḍā' al-Ṣirāṭ al-Mustaqīm* identifies several un-Islamic Christian borrowings that have infiltrated Islam, leading to practices such as the celebration of the Prophet's birthday and pilgrimages to the graves of Sufi saints. Hence, he seeks "perfect dissimilarity" between Muslims and Christians. Ibn Taymiyyah's *al-Jawāb al-Ṣaḥīḥ li-man Baddala Dīn al-Masīḥ* (The Correct Response to those who Change the Religion of Christ), was a particularly influential work, which became the standard for all subsequent Muslim works on Christianity. Hugh Goddard finds in it an intermediate position on Biblical corruption: Ibn Taymiyyah considers the text reliable in essence but corrupt in practice.[24]

Classical scholars also emphasized the irrationality of the Christian religion, as in 'Alī ibn Rabbān al-Ṭabarī's (died 855) *Al-Radd 'alā al-Naṣārā* (Response to the Christians). Al-Ṭabarī converted from Christianity when he was seventy years old. He was therefore very familiar with the Bible. He argues not for Biblical corruption, but uses the Bible as a proof against Christian doctrines, notably the incarnation.[25] Abū Ḥāmid Muḥammad al-Ghazālī (died 1111) takes a similar approach in his

22. Goddard, 35–36.

23. Ruthven, xi.

24. Ford, 19. Goddard, 35–37.

25. Ford, 8. Jean-Marie Gaudeul, *Encounters and Clashes: Islam and Christianity in History* (Rome: Pontificio Istituto di Studi Arabi e Islamici, 1990), I, 39–41.

Al-Radd al-Jamīl li-Ilāhiyyat ʿĪsā bi Ṣarīḥ al-Injīl (The Sublime Refutation of the Divinity of Jesus through the Plain Sense of the Gospel). He generally accepts the authenticity of Christian scripture, but stresses the essential irrationality of central Christian doctrines, notably the incarnation. Al-Ghazālī discusses the gospel texts in detail, using philosophical and linguistic arguments – the terms *ilāh* (god), *rabb* (lord) and *ibn* (son) are analyzed in detail – to pose an essential incompatibility between "humanity" and "divinity."[26]

Al-Ghazālī's *Iḥyā' ʿUlūm al-Dīn* (Revival of the Religious Sciences) was a seminal influence on Riḍā. This work, which seeks to harmonize Sufi mysticism with shariʿah-based formalism, includes a large number of sayings attributed to Jesus that highlight his austerity. While these sayings are based primarily on Islamic sources, they reflect, in Peter Ford's words, "distinct echoes" of the gospels.[27] Al-Ghazālī's work is also significant for its emphasis on immanence, seen as integral to Islamic universalism, just as Ibn Taymiyyah's emphasis on transcendence is integral to Islamic exclusivism. Ruthven comments:

> Islamic exclusivism is associated, historically and currently, with divine transcendence; Islamic universalism with the immanent "God within" and particularly with "higher" states of being or consciousness achieved by Sufi mystics and organised into emanationist hierarchies of Ithnaʿashari and Ismaʿili theosophies.[28]

Al-Ghazālī's theology opened the door for acceptance of religious experience outside an Islamic context, reflected in the poetic works of Jalāl al-Dīn al-Rūmī (died 1273) who, in his search for universal forms underlying material reality, deploys Jesus as the "Spirit of God" (showing some familiarity with the gospels). Rūmī's Islamic inclusivism is consistent with

26. Goddard, 28–31. Al-Ghazālī pays particular attention to the Gospel of John. Goddard notes that while this work is traditionally attributed to al-Ghazālī, it may have been written by one of his students, possibly a convert from Coptic Christianity.
27. Ford, 9. Goddard, 28–30.
28. Ruthven, xii.

Docetic rather than with Pauline or Nicaean theology. Docetic Christology might be reconcilable with the Islamic conception of an "ideal Christianity" but the materialization of the divine – whether attributed to Paul or the Church Council – is another matter.[29]

The Modern Period

Classical Muslim interpretations of Christianity, both accommodationist and rejectionist, were based on Muslim confidence, and self-awareness of its strength and superiority. Unquestionably, early scholars deemed Islamic civilization to be superior to its Christian counterpart. After the death of Ibn Taymiyyah, and particularly from the fifteenth century, there was a decline in Muslim interest in Christianity, but the traumas of confrontation with a technologically-superior Christian Europe at the end of the eighteenth century, and of colonialism, rendered superiority or indifference problematical, if not anachronistic.[30] Muslims were forced to re-evaluate.

Modern Muslim literature on Christianity, while less extensive than its classical counterpart, is still considerable. The modern period presented Muslims with new concerns, for example the relationships between Christianity and European imperialism and the threats of Christianity and secularism. Yet, to a considerable extent, Muslim concerns about Christianity remained framed by those of the medieval texts. This can particularly be seen in relation to the status of scripture and the doctrines of incarnation and Trinity.[31]

The Bible commentary of Sayyid Aḥmad Khān (died 1898) is particularly important. Khān was influenced by Raḥmat Allāh ibn Khalīl al-ʿUthmānī al-Kayrānawī (died 1898) and Wazīr Khān who, before the Indian mutiny of 1857, had engaged in theological argument with

29. Ruthven, xv–xvi. See also Lloyd Ridgeon, "Christianity as Portrayed by Jalāl al-Dīn al-Rūmī," in *Islamic Interpretations of Christianity*, 99–126.
30. On the impact of colonialism on the Muslim World in general, see Chapter Two below.
31. Lloyd Ridgeon, *Crescents on the Cross: Islamic Visions of Christianity* (Oxford: Oxford University Press, 2001), x.

Christianity. Khān's approach, in common with Riḍā's, emphasized the primacy of reason over literal acceptance of scripture. Khān gave preference to religious universalism over particularism. Like classical exegetes, he was highly selective in his use of Qur'anic references to Christians but, unlike them, highlighted Qur'anic praise of Christians. In his treatment of scripture, and his treatment of Christianity, he sought to demonstrate the two religions' compatibility. Knowledge of the scriptures of both traditions, Khān argued, would lead to Muslim–Christian *rapprochement.* Whereas al-Kayrānawī appropriated the work of Western philosophers and biblical critics such as T.H. Horne (died 1874) to deny the scriptural status of the Bible,[32] Khān was more interested in reconciliation. His three-volume commentary on the Bible holds much of value for Muslims.[33]

Khān distinguished between deliberate corruption and corruption in transmission, arguing for critical study of New Testament texts to determine Jesus' original revelation. He bent and extended the Islamic notion of revelation (*waḥy*) to incorporate the Gospel. However, as Ridgeon observes, his interpretation was inconsistent and he occasionally reverted to the orthodox denial of the gospels as revelation, restricting revelation to the Qur'an.[34] This inconsistency foreshadows Riḍā's, and is a common feature of Muslim efforts to accommodate Christianity.

The next decisively influential Muslim interpretation of Christianity is that of Riḍā's mentor, Muḥammad ʿAbduh (died 1905). ʿAbduh's views are set out in his book, *Islam and Christianity between Science and Civilization* and the Qur'anic commentary *Tafsīr al-Manār*, which he wrote with Riḍā. Both were first serialized in *al-Manār.*[35] In a parenthetical statement in the

32. Kayrānawī quotes the views of B. Spinoza (died 1677), J. Toland (died 1722), T. Woolston (died 1733), T. Paine (died 1809) and J. J. Rosseau (died 1778). On the depth of his actual comprehension of Biblical criticism, see Gaudeul, I, 261. See also Article One (*Shubuhāt*, 1).
33. Ridgeon, *Crescents on the Cross*, 5–7.
34. Ridgeon, *Crescents on the Cross*, 7.
35. On *al-Manār* and *Tafsīr al-Manār*, see Chapter Two below.

Tafsīr, 'Abduh commented: "We see in the Gospels that Christ's disciples themselves did not understand all that he told them in the way of admonitions, precepts, and glad tidings, which is the true gospel (*al-Injīl al-ḥaqīqī*) in our belief."[36] According to Ford, this indicates 'Abduh did not subscribe to the traditional doctrine that the gospels were textually corrupt. Goddard draws the same conclusion: for 'Abduh, the issue is corruption of meaning, not corruption of text. He goes on to contrast Khān and 'Abduh's positive evaluation of the Bible with Riḍā's dismissal.[37]

'Abduh's *tafsīr* does contain statements criticizing the traditional Muslim view of Biblical corruption. His commentary on the Qur'anic reference to the People of the Book "concealing" the scripture (2:159) is more explicit than the statement quoted above. Noting that some writers argue that Christians deleted gospel references to Muḥammad, he says: "This argument is unreasonable, as it is not possible that the people of the book could co-operate to that end in every area." Were it so, the European Bible would differ from the Arabic Bible.[38] However, when such statements are considered together with the views expressed in his other writings, the picture is less clear. In *Islam and Christianity*, he determines that the gospel message is ultimately errant and strongly expresses an extremely critical attitude towards various passages, particularly in the Gospel of Matthew. Unquestionably, 'Abduh considered gospel teaching theologically invalid, if not harmful.[39] In this light, the 'Abduh–Riḍā contrast becomes less appealing.

36. *Tafsīr*, ii, 160. Trans. author. Riḍā adds his own comment: "I say: but Christ informed them that he did not tell them everything . . . and he informed them of the Paraclete that will follow him . . . meaning Muḥammad."
37. Ford, 12. Goddard, 47, 56. Ford qualifies his assessment of 'Abduh's interpretation by noting that it does not necessarily apply to the historical material in the gospels.
38. *Tafsīr*, ii, 49. This is essentially the same argument advanced by Riḍā's opponent Niqūlā Ghibrīl, and Riḍā contests both. Unsurprisingly, when amending his mentor's view he is more respectful in his tone. See Chapter Three and Article Nine (*Shubuhāt* 38–39).
39. Ayoub, "Islam and Christianity: A study of Muhammad 'Abduh's view of the two religions," *Humaniora Islamica* 2 (1974): 126; 136.

After ʿAbduh, Muslim discourse on Christian scripture reverted to a more polemical, if not hostile, attitude. In Ford's view, the next instance of an irenic Muslim attitude towards the gospel is ʿAbbās Maḥmūd al-ʿAqqād's *ʿAbqariyyat al-Masīḥ* (The Genius of Christ), published in 1953.[40] Al-ʿAqqād is something of an exception, as Muslim treatment of Christian scripture throughout most of the twentieth century shows little of Khān's patience and effort at accommodation, however inconsistently applied.[41] Prominent examples of apologetic dismissals of the gospels include the works of Muḥammad Abū Zahrah (died 1974), Aḥmad Shalabī, Sayyid Quṭb (died 1966) and Mawlānā Mawdūdī (died 1979). The later dialogical works of Ismāʿīl Faruqī (died 1986) and Mahmoud Ayoub (1935–) represent a significant shift in attitude, returning to a neglected aspect of the Qur'anic paradigm and developing the potential of classical and modern Islamic thought into a more explicitly pluralistic vision. In particular, Ayoub treats Christian scripture with great deference.[42]

Modern Muslims remained as critical of Christian doctrine and ethics as their medieval counterparts, although the criticism was sometimes expressed in different terms. Khān was strongly influenced by the Enlightenment and natural philosophy (a point to which I shall return),[43] which led him to reject miracles and other unscientific elements in both Islam and Christianity. Similarly, based on rational criteria rather than Qur'anic prescription, he rejected Christian doctrine as irrational and Christian ethics as impractical. He embraced the ideology of universal progress to an ideal and pluralistic human society, a goal that would be facilitated by rationally based Muslim–Christian dialogue.[44]

40. Ford, 29.

41. Ford, 15.

42. On Abū Zahrah and Shalabī, see Ayoub, "Muslim Views of Christianity: Some Modern Examples" *Islamochristiana* 10 (1984): 60–70. On Quṭb, see Neal Robinson, "Sayyid Quṭb's Attitude Towards Christianity," in *Islamic Interpretations of Christianity*, 159–178 (especially 172–176). On the contrast between Khān's accommodationism and Mawdūdī's rejectionism, see Ridgeon, *Crescents on the Cross*, 1–32. On Faruqi, see David A. Kerr, "Islamic Daʿwa and Christian Mission: Towards a Comparative Analysis," *International Review of Mission* 89: 161–62. On Ayoub, see Ford, 20.

43. See Article Fourteen (*Shubuhāt*, 60).

44. Ridgeon, 10–12; 25–27.

'Abduh also stressed the deficiency of Christian doctrine and ethics. In *Islam and Christianity*, he drew on the thought of Renan, Spencer, and Tolstoy to argue that Christianity is incompatible with modern science. He went on to discuss the "fundamental principles" of Christianity and Islam, highlighting Islam's considerable rational, and practical, superiority.[45] 'Abduh's rejection of the incarnation returns us to the issue of scriptural corruption. Commenting on the Qur'anic "there is a party of them who distort the Scripture with their tongues" (3:78), he notes that the distortion referred to is an over-literal reading of references to Jesus as "Son" and "Father." Such expressions, 'Abduh argues, are metaphors. Christians err in reducing them to their apparent or literal meaning.[46]

45. Ayoub, *Islam and Christianity*, 122 on.
46. *Tafsīr*, iii, 345. 'Abduh's interpretation is scarcely that of a "fundamentalist literalist."

2

Muḥammad Rashīd Riḍā and his Environment

The Impact of Colonialism and Muslim Responses

The thinking of Rashīd Riḍā and his peers is intimately connected with the history of European colonialism in the Muslim world, particularly in the Middle East. Beyond there, the Indian sub-continent has significant influence in shaping Muslim responses to modernity, as indicated by the work of al-Kayrānawī and Sayyid Aḥmad Khān. Given the overriding influence of colonialism, Riḍā and his peers lack Christian counterparts. Whereas European and other Christians grappled with the relationship between tradition and modernity, but not in response to the humiliation and trauma of subjugation by a religious "other," Riḍā's writings reflect an overwhelming awareness of Muslim weakness relative to non-Muslim strength. The calm confidence of classical Islam is lacking in the works of Riḍā and his contemporaries.

The 1798–1801 incursion by the French into Egypt (where Riḍā spent almost all his professional career) is generally regarded as the event that opened Middle Eastern eyes to Muslim weakness and European strength. The timing of this event is significant; it coincides with the end of the Enlightenment, the movement synonymous with the beginnings of modernity.[1] The French

1. Some scholars suggest that the emphasis on 1798 is overstated and call for a different interpretation. See Peter Gran, *Islamic Roots of Capitalism: Egypt 1760–1840* (Syracuse: Syracuse University Press, 1998), xi–xxxvii.

incursion was followed in 1882 by Britain's military intervention in Egypt, to secure control of the Suez Canal. The period between saw the first efforts at modernization, under the leadership of Muḥammad ʿAlī, stagnation after his death in 1849, and the emergence of Rifāʿah Rāfiʿ al-Ṭahṭāwī (died 1873), perhaps the first significant Arab scholar to attempt seriously to engage with modernity within an Islamic frame of reference.

Although Egypt technically remained under Ottoman rule until the break-up of the Empire after the First World War, the British effectively controlled the country for several decades from 1882, and were not completely ousted until the nationalist revolution of 1952. For Muslims, who saw themselves as heirs of one of the world's greatest civilizations, colonial domination was a bitter pill. The humiliation suffered at British hands greatly influenced the intellectual development of many Muslim intellectuals, including Riḍā. For the colonizers, and many of the colonized, it was but a short step from Europe's technological and scientific superiority to its apparent superiority of civilization.

Muslims were very divided in their responses. In Riḍā's lifetime, and later decades, there were divergent Muslim engagements with the challenges of modernity and colonialism. This diversity has resulted in a variety of terms coined by Islamicists and other scholars to label certain trends in modern Islam: traditionalist, conservative, "establishment Islam," secularist, Islamic modernist, *Salafī*, fundamentalist, populist, activist, and Islamist. As they are applied inconsistently, this variety presents the student of Islam with some difficulty. To take a single, but telling, example, ʿAbduh is one scholar's "Islamic modernist" and another's "Islamic fundamentalist."[2]

Bringing some coherence to this variety is one of my goals. I contend that the numerous Muslim responses to modernity may be divided into four broad categories: traditionalist, secularist, modernist, and so-called

2. On ʿAbduh as a "modernist," see F. Denny, *An Introduction to Islam* (Englewood Cliffs, NJ: Macmillan, 1994), 330–331; J. Esposito, *Islam: The Straight Path* (New York and Oxford: Oxford University Press, 1998), 130; J. Schacht, "Muḥammad ʿAbduh," in *EI*. On ʿAbduh as a "fundamentalist," see Johannes Jansen, *The Dual Nature of Islamic Fundamentalism* (London: Hurst & Company, 1997), 40.

"fundamentalist." This is an imperfect categorization: first, because there are many more nuances of difference and second, because the categories are not discrete. However, I would argue that the first three can be delineated reasonably well. It is less clear whether the fundamentalist response can be defined satisfactorily. I shall examine the question of whether that categorization may legitimately be applied to Riḍā in Chapter Four.

The first category, the traditionalist, is synonymous with conservative, "establishment Islam," and would incorporate most Sufi Muslims. This response, especially as depicted by non-traditionalist Muslims, is not a rejection of modernity but an indifference to its opportunities. To its critics, the traditionalist mentality was one of *taqlīd*, understood as blind imitation or uncreative replication of tradition, witnessed at institutions such as al-Azhar University. Until the end of the nineteenth century, al-Azhar scholarship mainly consisted of rote learning and memorization of traditional materials, especially works on jurisprudence. Although significant reforms were undertaken after 1894 (largely due to ʿAbduh), a general lack of enthusiasm for engagement remained. A telling example is the teaching of European languages, which was not incorporated until the 1930s. Where modern subjects were introduced, they played a distinctly secondary role, reflecting a wider passivity to the challenges of modernity.[3]

The secularist is at the opposite end of the spectrum, wholeheartedly embracing modernity. Significantly, secularists understood modernity in culturally specific terms, that is, as specifically Western or European. Secularists felt that for the Middle East to become the scientific and technological equivalent of Europe, its inhabitants must adopt European culture completely – even to the extent of adopting a European styles of dress – something that would greatly diminish, if not eliminate, the role of Islam in public life. It is a commonplace that, among Middle Eastern countries, Turkey most enthusiastically adopted the secularist paradigm. After the break up of the Ottoman Empire, the Turkish nation-state was founded under the leadership of Riḍā's contemporary, Musṭafā Kemāl Ataturk (1881–1938). In 1928, Islam was officially abolished as the state

3. Kerr, 156.

religion and the Latin alphabet replaced the Arabic as the script for the Turkish language (a decision of which Riḍā was highly critical). Ataturk was personally involved in the propagation of the new alphabet. Four years later, Arabic and Persian were removed from the curricula of state education. These decisions reflect the cultural and ideological orientation of the secularist agenda. The Latin was adopted because it was European, and hence seen as more compatible with modernity than the Arabic.

Amongst Riḍā's Arab peers, prominent representatives of secularism include 'Alī 'Abd al-Rāziq (died 1966), of whom Riḍā was highly critical, and Aḥmad Luṭfī al-Sayyid (1872–1963), an early associate of both 'Abduh and Ataturk. 'Abd al-Rāziq caused a sensation with his 1925 essay, *Islam and the Bases of Power*, which called for a separation of the religious and political spheres.[4] Luṭfī al-Sayyid is deemed, by Bernard Lewis, to be the pre-eminent Arab proponent of European-style political liberalism. His thinking departed from Islamic precedent in several ways, including his focus on the individual rather than the community, his rejection of the notion of the pan-Islamic ummah in favor of the Egyptian nation-state (conceived according to a European paradigm), and his call for a separation of powers.[5] Another was Faraḥ Anṭūn (1874–1922), a personal friend of Riḍā. Although he was a Christian, Anṭūn's thinking had much in common with his secularist Muslim peers, especially in relation to the separation of civil and religious authority.[6]

The third category is the Islamic modernist; its pre-eminent representatives are al-Afghānī, 'Abduh and Riḍā, leaders of the modern *Salafiyyah* or *Salafī* movement (also known as *ḥarakat al-iṣlāḥ*). These terms derive from *salaf*, meaning "ancestors," or the first generations of Muslims. *Salafīs* sought to remove the accretions of tradition and return to the pure Islam of the early Muslims, which, according to some, ended in 855, on the death of Aḥmad ibn Ḥanbal. *Salafīs* upheld the examples of the pure

4. D. Sourdel, "Khilāfa" in *EI*. On Riḍā's critique of 'Abd al-Rāziq, see Emad Eldin Shahin, *Through Muslim Eyes: M. Rashīd Riḍā and the West* (Hendon, VA: International Institute of Islamic Thought, 1994), 67–68.
5. Bernard Lewis, "Ḥuriyya," in *EI*.
6. See Chapter Four and Articles Fourteen through Sixteen.

Muslims of history, who, unlike the majority, remained true to the Islamic ideal. Al-Ghazālī and Ibn Taymiyyah were given particular prominence.

Here again there is a degree of confusion: while many scholars date the modern *Salafiyyah* from the work of al-Afghānī and 'Abduh in the 1870s, some identify Riḍā as the first *Salafī* of the modern period.[7] The difference is significant. To those who name al-Afghānī and 'Abduh, the term is synonymous with "modernist;" to those who name Riḍā, it is synonymous with "fundamentalist."[8] This implies a different understanding of the relationship between al-Afghānī and 'Abduh and Riḍā: if Riḍā was the first "fundamentalist" *Salafī*, his work diverges from that of his modernist mentors. I would argue that Riḍā was a modernist, an interpretation which I shall defend later.

'Abduh's most significant work dates from 1884 when, both having been exiled from Egypt, he met his erstwhile mentor al-Afghānī in Paris. They founded an anti-British society, *al-'Urwah al-Wuthqā* (The Indissoluble Bond) and published a journal of the same name. Although it was only published for eight months, it was enormously influential in inspiring Riḍā and others to seek political independence through reform of Islam. Two of 'Abduh's other publications are especially noteworthy: *The Theology of Unity* (*Risālat al-Tawḥīd*) and *Islam and Christianity*.[9] These set down several themes later developed by Riḍā, including a call for the revival of independent reasoning (*ijtihād*) and a rejection of the mentality of blind imitation of tradition (*taqlīd*), a shift of emphasis from the traditional focus on jurisprudence (and adherence to a particular legal school) to modern fields of learning, and a gradualist approach to

7. On al-Afghānī and 'Abduh as founders of the *Salafiyyah*, see Emad Shahin, "Salafīyah," in *Encyclopedia of Modern Islam*. On Riḍā as the founder, see Chapter Four.
8. Those who define *Salafī* as fundamentalist stress the influence of Ibn Taymiyyah. Others note al-Ghazālī's influence on Islamic modernists. On the continuing relevance of these two classical scholars in general, see Ridgeon, *Islamic Interpretations of Christianity*, and especially Ruthven's comments, xi–xx.
9. *The Theology of Unity* was published in 1897. Riḍā quotes a lengthy passage in Article Fifteen (*Shubuhāt*, 80–83).

promoting the common good (*maṣlaḥah*) through mass education.[10] 'Abduh also argued for the primacy of reason over tradition. Like his secularist peers, 'Abduh sought to assimilate the Western approach to science and knowledge, but unlike them he wished to retain and reinforce Islamic cultural integrity. Secularists felt that modernity would weaken Islam: 'Abduh felt it would strengthen it.

The traditionalist, secularist, and modernist attitudes towards modernity can be differentiated with some clarity. The same cannot be said of fundamentalism. Fundamentalism is defined as an uncompromising, aggressive, and frequently violent rejection of modernity. Fundamentalists are said to reject the Enlightenment and regress to an alternative paradigm based on certain, pre-modern, "fundamentals," prominent among which are: resistance to rationalism, scriptural literalism, a dualistic world-view or "enclave culture," and eschatological expectations.[11] In my view, this definition is problematic: the theory of the first three is insufficiently supported by the evidence, and the fourth is insufficiently precise and describes monotheistic belief generally.

Those who question the utility of "fundamentalism," and I am one, must note that the term has a certain content. There is a discernible, if not universal, consensus as to *which* Muslims subscribe to fundamentalist Islam. Four names are prominent: Ḥasan al-Bannā' (died 1946), Sayyid Quṭb (died 1966), Mawlānā Mawdūdī (died 1979), and Ruhollah Khomeini (died 1989).[12] However, although there may be a consensus, it is one that struggles to withstand analysis. A cursory examination of the

10. 'Abduh's gradualism was his major difference from al-Afghānī, who advocated a more revolutionary approach.
11. See Gabriel A. Almond, R. Scott Appleby, and Emmanuel Sivan, *Strong Religion: The Rise of Fundamentalisms around the World,* (Chicago, University of Chicago Press, 2003), Karen Armstrong, *The Battle for God: A History of Fundamentalism,* (New York, Ballantine Books, 2001), Lawrence Davidson *Islamic Fundamentalism* (Westport, CT: Greenwood Press, 1998), 17 and Martin E. Marty and R. Scott Appleby, *The Glory and the Power: The Fundamentalist Challenge to the Modern World,* (Boston: Beacon Press, 1992), 29.
12. See the sample of notable Islamic fundamentalists given by Davidson in *Islamic Fundamentalism,* 87–111.

works of these authors reveals that they did not generally subscribe to the first three fundamentals and they also differ greatly in their interpretations of Islam. Hence, a monolithic term is of questionable value. "Fundamentalist" appears to over-simplify: it homogenizes important differences, for example, Mawdūdī's gradualism and disavowal of revolution with Khomeini's implementation of revolution. In my view, problems with this term have yet to be satisfactorily resolved.[13]

Apart from a brief overlap with al-Bannā', Riḍā's career pre-dates these others. Yet fundamentalism is certainly relevant to this study, as we shall see presently.

A Sketch of Rashīd Riḍā's Life and Works

This will be just a summary of the salient features of Rashīd Riḍā's life and career, which are detailed in many other sources.[14] By any measure, Riḍā was one of the most significant Muslims of the modern period and is still so regarded by Muslim intellectuals. He was born in Qalamun, a village near Tripoli in Northern Lebanon. The Muslim inhabitants of this area were exclusively Sunni and many, like Riḍā, claimed descent from the

13. In his recent, and acclaimed, book *Holy Terrors: Thinking About Religion After September 11*, Bruce Lincoln advocates replacing "fundamentalist" with "maximalist." While this would not address homogenization, Lincoln's interpretation is lucid, sophisticated, and deserving of serious consideration. "Maximalist" has one important advantage: unlike "fundamentalist," it does not connote a rejection of all modern ideas. Lincoln also persuasively argues for a more flexible and subtle understanding of modernity.
14. The definitive Arabic biography is Shakīb Arslān's *al-Sayyid Rashīd Riḍā aw Ikhā' Arba'īn Sanah* (Damascus: 1937). Useful sources in English include Emad Eldin Shahin's *Through Muslim Eyes: M. Rashīd Riḍā and the West* (Hendon, VA: International Institute of Islamic Thought, 1994), Zaki Badawi's *The Reformers of Egypt* (London: Croom Helm Ltd, 1978), Albert Hourani's *Arabic Thought in the Liberal Age* (London: Oxford University Press, 1962), 222–244, W. Ende's "Rashīd Riḍā," and A. Merad's "*Iṣlāḥ*" in *EI*.

Prophet Muḥammad. Juan Cole characterizes the local form of Islam as an austere Sunnism and notes its enduring influence on Riḍā.[15] The area also had a substantial Christian population. Relations between the two communities were better than in much of the Arab Middle East; in Riḍā's publications, deference to his Arab Christian neighbors was often clearly distinguished from critical appraisal of their European counterparts.

Riḍā received a typical education in the local *kuttab* and the Ottoman state school in Tripoli, where he demonstrated an early flair for Arabic. The school was directed by Shaykh Ḥusayn al-Jisr (1845–1909), an early modernist influence on Riḍā. His *al-Risālah al-Ḥamīdiyyah* is an early example of a cautious step towards Islamic modernism, arguing for the compatibility of Darwinism with the Qur'an.[16] In this environment, Riḍā was first exposed to the thinking of al-Ghazālī, whose *Iḥyā' 'Ulūm al-Dīn* (Revival of the Religious Sciences) left a distinct impression.[17] Al-Ghazālī's influence led Riḍā towards Sufism, at least in its "sober" manifestation. He joined the Naqshabandī order, and for some time was a *murīd*.[18] "Intoxicated" or antinomian Sufism was another matter; Riḍā was harshly critical of its rituals and popular practices. In *Al-Manār wa al-Azhar* (Al-Manār and al-Azhar), he describes his reaction to attending a performance of Mawlawī dervishes: "I could not control myself, and stood up in the center of the hall and shouted something like this: 'O people, or can I call you Muslims! These are forbidden acts.'"[19]

After completing his studies, Riḍā became a journalist and encountered the second decisively influential book, al-Afghānī's *al-'Urwah al-Wuthqā*. Although Riḍā had known of the journal since its first

15. J. R. I. Cole, "Rashid Rida on the Baha'i Faith: A Utilitarian Theory of the Spread of Religions," in *Arab Studies Quarterly*, 5 (1983): 290.
16. Hourani, 222–23. Riḍā cites this work in Article Fifteen (*Shubuhāt*, 72).
17. See Article Fourteen (*Shubhāt*, 62).
18. Badawi, 97.
19. Riḍā, *Al-Manār wa al-Azhar* (Cairo, 1934), 171–72. Quoted in Hourani, 225. The order takes its name from the title "Mawlānā," (Our Master), an epithet originally applied to Rūmī.

publication in 1884, he did not read it himself until 1892 (or possibly 1893). He describes his reaction:

> Every number [of the journal] was like an electric current striking me, giving my soul a shock, or setting it ablaze and carrying me from one state to another . . . no other Arabic discourse in this age or the centuries which preceded it has done what it did in the way of touching the seat of emotion in the heart and persuasion in the mind.[20]

Riḍā credited al-Afghānī's assessment of colonial policy and prescription for Islamic renewal with the profound redirection of his own thought. His greatest concern became communal well-being rather than individual salvation. He wrote to al-Afghānī stating his desire to study under him, but al-Afghānī died in 1897, before Riḍā could join him.

After being certified as an *ʿālim* (legal scholar) later that year, and inspired by al-Afghānī, Riḍā traveled to Egypt with Faraḥ Anṭūn. He joined ʿAbduh's modernist circle in Cairo while Anṭūn settled in Alexandria. Confirmed in his critical assessment of traditional Islam, Riḍā quickly became ʿAbduh's principal disciple. He founded the journal *al-Manār al-Islāmī* (The Islamic Lighthouse) to propagate the modernist agenda and expand the analysis of *al-ʿUrwah al-Wuthqā* beyond the scope of Egyptian politics. Riḍā edited it and wrote much of its content for thirty-seven years; most of his publications were first serialized in its pages. At first, it had only a very small circulation, but it grew to become hugely influential. Yusuf De Lorenzo, translator of Riḍā's *Al-Waḥy al-Muḥammadī* (The Muhammadan Revelation), describes it as "the most influential of all intellectual forums in the Muslim world."[21] Its influence extended from Morocco to Russia and even to Europe. It was especially influential in Southeast Asia; in Malaya, it fathered the journal *Al-Imam*, which contained translations of many important articles.[22]

20. Riḍā, *Ta'rīkh al-Ustādh al-Imām al-Shaykh Muḥammad ʿAbduh* (Cairo: Dār al-Manār, 1931), 303. Quoted in Hourani, 226.
21. Yusuf Talal De Lorenzo, translator, *The Muhammadan Revelation* (Alexandria, VA: al-Saadawi Publications, 1996), ix.
22. Badawi, 133.

Al-Manār viewed contemporary issues from a shari'ah perspective. This was not the overblown shari'ah of the legal schools, but a simplified version, based on the Qur'an and sunnah. The journal was strongly critical of partisanship in the law and, in Riḍā's formulation, of the elevation of the legal school to the level of the religion. Riḍā considered this tantamount to the advocacy of slothfulness in law and religion and a particularly objectionable case of uncreative imitation (*taqlīd*), something he emphasized at length in the series of fictional debates *Muḥāwarāt al-Muṣliḥ wa al-Muqallid* (Debates of the Reformer and the Traditionalist).[23] *Al-Manār* also argued against fatalism and Sufi excess and had a reputation for shunning discussions of philosophical issues (belied by Articles Fourteen and Fifteen).

Although Riḍā wrote most of the journal's content for four decades (1898–1935), he modestly claimed no originality in his ideas, professing to be merely his mentor's mouthpiece. He noted that there was little of significance in which he disagreed with his master. Hence, it is unsurprising that scholars have frequently noted their affinity and generally deem Riḍā's primary importance to lie in his continuation of 'Abduh's work, rather than in any original effort.[24]

The journal's most significant publication was the highly influential modernist Qur'an commentary, based on lectures delivered by 'Abduh at al-Azhar. It was first serialized and then published as a twelve-volume collection, *Tafsīr al-Manār*. In his introduction, Riḍā noted that it was the first commentary to combine "sound transmitted tradition" with "the plain sense of reasoned reflection."[25] It is distinguished by its pragmatism, and sets a precedent for discussing chapters as organic unities, in contrast to traditional atomistic exegesis.

At Riḍā's death, the *tafsīr* had reached chapter twelve of the Qur'an, making it approximately forty percent complete. Until recently, the work

23. The "debates" were serialized in *al-Manār* in 1901 and published as a short story in 1906. It is Riḍā's only published work of fiction. For a cogent analysis of this work, see Jakob Skovgaard-Petersen "Portrait of the Intellectual as a Young Man: Rashīd Riḍā's *Muḥāwarāṭ al-muṣliḥ wa al-muqallid*," in *Islam and Muslim–Christian Relations* 12 (2001): 93–104.

24. Badawi, 97 onwards.

25. *Tafsīr*, i, 1.

was attributed to 'Abduh but by far the greater part is Riḍā's: chapters one to four contain the commentary of both scholars, while Riḍā is solely responsible for chapters five to twelve.[26] Jane McAuliffe notes that at 'Abduh's death in 1905, only one and a half chapters were in print.[27] The first four chapters present the 'Abduh–Riḍā relationship in microcosm and clearly demonstrate that Riḍā was not only his mentor's mouthpiece. Adding his own comments immediately beneath those of 'Abduh, he shows no compunction in adding corrections where he finds it necessary. Riḍā made greater use of previous commentaries and hadith and was also more interested in questions of philology.

As well as promoting reform through writing and publishing, Riḍā was important in the development of pan-Arabism and Islamic education. He had been an early supporter of pan-Arabism through *al-Manār* and shortly before the First World War founded the pan-Arabist secret society *Jam'iyyat al-Jāmi'ah al-'Arabiyyah* (The Association of the Arab League). He traveled throughout the Middle East to promote its cause, and established relations with most rulers in the Arabian Peninsula. This complicated his relations with those of his followers who were closely connected to the Ottomans: his endeavors to improve relations between Arabs and Turks were frequently troubled. His efforts to promote Islamic education bore fruit in 1911, when he founded the Islamic university *Dār al-Da'wah wa al-Irshād* (Institute of Da'wah and Guidance) in Cairo, having earlier failed to found such an institution in Istanbul. Its curricula paid more serious attention to modern learning than those of al-Azhar, and sought to produce graduates who could defend Islam by modernist criteria.[28] The school was attended by many who later became important reformers at al-Azhar and elsewhere, but foundered after the First World War, a conflict that greatly undermined Riḍā's confidence in the West.

Riḍā is known for his critiques of other Islamic and related groups. He was harshly critical of Baha'ism. This is significant as, in Riḍā's own

26. J. J. G. Jansen refers to it as "Muhammad 'Abduh's Koran Interpretation." Jansen, *The Interpretation of the Koran in Modern Egypt* (Leiden: E. J. Brill, 1980).

27. McAuliffe, 79.

28. See *al-Manār*, xiv, 1911, 37–67; 785–800.

judgement, it was his only major point of disagreement with ʿAbduh, who felt that the young religion's success in winning converts must reflect a degree of genuine religious basis. In one respect, Riḍā considered Baha'ism more of a threat to the ummah than Christianity. Given its affinity to Islam, there was a greater danger that it would attract Muslim converts and in so doing encourage apostasy (Riḍā was not primarily concerned with Muslims converting to Christianity). Riḍā was infuriated that Baha'ism had penetrated the student body at al-Azhar, the very bastion of Sunni orthodoxy. He was inspired by al-Ghazālī's polemics against the Fatimid dynasty and considered his vigorous critique of Baha'ism to be essentially a recapitulation of that debate, although Baha'ism developed from Imāmī rather than Ismaʿili Shiʿism.[29]

Shubuhāt contains allusions to Riḍā's critical appraisal of Mahdism and Ismaʿili Shiʿism.[30] While he sometimes supported *rapprochement*, he was ultimately critical of Shiʿism, as seen in his late work *Al-Sunnah wa al-Shīʿah* (1930). In Hourani's view, here Riḍā departed from ʿAbduh, and even more from the Shiʿite al-Afghānī, questioning the viability of both Mahdism and Shiʿism as interpretations of Islam relevant to modern challenges.[31] The weakness of Islam, he felt, derived from Muslims themselves and therefore must be addressed by them (a major theme of *Shubuhāt*). Reliance on messianic figures such as the Mahdī and the hidden Imam was dangerous, as it encouraged passivity and inertia, rather than action.

Riḍā's negative assessment of Shiʿism was reinforced by his positive re-evaluation of Wahhābism after Āl Suʿūd took power in the Ḥijāz after 1924. As Ende notes, Riḍā joined those who argued that this development was historically legitimate, as in his collection of articles *al-Wahhābiyyūn wa al-Ḥijāz* (The Wahhābīs and the Hijāz, 1925–26), where he disclaimed and disavowed his earlier criticism of the Wahhābī movement. Riḍā's

29. According to Cole, this was not the only point on which Riḍā misread Baha'ism: see Cole, 287. Riḍā pays no special attention to Baha'ism in *Shubuhāt*.

30. See Article Sixteen (*Shubuhāt*, 87, 92).

31. Hourani, 230–31.

efforts included the promotion of Ḥanbalism and Ibn Taymiyyah (this shift post-dates *Shubuhāt*).

Throughout his career, Riḍā dedicated most of his resources to Islamic reform through publishing and other efforts. Consequently, he was rarely free of financial worries and he died poor and in debt. *Al-Manār* quickly foundered after his death. Riḍā's contemporary and enduring influence over Muslim intellectuals is beyond question but his ideas did not gain much of a following among common Muslims.

3

Riḍā's View of Christianity in *The Criticisms of the Christians and the Proofs of Islam*

Shubuhāt al-Naṣārā wa Ḥujaj al-Islām is not a monograph, containing a sustained argument. It is a collection of sixteen articles serialized in *al-Manār* from 1901 to 1903, published as a separate volume in 1905. Riḍā wrote the articles in response to missionary and secularist criticisms of Islam, criticisms he deemed fallacious. The specific publications he critiques include Niqūlā Ghibrīl's 1901 book *Abḥāth al-Mujtahidīn* (The Researches of the Mujtahids), the Protestant missionary magazines *Bashā'ir al-Salām* (The Glad Tidings of Peace) and *Rāyah Ṣahyūn* (The Standard of Zion), and *Al-Jāmi'ah* (1901–1904; 1906–1910), the humanist journal published by his friend, the Syrian secularist Christian Faraḥ Anṭūn.[1] As the criticisms ranged widely, so did Riḍā's responses.

1. Riḍā wrote numerous articles for *al-Manār* on religious mission (for example, ii, 1899, 140–43; iii, 1900, 457–63, 481–90; xxvii, 1914, 147–47). Many stressed the need for Muslims to resist the Christian mission in areas such as Egypt (xvi, 1913, 878–79; xxxiii, 1933, 231–37), the Sudan (xiv, 1911, 311–13), Arabia (xxviii, 140–44), Syria (xxii, 1909, 16–26, 637–40; xiii, 1910, 441–44 and numerous other articles), Cyprus (ix, 1906, 233–34), Russia (xiii, 1910, 853–56), Iraq (xxiv, 1911, 914–22), and other parts of the Middle East. He also wrote many articles critical of secularism or imitative Westernism, for example xvii, 1914, 156–60; xx, 1918, 34–45. See also the series "The Attack upon the Muslim World (*Al-Ghārah 'alā*

Prominent among the criticisms were: Islam is inherently inferior to Christianity; Islam is an irrational religion; the Qur'an is inconsistent and inharmonious; Muḥammad is inferior to Moses and Jesus; Muslims do not adhere to the requirements of their own scriptures, notably the requirement to believe in the veracity of the Bible; European technological superiority is based on the superiority of Christian civilization; and the Islamic union of religious and political authority is an anachronistic barrier to progress.

Riḍā characterizes his opponents' arguments as *shubuhāt*, and he rebuts them with *ḥujaj* of Islam; both terms were carefully chosen. *Shubuhāt* (sing. *shubhah*) are, literally, "resemblances." The word derives from the trilateral SH-B-H, the verbal forms of which mean "to resemble" or, the sense that applies here, "to make (something) resemble (something else)." In law, *shubuhāt* are illegal acts that have been modified to resemble legal ones. In theology and philosophy, *shubuhāt* are invalid arguments contrived to resemble valid arguments. A common rhetorical technique in Muslim scholarly discourse is to juxtapose an author's arguments against an opponent's *shubuhāt*, and thereby demonstrating the superiority of the former. *Ḥujaj* is the plural form of *ḥujjah*, a Qur'anic term meaning "proof." This includes both the demonstration of what is true and (the sense that applies here) the refutation of what is false. *Ḥujjah* differs slightly in meaning from *burhān* (evidentiary argument) and *dalīl* (indication). Whereas *burhān* and *dalīl* connote "evidence" and "indication" of what is certain, *ḥujjah* connotes also the further sense of a *contrary* argument, one that leaves an opponent without a response, "dialectical proof" therefore being the most technically correct translation. I shall shorten this to "proof".[2]

al-'Ālam al-Islāmī)" *Al-Manār*, xv, 1912. It reproduces in Arabic translation materials from a French magazine on Christian mission to the Middle East during the early years of the twentieth century. Sources include the writings of Samuel Zwemer, and reports from missionary conferences held in Cairo (1906), Lucknow (1911), and Edinburgh (1912).

2. On *shubhah* and *ḥujjah* in Islamic discourse, see E.K. Rowson's "Shubha" and L. Gardet's "Ḥudjdja" in *EI*.

While Riḍā's title, *Shubuhāt al-Naṣārā wa Ḥujaj al-Islām*, is translatable as *The Criticisms of the Christians and the Proofs of Islam*, we should note that these are criticisms of a particular type: fallacies or willful deceptions. Riḍā felt his Christian opponents had deliberately and often hypocritically contrived their arguments to mislead uneducated Muslims, the "common folk who do not investigate carefully" (Article Five, 20). His opponents understood only too well that uneducated Muslims, and even the traditionalist ulama (Preface, *jīm*), unlike Riḍā, lacked the means to distinguish a valid argument from an invalid one. This was especially so when the invalid argument had been "made to resemble" the valid. Such fallacies instilled "doubts" in Muslim minds, ("doubts" connoting another sense of the multivalent *Shubuhāt*) and these needed eliminatng. To achieve the twin goals of debunking *Shubuhāt* (Christian fallacies concerning Islam) and eliminating *Shubuhāt* (Muslim doubts concerning Islam), Riḍā follows Kayrānawī's example in juxtaposing his opponents' claims with *ḥujaj*, clear proofs or "that which cannot be repelled" (Article One, 1).

Riḍā's title holds a further point. In the original *Al-Manār*, series Riḍā had opposed Christian Criticisms with "the proofs of Islam" (Articles Three – Six) and "the proofs of the Muslims" (Articles Seven – Eleven, Fourteen).[3] On the 1905 collected edition, he notes: "We named it *The Criticisms of the Christians and the Proofs of Islam*, signifying that the Christian religion itself does not criticize the Islamic religion, rather the Christians themselves criticize it, and that the right proofs against them are not those of those Muslims who have become a proof against their religion, but rather those of the religion of Islam itself" (Preface, *dāl*). Riḍā's explanation reflects his view that the ideal forms of Christianity and Islam are not opposed, an "innate" or "ultimate" religion underlying both. But ultimate religion is not represented by the agents of Christian mission or by traditionalist Muslims, who through intellectual stagnation and political passivity had effectively become an argument or proof against Islam.

3. *Al-Manār*, iv, 411-417; 448-453; 536-539; 574-578; 619-627; 654-659; 743-749; 816-820; v, 98-101; 759-770.

"Calling to the Good": Islamic Da'wah and the Religion of the Other

In light of the Qur'anic ambivalence towards Christians, it is notable that Riḍā introduces *Shubuhāt* with a Qur'anic injunction that enjoins Muslims to engage Christians positively:

> Call unto the way of thy Lord with wisdom and fair exhortation, and reason with them in the better way . . . (16:125); And argue not with the People of the Scripture unless it be in (a way) that is better, save with such of them as do wrong; and say: We believe in that which hath been revealed unto us and revealed unto you; our God and your God is One, and unto Him we surrender (29:46)
>
> Preface, *bā'*

Riḍā comments: "Verily, the lifeblood of religions is da'wah, and the power of truth is in truth itself, while the persistence of untruth occurs when the truth is neglectful of it" (Preface, *bā'*). The selection of verses and commentary places da'wah prominently while linking it with a positive conception of Muslim–Christian relations. In classical Islam, da'wah was a foundational concept, meaning "call" or "invitation," linked to notions of the "abode of Islam" and its expansion into the "abode of war." As the religious community grew and expanded, da'wah operated both externally and internally: non-Muslims coming under Muslim rule were "called" to accept Islam, while Muslims were "called" to renewed commitment. However, the primary impetus for da'wah was external. As the classical expansionist world-view became untenable when most of the Muslim world fell under colonial rule, the concept of da'wah fell into neglect. Riḍā played a role in its rehabilitation by reversing the classical world-view and emphasizing internal da'wah over external.[4] That is, he deploys da'wah centripetally and understands it as primarily an intra-Muslim affair. While on occasion in *Shubuhāt* Riḍā alludes to the

4. On Riḍā's rehabilitation of Islamic da'wah in general, see Ary A. Roest Crollius, "Mission and Morality: *Al-amr bi-l-ma'rūf* as expression of the communitarian and missionary dimensions of qur'ānic ethics," in *Studia Missionalia* 27 (1978): 257–283 (especially 277–82), and Kerr, 150–171.

desirability of Christian conversion to Islam, it is clear that in this book his priority is the call for Muslim "conversion" to Islam.[5]

Riḍā's discussion continues:

> Truth is concealed when its people abandon it . . . but it was not long before its people forsook it, its party split into factions, the greedy strove against them, and the liars themselves dared to attack Islam. Thus did paganism assail divine oneness, blind imitation (*taqlīd*) exceed rational proof, and the worshipers of the son of man argue against the worship of the Merciful.
>
> (Preface, *bā'*)

In Riḍā's view, after the age of the first generations – known as "the pious ancestors" – Muslims abandoned true Islam and weakened their community.[6] This enabled Europeans to subjugate Muslim peoples and disperse missionaries throughout their lands (Preface, *jīm*). Riḍā's discussion sets up parallels between divine unity, rationalism, and true worship on the one hand and paganism, imitation, and Christian worship on the other. This links an analysis of contemporary Islam with comment on Christian mission. In limiting scholarship to imitation – uncreative recycling of an unchanging body of material – the ulama have left the community vulnerable to "pagan" Christian propaganda: Muslims lack the skills of rhetoric and debate. Riḍā considers this but one specific instance of a wider Muslim failure to engage modernity.

This traditionalist mentality, Riḍā argues, has obscured Islam's rational character. Consequently, Muslims living under European rule at the turn of the twentieth century lacked the wherewithal to engage missionary and secularist critics in debate and discourse. What, Riḍā asks rhetorically, does the feeble traditionalist (*muqallid*) do when he is presented with missionary propaganda and told, "these are teachings of your school's ulama"? The shaykh is thrown into shock and disarray, unable to

5. Riḍā considered Western conversions to Islam to be significant. See for example *al-Manār*, xxiii, 1922, 268, xxvi, 1925, 60–64; xxviii, 1927, 705–09; xxix, 1928, 153–54.

6. Riḍā does not provide a chronology for the age of "the pious ancestors".

distinguish the two (Preface, *jīm*). Clearly, common Muslims could not look to such leaders for guidance. Lost in a web of juristic works, written in highly technical and difficult Arabic, the ulama have allowed the science of logical proof to fall into neglect. Following 'Abduh, Riḍā does not waver from the theme of conflict between imitation (*taqlīd*) on the one hand and independent reasoning and logical demonstration (*burhān*) on the other. Islamic da'wah entails Muslim "conversion" from the religion of imitation to the religion of independent reasoning and logical demonstration, which Riḍā deems the foundation of both Islam and Western modernity. To this end, he directs his readers towards 'Abduh and al-Ghazālī, not the contemporary traditionalist ulama (Articles Fourteen and Fifteen).

Missionary Criticisms

Drawing an explicit connection between evangelism and imperialism, Riḍā argues that missionaries were fully conscious of traditionalist stagnation and the Muslim abandonment of the Qur'an. He notes that they capitalized on the opportunity this presented to mislead ordinary Muslims about their own religion: "they hit them where they were most vulnerable" (Preface, *jīm*). The chronology of these missionary attacks or criticisms is important. Jane Smith has shown that, during the late nineteenth and early twentieth centuries, missionary portrayals of Islam generally emphasized its putative defects – particularly with regard to the Qur'an and the personality of Muḥammad – and contrasted it with Christianity. In the 1930s came a shift from hostility towards deference, and from contrasting towards comparing the two religions. Missionaries such as Samuel Zwemer began to show an appreciation for the good qualities of Muslims and their affinity with Christians as fellow seekers of God.[7]

It is clear that this turn postdates the period I am examining. In Riḍā's view, little deference is evident in missionary publications and other missionary activities. He repeatedly refers to their excessive zeal and open

7. Jane Smith, "Christian Missionary Views of Islam in the 19th and 20th Centuries," *Islam and Muslim–Christian Religions* 9 (1998): 361.

enmity to Islam. Not content with spitting out "their hostile poison" in religious publications, they even attacked Islam in academic and political journals and newspapers. He also refers to missionaries "making gatherings" to spread their slanders against Islam verbally (Article One, 1). Among the publications Riḍā criticizes in *Shubuhāt*, enmity towards Islam is perhaps most apparent in the magazine *The Glad Tidings of Peace* (Articles Seven, Eleven and Twelve). The claims made in this and other publications reflect the general missionary thesis that Islam is an inherently inferior and irrational religion. Specific criticisms include: the Qur'an is inconsistent and inharmonious, Muḥammad is inferior to Moses (and the Israelites generally), Ismā'īl is inferior to Isaac, and Muslims do not adhere to the requirements of their own scriptures (namely, that they should believe in the Bible).

Riḍā did not see the missionary goal as Muslim conversion to Christianity, nor did he fear this from their efforts. Rather, he felt that calls for conversion were insincere and obscured the real agenda, which was not to turn Muslims to another religion, but away from religion in general. Recalling al-Afghānī's comments about the Dahrī school in India (Article Fourteen, 60–61), Riḍā comments:

> I do not fear from the missionaries that the Muslim will become a Christian. Rather, I fear that he will [be led to] doubt the fundamental essence of religion and become a libertine. Yet, however much the winds of paganism sway him, he would not ascribe divinity to other than God, as do the Christians.
>
> (Preface, *jīm*)

Riḍā felt that the missionaries' efforts might be counter-productive. The degree of their hostility was such that their attacks might be a blessing in disguise, awakening the sleeping Muslims from their slumber. Riḍā comments (to paraphrase): "And perhaps the missionary who awakens the Muslims undermines his own cause through that which they to turn to their own advantage, since he induces them to return to the Qur'an and hold fast to its strong rope" (Preface, *jīm*). Hence, he embraces this opportunity, urging the Muslim public not to consider missionary attacks among the evils of a free press but rather one of its greatest benefits. Provoked by missionaries to re-examine their own religion and carefully guided by Riḍā and other like-minded individuals, Muslims will return to the long-neglected fundamentals of Islam (Article Twelve, 54).

Responding to Criticisms: Dialogue or Polemics?

What posture does Riḍā adopt in guiding his readers through the terrain of missionary criticism and Islamic rebuttal? Do these articles represent cautious steps towards Muslim–Christian dialogue, laying the ground for the more explicitly dialogical approaches of Faruqi and Ayoub or, in contrast to Aḥmad Khān, does Riḍā represent a reversion to unqualified polemics?[8] In which case, Riḍā is rather the predecessor of Muḥammad Abū Zahrah, Aḥmad Shalabī, and Sayyid Quṭb.

These questions do not have clear and unambiguous answers. Riḍā's attitude towards the project he undertakes in *Shubuhāt* is ambivalent and his tone inconsistent. His comments about the blessings of a free press suggest a certain enthusiasm for taking on his opponents. As for his tone, the reader will quickly observe that the articles are not free of traditional anti-Christian polemics. In much of Article Two, Riḍā simply dismisses Christianity and makes little attempt seriously to understand or engage Christian interpretations of Christian scripture. He deems the religion utterly incompatible with the development of culture and civil society; its ethics, if implemented, would bring about its ruin and condemn humankind to "an animal-like existence" (Article Two, 7).

Although the polemical element is quantitatively predominant, Riḍā's effort to adopt a dialogical posture is also clear. He disclaims his critique on numerous occasions, and in his introduction suggests that it is material he would have preferred not to print, at one point implying that his initial reaction to his opponents' claims was amusement (Preface, *dāl*). He stresses that he did not initiate the debate (Article Fourteen, 60), but that his involvement is mandated by Islamic law: if a Muslim sees another

8. On the link between Riḍā and Faruqi, see Kerr.

Muslim doubting his own religion, he must, if capable, strive to eliminate the doubt. Riḍā indicates that he came to the project reluctantly, commenting that for some time he bore missionary hostility with patience and only responded in writing when urged to do so by "the questioners among the people of our own religion" (Article One, 1). When materials sent to the offices of *al-Manār* by missionaries were supplemented by letters from Muslim readers apparently influenced by them, Riḍā felt compelled to act. The Muslim understanding of Islam is his greatest concern.

Riḍā imposed conditions upon himself, including defending Islam without attacking Christianity, and going no further than addressing Muslim readers' questions. He comments that, in light of these limitations, responding to his opponents "measure for measure" is impossible (Article Two, 5). He stresses that the articles are one aspect of a wider drive to eliminate resentment between the two communities and spread a message of harmony, agreement, and concord (Articles One, Two, Ten). He also expresses the desire that Muslims and Christians should reach a consensus as to the best way for the country to progress and refers to face-to-face meetings with his opponents (Article Two, 5). Finally, he expresses his desire that each religion be upheld through the manifestation of its good qualities and not by attacking the other's defects: "We desire that no one slanders the religion of the other, neither through speech nor writing" (Article One, 1). It seems likely that Riḍā's upbringing in a region where Muslim–Christian relations were generally better than in much of the Arab world influenced his approach.

Riḍā's success in adhering to his self-imposed conditions was mixed, and we must note both the polemical and dialogical elements in the articles. So far as polemics are concerned, Riḍā's tone should be set against that of his opponents, and the general context of imperial and missionary hostility towards Islam.[9]

9. See Ayoub, "Muslim Views of Christianity: Some Modern Examples," *Islamochristiana* 10 (1984): 55.

The Religion of Innate Disposition (*dīn al-fiṭrah*)

An important aspect of Riḍā's dialogical understanding of religion is his universalism. This is seen in his emphasis on the common basis of the three monotheistic religions and, in fact, religions generally. It is expressed in several formulations, of which "the religion of innate disposition" (*dīn al-fiṭrah*) and "ultimate religion" (*al-dīn al-muṭlaq*) are especially important.[10] *Fiṭrah* refers to a disposition with which God has endowed his creatures, Muslim and non-Muslim, human and non-human. Its cognates occur some eighteen times in the Qur'an, usually verbally. However, its Qur'anic meaning is not completely clear, and remained obscure to the Prophet's Companions.[11] In Islamic discourse, the term is also associated with two others of particular relevance: *'aql* and *ḥanīf*. *'Aql* means reason or intellect. In connection with *fiṭrah*, it refers to a natural intelligence that, so long as it is uncorrupted by unrestrained desire, should be pursued and developed with certitude. Ibn Rushd refers to this as "a keen sense of the truth" (*dhakā' al-fiṭrah*) and asserts that the prevention of its use is forbidden, so long as it is accompanied by the necessary legal and ethical requisites.[12] *Hanīf* refers to the generic sense of submission to divine oneness and is often mentioned in connection with Islam's Abrahamic foundation, Abraham being upheld as a pre-Muhammadan paradigm of pure submission. This is the sense in which Riḍā uses it when advocating the religion of "the community of pure submission" (Article Fifteen, 75).

In his *tafsīr*, Riḍā outlines his teaching on *fiṭrah* in *al-Islām dīn al-fiṭrah al-salīmah wa al-'aql wa al-fikr wa al-ḥikmah wa al-burhān wa al-ḥujjah* (Islam is the religion of pure innate disposition, thought, wisdom, rational demonstration and proof), which discusses the relationship of reason and *fiṭrah*. Drawing on the notion of *dīn al-fiṭrah*, he avers that Muslims have

10. Riḍā refers to "innate disposition" and "ultimate religion" on several occasions in *Shubuhāt*. On the former, see Article Two, 5; Article 4, 19; Article Seven, 32; and Article Sixteen, 88. On the latter, see Article Two, 10; Article Ten, 47; Article Fourteen, 60; and Article Fifteen, 77.
11. D. B. MacDonald, "Fiṭra" in *EI*.
12. R. Arnaldez, "Ibn Rushd" in *EI*.

become an example against their own religion, and calls for uniting or finding common ground between Islam and Christianity. In a conversation with Niqūlā Ghibrīl, one of his opponents, he comments that the difference between Muslims and Islam is equal to or greater than that between Christians and Christianity (Article Two, 9). The difference is between *dīn al-fiṭrah*, or true Islam, and the empty shell to which it has been reduced by the mentality of imitation (*taqlīd*). Similarly, Christianity does not challenge Islam, as the religion of innate disposition underlies both. Riḍā's interpretation implicitly employs the notion of *islam* – as opposed to *Islam* – or generic submission to divine oneness. He notes that he writes in the service of ultimate religion, so that not only Islam, but Judaism and Christianity – ideally conceived – may also be truly known: "for if the religion of innate disposition (*fiṭrah*) is not established, no religion may be established" (Article Two, 5–6).

Riḍā's universalism is rational rather than Sufistic or emanationist, an approach that has more in common with Aḥmad Khān than Rūmī. Riḍā, however, was more successful in reconciling his rationalism with Islamic orthodoxy than Khān. His argument also recalls the Qur'anic notion of an "ideal Christianity." Commenting on 'Abduh's *Theology of Unity*, he instructs: "let no one imagine that Muslims believe that in Christ's religion itself there is something that, in its essence, is harmful" and goes on to say "Muslims believe in the true nature of the Christian religion" (Article Fifteen, 82, 85). This raises interesting questions: is there any difference between ideal or true Christianity and ideal Islam? That is, is *dīn al-fiṭrah* unitary or manifold? May generic submission, *islam*, be manifested in a variety of forms in diverse historical and geographical contexts? Or is "ideal Christianity" merely a veneer for Islam, repackaged for Christian consumption? Riḍā is not fully consistent and leaves these questions open.

Christian Scripture and Doctrine

In discussing the Torah, consistently with Islamic teaching and Kayrānawī's *Iẓhār al-Ḥaqq* (Demonstration of the Truth), Riḍā affirms that the Bible suffered textual corruption (*taḥrīf*), a point he found confirmed by insights derived from Biblical criticism. He presents his critique in terms of contractions between the text and facts known by way of modern science ("the snake does not eat earth," Article One, 2–3). In addition, he highlights logical incompatibilities in his opponents' arguments. There are three main issues that Riḍā addresses: the question of the Torah's authenticity, particularly in light of the Qur'anic corroboration of it, the claim that this confirmation mandates Muslim faith in the Torah, and the Christian stance towards the Torah.

On corroboration, Riḍā asserts that the Qur'anic Torah is *precept*. That is, it consists of certain unspecified rulings attributed to Moses and established by those who succeeded him. The Qur'an does not support the Jewish or Christian identification of the Torah with the Pentateuch or entire Hebrew Bible. Clearly, that Torah testifies to its own falsity through internal inconsistency, attribution of unbefitting qualities to God, and inclusion of statements disproved by logical analysis and experience, and archeology, geology, history and other sciences. Riḍā is fairly explicit as to where the true Torah may be found:

> Yes, we favor our understanding that all or most of the rulings attributed to Moses in the books of Exodus, Numbers, Deuteronomy and Leviticus are from Torah, because if they are not, then where is it?
>
> (Article One, 4)

> The Qur'anic Torah consists of the precepts that Moses brought, peace be upon him, and they are – that is, some of them are – in the five books attributed to Moses, except the book of Genesis, which include his history and mention his death.
>
> (Article Four, 16)

Genesis, Isaiah, Ezekiel, Daniel and "the numerous historical books" are unambiguously rejected, as they are not corroborated by the Qur'an, in Riḍā's view. While, Genesis apart, he makes a point of distinguishing the five books of Moses on more than one occasion, he does not simply identify them with the Torah or deem them fully sound. For example, he makes highly critical readings of passages in Exodus and Deuteronomy, which he contrasts with equivalent Qur'anic passages to emphasize its theological superiority. He asks, rhetorically: how may the two even be compared (Article Three, 14)?[13] Overall, a reasonably clear picture of the Torah emerges in the articles. In its present form, Riḍā deems the Torah neither fully corrupt nor fully sound, but beyond distinguishing Exodus, Leviticus, Numbers and Deuteronomy, makes no effort towards a more precise determination. In his view, no criteria exist for making one. Riḍā compares the Torah with biographical sources on Muḥammad such as *Sīrat al-Ḥalabiyyah*, which contain a mixture of divine revelation and historical accretion. In the case of the Torah, the revealed and the historical cannot be distinguished.

In a second line of argument, Riḍā emphasizes what he deems to be the logical incongruity of his opponents' case that the Qur'anic corroboration of the Torah mandates Muslim faith in it. This is the thesis advanced by Ghibrīl in *Researches of the Mujtahids*, a book Riḍā critiques in detail in Articles Five, Six, Eight and Nine. Ghibrīl's claim was not new. Amongst others, the German missionary Karl Gottlieb Pfander (died 1865), drew the same conclusion in *Mizān al-Ḥaqq* (The Balance of Truth, 1829) and his famous debate with Kayrānawī in Agra in 1854, a debate he was judged to have lost. Riḍā retorts that Ghibrīl is arguing from a source in which he does not believe, a technique he deems illegitimate. Taken to its logical conclusion, Ghibrīl's proposition results in the invalidation of both scriptures – if, as Ghibrīl believes, the Qur'an is invalid, then the Torah is likewise invalid, as it is corroborated by the Qur'an – and therefore does nothing to advance interreligious dialogue and understanding. On this point, Riḍā articulates his thesis with care and clarity (in Article Three, he advances the apologetic proposition that Christians should embrace the Qur'an and deny Christ's divinity). He also analyzes Ghibrīl's highly selective use of Qur'anic quotation, drawing attention to questionable interpretations, if not actual errors. Articles Five, Six, and Eight give a thoughtful defense of the Muslim position.

Third, Riḍā addresses the Christian attitude towards the Torah, arguing that, due to the efforts of Saint Paul, Christians have relinquished the Torah altogether. Thus, the missionary demand for Muslims to embrace it

13. The passages in question are Ex 20:16, Deut 4:30 and Deut 14:26.

is doubly hypocritical (Article Three, 16; Article Five, 21). Riḍā critiques a Protestant understanding of the relationship between law and grace; unsurprising, given the general context of Protestant mission (Riḍā identifies *The Glad Tidings of Peace* and *The Standard of Zion* as Protestant).

Generally, Riḍā's verdict on the gospel parallels his verdict on the Torah. Just as the latter consists of precepts attributed to Moses, the former consists of "warnings, wisdom, and precepts that God Almighty revealed to Christ . . . and with which he exhorted and taught the people" (Article One, 3). However, certain of these original warnings and precepts have been lost, while the remainder has been supplemented with historical and other materials. As with the Torah, Riḍā asserts that no criteria exist for distinguishing the one from the other. Following Kayrānawī, he asserts that the gospels lack the requisite uninterrupted "chains of transmission" (*asānīd*) that would make them trustworthy. For this reason, Muslims should follow the prophetic hadith and neither adopt an attitude of belief nor disbelief towards them.[14] There is only one instance where Riḍā offers any specific comment as to where sound material might be found in the gospels when, immediately following his statement indicating preference for Exodus, Leviticus, Numbers and Deuteronomy, he indicates similar preference for the Sermon in the Mount as reported in Matthew's gospel. He also approvingly cites an opinion that a major part of the "true gospel" became incorporated into the book of Isaiah (Article One, 4).

Riḍā's comments may be taken together with his discussions of the same in other publications. In his *tafsīr*, on one occasion, he feels impelled to qualify and amend 'Abduh's skepticism about the Muslim claim that Christians deleted gospel passages describing the coming of Muḥammad.[15] An interesting and provocative piece is his short introduction to the Arabic translation of the Gospel of Barnabas, which he commissioned and published in 1908 under the title *The True Gospel* (*al-injīl al-ṣaḥīḥ*). After a brief summary of the process whereby the four canonical

14. Bukhārī, *Tawḥīd*, 51, *I'tiṣām*, 25.

15. *Tafsīr*, ii, 49.

gospels were selected, he advances the case for Barnabas, which, however, is unquestionably a forgery dating from the sixteenth century. It presents an entirely Muslim Jesus, who brings news of "the one to follow him who will perfect God's religion."[16]

In a work entitled *'Aqīdat al-Ṣalb wa al-Fidā'* (The Doctrine of Crucifixion and Redemption), Riḍā presents "evidence for lack of confidence in the gospels." Drawing on Kayrānawī, he comments that the gospels and Paul's letters lack the requisite conditions for their characterization as *tawātur* (something in which one may have complete confidence). He raises questions about the gospels' and letters' veracity on a variety of grounds, and also notes variations between differing translations identified as "Protestant," "ancient" and "Jesuit" (he cites three different renderings of a single verb in Gal 1:7). He provides a lengthy critique of the doctrine of crucifixion, which upholds the orthodox Islamic denial, which includes a discussion of "mutual contradictions" between accounts of the crucifixion found in the canonical gospels.[17]

Riḍā criticizes what he understands to be the teaching of the canonical gospels (Articles Two and Three). His interpretation is rather superficial and undeveloped, standing in sharp contrast to his detailed analysis of the science of Islamic exegesis. In broad terms, he regards gospel teaching as excessive, exaggerated, destructive of social and civil development and generally impractical. This is seen in his comments on the injunction to "pray for those who persecute you" (Mt 5:44) and "offer the left cheek" (Article Three, 14 – he paraphrases Mt 5:39); to Riḍā, such teachings lower and debase human dignity, in contrast to the Qur'anic message of moderation and elevation. Riḍā is equally dismissive of excessive hatred, as seen in the requirement that one "hate his father and mother" (Lk 14:26). He finds the notion that one should not worry about livelihood, food or drink (Mt 6:25) (Article Three, 14–15) simply incomprehensible. This notion might make for an interesting comparison with al-Ghazālī's teaching on trust in God (*tawakkul*), although Riḍā does not explore the connection (Article Fourteen).

16. Riḍā, ed., *Injīl Barnābā* (Cairo: Maṭba'at al-Manār, 1908), *qāf*.
17. Riḍā, *'Aqīdat al-Ṣalb wa al-Fidā'* (Cairo: Maṭba'at al-Manār, 1934), 33–47.

Perhaps the most detailed discussion Riḍā gives on the gospels in *Shubuhāt* is his critique of Ghibrīl's claims about the "Qur'anic gospel" (Articles Five, Six and Eight). He largely follows his opponent in treating the Torah and gospel together. As with his treatment of the "Qur'anic Torah," he generally offers a strong defense of the Muslim reading of the Muslim scripture. His discussion of Qur'an 5:47 and 5:46, for example, is highly detailed and includes an analysis of two variant readings of the passage, neither of which would appear to offer any support to Ghibrīl's claim that Muḥammad submitted to the Gospel's precepts (Article Five, 22–23). Riḍā also draws his readers' attention to historically dubious claims made by his opponent, such as that of the pre-Islamic Meccans being well-versed in the Torah and Gospel (Article Six, 25). Finally, Riḍā's critique of Ghibrīl's partial and selective, if not outright dishonest, quotation of the Qur'anic references to the Gospel is sober and lucid, such as Ghibrīl's reading of Qur'an 28:49 and Riḍā's critique of it (Article Six, 25).

Riḍā does not discuss the doctrine of Trinity in great detail. His fullest explanation is offered in his criticism of the missionary magazine *The Glad Tidings of Peace.* He comments that the doctrine entails accepting:

> That God is composed of three fundamentals (*uṣūl*), each identical to the other two, so that the three are one. That one of the three, the son, became incarnate in a human body by means of another, the holy spirit. Thus, this human being became God, the son of God, a human being, and the son of a human being who became God.
>
> (Article Twelve, 52)

The accuracy of Riḍā's language (or the extent to which it accurately reflects Christian doctrine) might be questioned: the description could be read as a summary of Tritheism rather than Trinity. That said, Riḍā finds the summarized doctrine self-evidently irrational, and would appear to deem further elaboration unnecessary. He makes clear on several occasions that, from the Islamic perspective, full understanding of all doctrine (such as that of the afterlife) is neither mandatory nor possible: "Our statement that the religion of Islam is rational does not mean that all of its issues may be comprehended by way of independent reason" (Article Fifteen, 77).

However, belief in an idea that is not fully understood differs from belief in an idea such as Trinity, which is clearly irrational or logically inconsistent. For Muslims, faith in the latter is impossible. Hence, accepting such a proposition as "three is one" would "banish the independence of thought" and "extinguish the light of the mind" (Articles Two and Three). In Riḍā's view, this doctrine is upheld entirely on the basis of unquestioned acquiescence to the teachings of church leaders. No reference is made to Christian attempts to explain it in rationally acceptable terms.

Riḍā also rejects the doctrine of the Incarnation for its irrationality. The Christian position is doubly ironic, as it denies Muḥammad's prophecy, which has been established by "the strongest rational proofs" (Article Three, 12). Riḍā goes on to deem incarnationism a form of paganism and note its lack of originality. He quotes a lengthy passage from 'Alī Pāshā Mubārak's *The Standard of Religion*, which includes the views of a French philosopher who comments:

> They were not the first to speak of incarnation. Rather, it was said earlier of Jazākā and Brahma, in India's holy city, and it was said that Vishnu became incarnate five hundred times. The inhabitants of Peru in America said that that the true God became incarnate in their god Ūdīn. The birth of Jesus from the Virgin Mary through the triumph of the Holy Spirit resembles the statement of the people of China that their god Fuwah was born of a virgin girl who was impregnated with him by the rays of the sun.
>
> (Article Four, 18)

In its original form, like the religions of India and China, Christianity was monotheistic. Thereafter, Christians, Hindus and Chinese mingled pure faith with "inherited pagan customs," worshiping Christ, his mother and other humans (Article Eight, 35). Riḍā also repeats the traditional Islamic view of the inconceivability of God suffering the humiliation of being cursed, tormented and crucified for the salvation of mankind from the un-Islamic doctrine of original sin (Articles Eleven and Twelve). Finally, Riḍā addresses the related issue of anthropomorphism in the Qur'an. As this involves his theory of language, I shall examine this in Chapter Four.

To summarize, Riḍā's interpretation of Christianity is ambivalent. Notwithstanding his more positive evaluation of the Pentateuch (excluding Genesis), he follows his classical and modern predecessors in deeming the Bible inauthentic and Christian doctrine invalid. Yet we have also seen his effort towards Christian–Muslim *rapprochement*. His reworking of Islamic da'wah is probably his most significant contribution. Since Riḍā's time, most influential Muslim thinkers have staunchly upheld the traditional supersessionist rejection of religious pluralism in general, and Christianity in particular, as seen in the works of Sayyid Quṭb, Muḥammad Abū Zahrah, and others.

4

Rashīd Riḍā and the Origins of Islamic Fundamentalism

Islamic fundamentalism may appear a surprising theme to discuss in this study. First, fundamentalism is generally depicted as post-dating Riḍā. The 1967 Six-Day War is frequently cited as the watershed, precipitating the 1970s turn to fundamentalism which culminated in the Iranian revolution.[1] Fundamentalism is sometimes traced earlier, to the rise of the Muslim Brotherhood in the 1930s. According to this view, the 1930s and 1970s mark two "waves" of fundamentalist activism, the first wave losing its momentum with the rise of nationalism in the struggle for political independence throughout the Muslim world. Riḍā died in 1935 so his career mainly precedes both these developments. Second, fundamentalism is defined as a rejection of modernity. Yet Riḍā, as we have seen, was intimately connected with 'Abduh, a paradigmatic Islamic modernist. Third, fundamentalism is understood to operate at the level of mass movements, whereas Riḍā was very much an intellectual, outside a formal organization.

1. Marty, 157. John Voll, "Fundamentalism in the Sunni Arab World: Egypt and the Sudan," in *Fundamentalisms Observed*, eds Martin E. Marty and R. Scott Appleby (Chicago: University of Chicago Press, 1991), 376. On the relevance of the Six-Day War to the emergence of Jewish fundamentalism, see Marty, 177.

Against this background, the characterization of Rashīd Riḍā as an Islamic fundamentalist might appear strange, if not oxymoronic. Yet several scholars, including scholars of note such as John Voll and Johannes Jansen, identify Riḍā not only as a fundamentalist, but a significant one. Riḍā's importance is also noted by Gabriel Almond, R. Scott Appleby, and Emmanuel Sivan in *Strong Religion: The Rise of Fundamentalisms around the World.* This important recent work summarizes and updates the theses advanced in the groundbreaking five-volume *Fundamentalism Project* (1991–95). *Strong Religion* traces fundamentalism's genealogy from Riḍā through Mawdūdī to Quṭb.[2]

Here, a qualification must be added. A significant shift occurred in Riḍā's thought after the First World War. This became particularly pronounced after 1924–26, during which Āl Su'ūd established a larger Wahhābī kingdom in much of Arabia. As noted above, this development inspired Riḍā to became a spokesman for Wahhābism, Ḥanbalism and the school of Ibn Taymiyyah, all of which, predating modernity, are often considered examples of "proto-fundamentalism," rather than fundamentalism proper. Significantly, Ibn Taymiyyah, Ibn 'Abd al-Wahhāb and Aḥmad ibn Ḥanbal are never mentioned in *Shubuhāt.*[3] This stands in contrast to the careful attention Riḍā pays to al-Ghazālī.

The tension between Riḍā's early association with modernism and late association with fundamentalism might be eliminated simply by dividing his career into two halves: before and after 1918, or before and after 1924. Yet the scholars who identify Riḍā as a fundamentalist make no such division: Riḍā's fundamentalism is traced to 1905 and earlier. Jansen emphasizes Riḍā's rediscovery and rehabilitation of Ibn Taymiyyah – Riḍā began to re-edit his works in 1925 – yet deems al-Afghānī, 'Abduh and Riḍā the "founding fathers" of Islamic fundamentalism, and notes the critical role played by Riḍā from 1897

2. Gabriel A. Almond, R. Scott Appleby, and Emmanuel Sivan, *Strong Religion: The Rise of Fundamentalisms Around the World,* (Chicago: University of Chicago Press, 2003), 24–25.
3. Among the founders of the legal schools, only Abū Ḥanīfah is mentioned. Article Sixteen (*Shubuhāt,* 99).

onwards.[4] Similarly, in Volume One of the *Fundamentalism Project*, Voll identifies Riḍā as perhaps the first thinker to develop fundamentalist ideas. This comment is immediately followed by a sub-heading entitled: "The Beginnings of Modern Fundamentalism: 1905–1928."[5] Voll explains the reasoning behind his selection of the two dates: 1905 marks the year of 'Abduh's death and Riḍā's assumption of the leadership of the *Salafī* movement and 1928 marks al-Bannā"s foundation of the Muslim Brotherhood, a paradigmatic fundamentalist movement for Voll and other scholars of his persuasion.[6] Hence, Voll revises the view that fundamentalism begins with al-Bannā', tracing it instead to Riḍā. By coincidence, *Shubuhāt* was published in 1905. Therefore, it would presumably be a good place to seek evidence of fundamentalist leanings. This assumption is strengthened by the fact that Voll, Jansen, and others do not limit Riḍā's putative fundamentalism to his support of Ḥanbalism, Ibn Taymiyyah and Wahhābism, but is in fact discussed in terms of the very issues Riḍā addresses in *Shubuhāt*.

It is important to note that fundamentalism is a controversial issue in contemporary religious studies, particularly in connection with Islam. Most scholars find that the term provides a useful model or framework within which to conduct analysis. Prominent proponents of its use include Martin E. Marty, R. Scott Appleby, Emmanuel Sivan, and Bruce Lawrence. On the other hand, a minority of scholars are either skeptical of its utility or reject it outright, considering it imprecise and/or offensive. This group includes Khalid Blankinship, Bruce Lincoln, Ervand Abrahamian, and David Watt, who describes it as "a dead metaphor."[7] The term is considered imprecise because the criteria that would clearly distinguish fundamentalist Islam from non-fundamentalist are felt to be lacking; it is considered offensive because it almost invariably describes "the other," not the self.

4. Jansen, 29–40.

5. Voll, 356.

6. The movement did not attain a significant following until after al-Bannā' moved from Isma'iliyyah to Cairo in 1932. Hence, the 1930s rather than the 1920s is seen as marking the first wave of fundamentalist activism.

7. See for example Watt's "Meaning and End of Fundamentalism," *Religious Studies Review* 30 (October, 2004): 271–274, and Lincoln's *Holy Terrors*.

In light of this controversy, it is important to state my objectives clearly. Beyond the concerns expressed in Chapter Two and a specific point pertaining to Arabic terminology (below) I offer no detailed critique or general theory of the fundamentalist model. Rather, I simply argue that that model does not fit in the case of *Shubuhāt*'s sixteen articles and certain related texts. The evidence does not support the theory. On the other hand, I make no definitive claim about Riḍā's theory of the caliphate or his general rehabilitation of Ibn Taymiyyah and support of Wahhābism in *al-Manār* from 1924 onwards, as this material is not the focus. That said, my study is not entirely exclusive of Riḍā's late writings, nor those dealing with political issues.

Non-Equivalence between English and Arabic Terminology

In his book *Islamic Fundamentalism*, Lawrence Davidson, noting the objections of some critics, defends the fundamentalist model by asserting that the English "Islamic fundamentalism" and "fundamentalist" correspond to the Arabic "*al-uṣūliyyah al-islāmiyyah*" and "*uṣūlī*".[8] Based upon this claim, the full correspondence between Arabic and English would appear straightforward: "*aṣl*" corresponds to "fundamental," "*uṣūl*" to "fundamentals," "*uṣūlī* " to "fundamentalist" and "*uṣūliyyah*" to "fundamentalism." As a fundamentalist is a person who upholds or emphasizes "the fundamentals of religion," an *uṣūlī* is a person who emphasizes "*uṣūl al-dīn*." For Davidson, this correspondence with Arabic forecloses any potential or other methodological problems with the English terms. This is an interesting argument and one highly applicable to Riḍā, as he has much to say about *usūl al-dīn*, or the fundamentals of religion.

As to this putative linguistic equivalence, I make a general criticism of the fundamentalist model. In Islamic discourse in Arabic, *uṣūlī* does not mean "fundamentalist." Literally, it means "one who goes back to first principles;" an individual who has studied *uṣūl al-dīn* or the principles of religion, and this is precisely the sense in which Riḍā uses the term. More

8. Davidson, 16.

specifically, it refers to a specialist in *uṣūl al-fiqh* or the principles of jurisprudence. The reference is to an academic specialization, whereas "fundamentalist" refers to a political or religious orientation. In Shiʿite Islam, *Uṣūlī* is a legal term synonymous with "rationalist." It refers to the anti-literalist *Uṣūlī* branch of Shiʿite jurisprudence, as distinct from the "traditionist" *Akhbarī* branch. These meanings have been standard since the medieval period. In my view, it is difficult to find any equivalence between an Arabic term that predates modernity by several centuries and an English term that denotes a particular reaction to modernity.

Turning from Islamic discourse to Modern Standard Arabic, *uṣūlī* means "traditional," "normative," or "based upon the prevailing principles." This is clearly something very different to fundamentalist. As stated in Chapter Two, "traditional" Islam responded to modernity with quiescence, passivity, and inertia, whereas "fundamentalist" Islam responded with activism and reactionary rejection, if not violence. Since the 1970s, there has been a colloquial appropriation of *uṣūlī* as fundamentalist in Egypt and some other Arab countries, where it is frequently synonymous with *islāmiyyūn* ("Islamists") or *al-sunniyyah* ("Sunnites"). However, this use may have little currency in scholarly publications. In discussing this recent usage in the *Encyclopedia of Islam*, A.J. Newman and Jansen contrast it with the earlier meaning connected with *uṣūl al-dīn*. They cite as an example of the latter the works of, of all people, Rashīd Riḍā.[9] In a different publication, Jansen labels Riḍā a fundamentalist on other grounds. In any case, labeling Riḍā fundamentalist solely on the basis of this putative equivalence is clearly untenable. But more generally, to defend an English term on the basis of its colloquial appropriation in Arabic – or, for that matter, its colloquial appropriation in any other language – is to advance entirely circular argument. My argument here recalls that of Ervand Abrahamian, who rejects defending the term fundamentalist through a putative Persian equivalent, which he identifies as *bonyadegar*.[10]

9. Newman and Jansen, "*Uṣūliyya*," in *EI*.

10. E. Abrahamian, *Khomeinism: Essays on the Islamic Republic* (Berkeley: University of California Press, 1993), 13.

Uṣūl al-Dīn

If the thesis of equivalence between Arabic and English terminology is generally unpersuasive, Riḍā's deployment of *aṣl* and *uṣūl* (and, for that matter, *asāsī*) offers no evidence of a fundamentalist persuasion. I have already noted Riḍā's fear that missionary propaganda will induce common Muslims "to doubt the fundamental basis (*aṣl*) of ultimate religion." This recalls al-Afghānī's claim that missionaries in India strove to turn Muslims towards the materialistic Dahrī school by "sowing doubts about the fundamental basis (*aṣl*) of ultimate religion" (Article Fourteen, 60). In both cases, the fundamental in question is simply identified with faith and contrasted with free-thinking, libertinism or materialism. This is an interpretation contrasting religious and non-religious mentalities, rather than one contrasting differing religious orientations or attitudes towards modernity.

Elsewhere, Riḍā uses the term *uṣūl* to refer to normative Islamic doctrine. For example, he argues against the Bible's authenticity on the basis that it contradicts the religion's fundamental principles and specific provisions (*uṣūl wa furū'*). He cites Christian anthropomorphism as an example of such a contradiction, contrasting it with the Islamic principle of dissociation (Article Eight, 36). Riḍā also refers to dissociation as the "essential foundation" (*al-qā'idah al-aṣāsiyyah*) of faith (Article Seven, 30). This is no more than a re-statement of an orthodox Islamic critique of incarnationism; a critique with a long history in classical Islamic discourse, and serves to highlight what remains the most prominent theological difference between Islam and Christianity.

Riḍā also refers to scripture as religion's *aṣl* or fundamental basis. He critiques the missionary claim that Muslims regard the Qur'an and hadith as equivalent sources of authority and responds that "the Qur'an is the fundamental basis (*aṣl*) of the religion, while the sunnah elaborates it." Riḍā goes on to discuss certain of the Qur'an's distinguishing characteristics that the hadith or sunnah lack, including the recitation of its verses during the salat (*ṣalāh*). He concludes by urging his readers to "let the Muslims see how the Christians invent their religion's fundamentals (*uṣūl*) for them" (Article Thirteen, 56). Riḍā's interpretation re-affirms Islamic orthodoxy. He does not grant the hadith the Qur'anic status of "fundamental," but neither does he reject it outright. He does not accept traditions he deems weak, even if validated through citation by a figure of al-Ghazālī's stature. On the other hand, he staunchly defends the integrity of sound traditions (Article Twelve, 53). Certainly, there is nothing in this or his pithy description of the Qur'an–hadith relationship that could be characterized as fundamentalist.

Altogether, Riḍā's discourse on the above *uṣūl* or fundamentals represents no more than Islamic normativity and provides no basis for a fundamentalist/non-fundamentalist division and his location in the fundamentalist category.

The Fundamentals of Fundamentalism

Davidson offers a second defense of the fundamentalist model: "The term fundamentalist is sufficiently accurate to describe those who see themselves as adhering to the ultimate fundamentals of Islam."[11] Fundamentalists are people who adhere to "ultimate fundamentals." The reader is left to speculate as to what a "non-ultimate fundamental" might be. Davidson's definition is not original, but follows those frequently forwarded by leading scholars in the field, including Martin Marty and R. Scott Appleby.[12] This definition is certainly viable, provided two conditions are met. First, its proponents must clearly define the "ultimate fundamentals" in question and second, they must furnish evidence that fundamentalists uncompromisingly adhere to these fundamentals, whereas

11. Davidson, 17.
12. Davidson's implicit division of fundamentals into ultimate and non-ultimate categories recalls Marty's division into those that may be compromised and those that may not. For example, he characterizes the Muslim Brotherhood's Adel Hussein as representative of "the rational, compromising face of Islamic fundamentalism." Marty, 136.

non-fundamentalists do not, enabling the reader to differentiate fundamentalism from non-fundamentalism. If the two cannot reasonably be clearly distinguished, the term has no meaning. I will argue that, in the present case, the first condition is met but the second emphatically is not.

Scholars have identified many fundamentals or "ultimate fundamentals" of fundamentalism. I shall focus on three attributed to fundamentalists in general and Riḍā in particular: resistance to rationalism, literalism or scripturalist fundamentalism, and "the enclave culture," which refers to an exclusivist and dualistic world-view. The three are linked by the common theme of a negation or rejection of modernity, particularly as conceived in the Enlightenment paradigm.

Resistance to Rationalism

Voll prefaces his claim that fundamentalism originates with Rashīd Riḍā in 1905 rather than with al-Bannā' in 1928, commenting:

> The fundamentalist potential in Islamic modernism was developed by one of 'Abduh's principal students, Rashid Rida (1865–1935) . . . Rida became increasingly distrustful of the rationalist tendencies in the thinking of other modernists. He was concerned by the secularist aspects of the thought of Egyptian liberals who considered themselves followers of 'Abduh.[13]

Voll identifies the liberals in question as Qāsim Amīn (died 1908), who had written a book calling for the liberation of women, and Aḥmad Luṭfī al-Sayyid, whose importance has already been noted. Riḍā's distrust of rationalism and secularism, Voll writes, led him "toward a more fundamentalist articulation of Islam." Voll makes Riḍā an intermediary linking 'Abduh's modernism with al-Bannā''s fundamentalism. But making this argument persuasively would entail indicating which of Riḍā's publications support it: where in *al-Manār*, or elsewhere, is one to find Riḍā articulating fundamentalist Islam? This question is unanswered. Voll also conflates secularism with rationalism, distrust of the one, *ipso facto*, distrust of the other.

13. Voll, 356.

The evidence against the claim that Riḍā distrusted rationalism is clear. In *Shubuhāt*, Riḍā not only embraces rationalism, but advances as his strongest critique of traditional religion – in both its Muslim and Christian forms – its failure to do so. Riḍā refers to "speaking with the tongue of pure reason, not that of Islam" so that his arguments are more acceptable both to Muslims and non-Muslims (Article Seven, 28). (See Article Fifteen in particular, where Riḍā explains the basis for giving preference to rational evidence over transmitted evidence.)

Riḍā's advocacy of rational inquiry parallels the secularist embrace of Enlightenment, while retaining a self-consciously religious identity. Seen in this light, he may be labeled not as a fundamentalist but as a modernist "reformer" (*muṣliḥ*), as opposed to the secularist "thinker" (*mufakkir*), both terms denoting a general modernist orientation.[14] As to Riḍā's critique of secularism – represented by Qāsim Amīn and Aḥmad Luṭfī al-Sayyid – I find Voll's analysis inadequate, a point I address in relation to "the enclave culture."

Literalism or "Scripturalist Fundamentalism"

Literalism is perhaps the best-known fundamental of fundamentalism. The expression "fundamentalist literalism" has become a commonplace in academic and non-academic discourse on contemporary religion. It derives from a specifically Protestant and American context that is contemporary with Riḍā. If the criterion is literalism, Riḍā is no fundamentalist.

In *Shubuhāt*, Riḍā rejects literalism in no uncertain terms. In fact, he explains the science of allegorical interpretation in some detail (especially in Article Fifteen), drawing on both classical and modern discourse for support, citing the works of al-Rāzī, al-Ghazālī, Ibn Rushd, al-Laqānī (died 1631) and ʻAbduh. The following statements are characteristic:

14. On the significance of terms *muṣliḥ* and *mufakkir*, see Petersen, 99 onwards.

> In the Muslim view, the fundamental base of faith is God Almighty's utter dissociation (*tanzīh*) from resemblance to created beings. Thus, if an expression is related in revelation whose apparent meaning contradicts God's dissociation, they divert it from its apparent meaning by way of metaphorical and allegorical interpretation (Article Seven, 30).

> Contradictions between rational evidence and transmitted evidence: We have mentioned more than once in *al-Manār* that . . . if there is related in the apparent revealed law that which contradicts clear-cut rational evidence, then acting in accordance with the rational evidence is the imposed duty. For transmitted texts, we have the science of allegorical interpretation (*ta'wīl*) or delegation (*tafwīḍ*) (Article Fifteen, 71).

The principle of *tafwīḍ* enables Muslims to solve problems of interpretation by "delegating" or "entrusting" the matter to God.[15] This approach is also referred to as "handing over" or *taslīm*. Hence, Muslims may accept the non-literal truth of a verse that, in its literal meaning, is incomprehensible or appears to contradict an Islamic doctrine, such as that of God's utter dissociation (*tanzīh*).

Riḍā places limits on allegorical interpretation. In his *tafsīr*, he comments on its danger[16] and criticizes excessively speculative Sufi and Bāṭinī Shi'i exegesis,[17] while he corroborates Ibn Rushd's view that *ta'wīl* should not be attempted other than by specialists who are firmly rooted in knowledge (Article Fifteen, 80). Similarly, he finds that anthropomorphic Christian doctrine is based upon unjustifiably creative exegesis (Article Seven, 30). Conversely, he argues that missionaries have misrepresented the *mutashābihāt*, namely the ambiguous Qur'anic verses that need of *ta'wīl*, *tafwīḍ* or *taslīm*. He avers: "they represented their consistency as inconsistency and their harmony as disharmony" (Preface, *jīm*). Such a critique would certainly be intelligible if written in response to inappropriately literalistic readings. Riḍā's approach to exegesis is complex: he criticizes overly creative readings on the one hand and overly literal

15. On the emphasis placed on *tafwīḍ* by 'Abduh and Riḍā, see *Tafsīr*, i, 252.

16. *Tafsīr*, iv, 17.

17. *Tafsīr*, iv, 191.

readings on the other. His attitude depends on the case in question and demonstrates the limited utility of such glib terms as "literalist" or "fundamentalist literalist."

Said Amir Arjomand, who identifies Riḍā rather than al-Afghānī or 'Abduh as the founder of the Salafī movement, characterizes Riḍā's thought not as an instance of "fundamentalist literalism," but as "scripturalist fundamentalism," distinguishing it from Ḥasan al-Bannā"s "political fundamentalism." "Scripturalist fundamentalism," Arjomand writes, consists of the belief that the Qur'an is the uncreated word of God, the belief that the first generations of Muslims – *al-salaf al-ṣāliḥ* – were the soundest authorities on hadith or prophetic tradition and the legal position that consensus be limited to that of the Prophet's Companions (consensus being the fourth source of law in Sunni Islam).[18]

The Uncreated Qur'an

In my view, the belief that the Qur'an is the uncreated word of God fails to meet the criterion of being a fundamental of fundamentalism because it represents a normative and orthodox Islamic belief, not the belief of a fundamentalist minority. God's attributes, of which God's speech and therefore the Qur'an is one, are believed to share God's qualities. As God is eternal, His speech is eternal and therefore uncreated. To limit the eternity of God's speech would be to limit the eternity of God. For this reason, the Mu'tazilī position that the Qur'an was created was rejected by the majority. Therefore if Riḍā upheld the notion of the uncreated Qur'an this would not be a point of particular significance, nor would it justify categorizing him as a fundamentalist.

Riḍā does not address this issue in *Shubuhāt.* His comments elsewhere in *al-Manār* reflect a reticent, not a fundamentalist stance. In a 1909 fatwā, Riḍā responds to a Saudi questioner who expresses his surprise that, until then, the issue had not been addressed in *al-Manār*. Riḍā emphasizes

18. Said Amir Arjomand, "Unity and Diversity in Islamic Fundamentalism," *Fundamentalisms Comprehended* (Chicago: University of Chicago Press, 1991), 180.

two points in his response. First, he upholds the orthodox position, characterizing the opinion that the Qur'an was created as a reprehensible innovation, unsanctioned by the Prophet. However Riḍā prefaces this affirmation by explaining his reticence. Sometimes, he notes, "ignorance on an issue accompanied by unity is preferable to knowledge accompanied by disagreement." It is a matter he would prefer to avoid discussing. Such discussion too easily becomes "meaningless debate" that is disliked by God, and that leads to madhhabism or legal partisanship, which Riḍā contrasts with the non-partisan practice of the *Salaf*.[19] Riḍā's reticence is also seen in *The Muhammadan Revelation* (1934):

> The controversy between the theologians in regard to whether or not God's speech was created was completely a matter of philosophy and invented speculative opinion that was never addressed in either the Qur'an or the sunnah. In fact, it has nothing to do with analytical inquiry into the nature of God's essence and the attributes and, as such, it only serves to call up doubts and the whisperings of Satan. *Therefore, it should be avoided.* Rather, it should suffice us to believe that speech is one of the attributes of God's perfection and that it is connected to God's knowledge.[20]

To me, such statements do not support the thesis that Riḍā was a fundamentalist.

Prophetic Tradition

In my view, the belief that the first generations of Muslims were the soundest authorities on prophetic tradition or hadith also fails to meet the criterion of being a fundamental, as it also represents a normative and unexceptional position. The further question might be asked, if not the first generations, who would be the soundest authorities on this material? I find nothing, either at a general level or in Riḍā's own views, that would support the fundamentalist model.

19. *al-Manār*, xii, 1909, 182–184.
20. Riḍā, *Al-Waḥy al-Muḥammadī* (Cairo: Dār al-Manār, 1948), 46. DeLorenzo, 4. Emphasis added. Trans. author (adapted from DeLorenzo).

The Consensus of the Companions (*ijmāʿ al-ṣaḥābah*)

The third belief that Arjomand lists – the limiting of consensus as a source of law to that of the Companions – refers to a debate with a long history, juridical rather than ideological in nature. Arjomand's definition appears to identify fundamentalism with Ḥanbalism (a feature of Ḥanbalī doctrine is the assertion that only the Companions' consensus is of value). This concerns the interrelationship between the terms *jamāʿah* (community) and *ijmāʿ* (consensus), both deriving from the same trilateral root (J-M-ʿ). *Ijmāʿ* is the agreement of the *jamāʿah*, Ḥanbalī doctrine restricting the community in question to the Companions.

Arjomand does not indicate where in Riḍā's writings one might find a fundamentalist interpretation of consensus. In *Shubuhāt*, the handful of references to "that upon which the Imams are agreed" or "that upon which the Imams are in consensus" do not limit or restrict the Imams in question to the Companions or any other group. This statement is typical:

> If we find in revelation something whose apparent meaning contradicts rational clear-cut evidence, we reconcile it with the rational clear-cut evidence through allegorical interpretation, or we entrust the matter to God, together with accepting the rational evidence. This is that upon which the Muslim Imams are in consensus, as stated previously (Article Fifteen, 79).

The Imams Riḍā cites in support of this view include al-Rāzī, Ibn Rushd, and ʿAbduh: little indication of fundamentalist limitation.

Riḍā's commentary on *jamāʿah* and *ijmāʿ* in his other writings is extensive, and worthy of a separate study. His thinking on this issue was both developed and original and while his views reflect a certain tension, this is carefully resolved. Riḍā's understanding of religious essentials might appear to support Arjomand's claim. In his *tafsīr*, Riḍā upholds the restriction of *canonical* consensus to that of the Companions: "no one shall be excused for opposing the consensus of the Companions."[21] Significantly, this injunction falls under the heading "the need to

21. *Tafsīr*, vii, 198.

abide by texts in matters of worship." Similarly, drawing evidence from his short story, Hourani comments that in Riḍā's view: "[The] Islam of the 'Elders' is that of the first generation who had known Muḥammad, and the only *ijma'* which is valid is that of this generation" and further, "[in matters of worship] the *ijma'* of the first generation ... is binding."[22]

However, in his book *al-Khilāfah aw al-Imāmah al-'Uẓmā* (The Caliphate or the Great Imamate), Riḍā approvingly cites al-Ṭabarī's assertion that consensus should not be historically limited, but defined "without reference to any particular period." L. Gardet and J. Berque note that Riḍā "does not hesitate to expand the strict sense given to [*jamā'ah* and *ijmā'*] by the Ḥanbalīs."[23] Riḍā argues that the guardians of consensus in any age are "those who bind and loosen" – a generic expression referring to those in authority – who must be followed by the community whenever they are in consensus (*ijmā'*).[24] Similarly, in his *tafsīr*, Riḍā refers to the consensus of those in authority as "the true consensus that we consider among the fundamentals of our shari'ah."[25] Commenting on this sense of *ijmā'*, Hourani notes that Riḍā was distinctly modern in elevating the notion of common social interest (*maṣlaḥah*) from a subordinate to a guiding principle – an elevation clearly evident in *Shubuhāt*. Riḍā asserts that as the social interest varies according to circumstance, "there is and in fact can be no *ijma'*, *even that of the first generation*, in matters of social morality." Hourani summarizes Riḍā's position thus: "[H]aving rejected the old conception of *ijma'*, he is introducing a new one: the *ijma'* of the *'ulama'* of each age, a legislative rather than a judicial principle, working by some sort of parliamentary process."[26] It is clear that Riḍā's interpretation was something considerably more involved than a "fundamentalist" regression to the tradition or consensus of the Companions.

22. Hourani, 230 and 233. See Riḍā, *Muḥāwarāt*, 58 and 126.
23. L. Gardet and J. Berque, "Djamā'a," in *EI*.
24. Riḍā, *al-Khilāfah aw al-Imāmah al-'Uzmā* (Cairo: 1923), 14.
25. *Tafsir*, v, 190.
26. Hourani, 234. Emphasis added.

The Enclave Culture

In his book *The Glory and the Power: The Fundamentalist Challenge to the Modern World,* Martin Marty characterizes this culture as a dualistic worldview that divides the world into fellow defenders and enemies and tolerates "no shades of gray between light and darkness."[27] Emmanuel Sivan, a writer who notes that Riḍā's "alarmist theories" provided the bare bones for Ḥasan al-Bannā''s fundamentalist agenda, characterizes this as "the enclave culture."[28] Islamic Fundamentalists, he writes, seek social and symbolic separation from non-Muslims in general and in particular from liberal Muslims who would adapt Islam to modernity. Fundamentalists stress *difference.* They emphasize how their interpretation of religion contrasts with that of others and seek to create barriers and boundaries. Their attitude parallels that of those Jews and Christians who seek separation from Reform and Zionist Jews and liberal Christians. Related to this is a dualistic understanding of knowledge as divided into that of the Muslims and that of non-Muslims, the latter being unacceptable, in the fundamentalist view.

While Sivan refers to Riḍā's enclave mentality, he does not support this interpretation by reference to Riḍā's works. In my view, the enclave mentality is indeed present in Riḍā's work, as a mentality that he not only criticizes and challenges, but parodies and lampoons. I have already noted his caustic reference to the feeble traditionalist shaykh, whose closed-mindedness to non-Islamic knowledge renders him impotent in the face of missionary critique. This theme is elaborated in *Debates of the Reformer and the Traditionalist.* The fictional reformer – clearly Riḍā himself – constantly befuddles the inept shaykh, who vainly strives to resist the encroachment of Western thought and remain in an isolated and self-contained Islamic enclave. The shaykh will neither take Christians or other non-Muslims as friends, nor will he accept information deriving from a non-Muslim source. Would the shaykh, Riḍā's reformer asks, refuse to accept a British report about the Boer War in South Africa, simply because the reporter is

27. Marty, 29.

28. Almond, Appleby and Sivan, *Strong Religion: The Rise of Fundamentalisms Around the World,* 46; Sivan, "The Enclave Culture," in *Fundamentalisms Comprehended,* 27.

not Muslim? The reformer avers that any report, Muslim or non-Muslim, may be accepted, provided it is properly attested or *mutawātir* (a term to which we shall return). Riḍā deploys a technical juristic term as a metaphor for modernity, in a context having nothing to do with Islam.[29] I find little support in this for Sivan's thesis of enclave "alarmism".

Riḍā's attitude is also seen in his discussion of education. He calls for the Muslim ulama to follow the example of their European counterparts and, in addition to Islamic learning, pursue education in "the universal sciences" (Article Four, 20). This involves a general embrace of secular education. In his *tafsīr*, Riḍā goes into considerable detail, listing the subjects educated Muslims need to master: universal history, argument and discourse, geography, psychology, moral science, sociology, political science, and the arts, sciences and religious sects of non-Muslim nations. Last, and particularly significantly, Riḍā advocated instruction in languages other than Arabic, drawing on the example of the Prophet's advice to some of his Companions to study Hebrew. Unsurprisingly, Riḍā's promotion of foreign languages was resisted by Al-Azhar.[30]

This returns us to Voll's reference to Riḍā's distrust of secularism. Article Fourteen shows that Riḍā was opposed to certain secular political ideas favored by Faraḥ Anṭūn and Aḥmad Luṭfī al-Sayyid. (Although Riḍā's attitude is not of blanket opposition to all Western political thought. But this is beyond the scope of this study.) However, Riḍā's attitude to education clearly demonstrates that his thought cannot be legitimately characterized as distrust of all things secular. As for Voll's reference to Riḍā's distrust of Qāsim Amīn, who had called for women's liberation, we also note the findings of Emad Eldin Shahin, who has examined Riḍā's writings in considerable detail. While duly noting that Riḍā had his own ideas on gender, which he published in *al-Manār*, Shahin comments: "Riḍā was among the supporters of Amīn, as he honored, defended, and quoted parts of Amīn's books in his journal."[31]

29. Petersen, 101.
30. *Tafsīr*, iv, 30–36. Crollius summaries the relevant passages. Crollius, 278–280.
31. Emad Eldin Shahin, "Muhammad Rashid Rida's Perspectives on the West as Reflected in *al-Manar*," *Muslim World* 79 (1989): 120. See *al-Manār*, iii, 1900, 850

I find, then, that Voll, Jansen, Sivan, Arjomand and others who characterize Riḍā as an Islamic fundamentalist fail to make a persuasive case. In my view, if Riḍā articulated a fundamentalist interpretation of Islam, he did not do so in discussing his views on the fundamental principles of religion, rationalism, scriptural exegesis, or by advocating Muslim withdrawal into a self-contained Islamic "enclave." Riḍā's position on these matters is unambiguous. It is a modernist rejection of traditionalism, not a fundamentalist rejection of modernism.

and iv, 1901, 26–34. On Riḍā's views on the status of women, see Shahin, 120–122 and Riḍā's 1932 book *Nidā' Ilā al-Jins al-Laṭīf* (A Call to the Fair Sex), which was originally published in *al-Manār*.

5

A Translation of the Criticisms of the Christians and the Proofs of Islam

Preliminary Note on Translation Theory

As Khalid Blankinship notes, translation "is much done but, until recently, not much studied." Translation is nearly as old as writing itself, as indicated by bilingual dictionaries in Sumerian and Akkadian. Yet a typical translation of a classical or modern Arabic text provides no information on the translator's method. The reader is left with the impression that the translator has aimed for "accuracy," but no more. Given the highly subjective and arbitrary nature of translation, this may seem surprising.

Following Lawrence Venuti, a leading authority, we may observe that approaches towards translation are divisible into two categories: those aiming for fidelity and those aiming for domestication. The former retains "the foreignness of the foreign text." It seeks to stay as close to the meaning of the original language as possible, provided a basic standard of coherence in the target language is maintained. The latter aims at "dynamic equivalence" and makes intelligibility in the target language the guiding principle. This approach sanctions the translator to take far greater liberties with the text. The division goes back at least as far as classical Greece and Rome, while in the field of religious studies the most prominent representatives of the two approaches are probably Schleiermacher and Martin Luther. Schleiermacher presented the case for fidelity in his famous 1813 lecture "On the Different Methods of Translation," but Luther's advocacy of domestication has been more influential. It is, for example, the approach currently favored and promoted by the American Bible Society.

In this translation, I have chosen fidelity rather than domestication. This brings both advantages and disadvantages. The major disadvantages are stylistic: fidelity to the Arabic can result in convoluted and repetitive language, a feature many translators simply "smooth over" so that, in some cases, the result is effectively a paraphrase rather than a translation, albeit one that results in a superior style of English. However, fidelity better preserves the author's original meaning: for example, it is common for the word "shari'ah" to be translated as "religion," a clear example of domestication. In my view "law" is preferable. Better still, as this word has now become incorporated into English, it may be left untranslated, as I have done.

The Criticisms of the Christians and the Proofs of Islam

Title Page and Preface

Sixteen articles published in the fourth and fifth volumes of the journal *al-Manār al-Islāmī* (The Islamic Lighthouse) in response to the book *Abḥāth al-Mujtahidīn* (Researches of the Mujtahids) and the periodicals *Bashā'ir al-Salām* (The Glad Tidings of Peace) and *al-Jāmi'ah*. Herein: demonstration of the meaning of the Torah and Gospel; comparison of Moses, Jesus and Muḥammad (God's blessing and peace be upon him); comparison of Islam with Christianity; demonstration of Christianity's character as a form of paganism; inquiry into the prophets' sinlessness, salvation, faith, works, and God's ways in creation; demonstration of Islam's character as the religion of reason and knowledge; inquiry into civil and religious authority, the shari'ah and the religion, and other topics.

By Sayyid Muḥammad Rashīd Riḍā, Founder of *al-Manār*, God, be He exalted, have mercy upon him.

Second Edition published by Dār al-Manār, 14 al-Inshā' St, 1367 AH (1947)

In the name of God, the Compassionate, the Merciful

> [*bā'*] Call unto the way of thy Lord with wisdom and fair exhortation, and reason with them in the better way. Lo! Thy Lord is best aware of him who strayeth from His way and He is Best Aware of those who go aright (*Sūrat al-Nahl*, [16:125]).

> And argue not with the People of the Scripture unless it be in (a way) that is better, save with such of them as do wrong; and say: We believe in that which hath been revealed unto us and revealed unto you; our God and your God is One, and unto Him we surrender (Sūrat al-'Ankabūt, [29:46]).

Verily, the lifeblood of religions is mission (da'wah), and the power of truth is in truth itself, while the persistence of untruth occurs when the truth is neglectful of it. Truth is concealed when its people abandon it, while untruth is made manifest by its people gathering together upon it.

And never have truth and falsehood wrestled with one another but that truth is the victor and falsehood the defeated.

> Nay, but We hurl the true against the false, and it doth break its head and lo! It vanisheth [21:18]; Then, as for the foam, it passeth away as scum upon the banks, while, as for that which is of use to mankind, it remaineth in the earth. Thus Allah coineth the similitudes [13:17].

Islam appeared and wrestled with all the religions and threw them down. Its party fought all the sects and vanquished them. Its doctrines brought the people from the darkness to the light, while its precepts directed them towards the shade when they were in a hot wind. Thus did its truth overcome all falsehoods, the morning appearing by it and extinguishing every candle. But it was not long before its people forsook it, its party split into factions, the greedy strove against them, and the liars themselves dared to attack Islam. Thus did paganism assail divine oneness (*tawhīd*), blind imitation (*taqlīd*) exceed rational proof and the worshipers of the son of man argue against the worship of the Merciful (*al-Raḥmān*).

> Unto Him is the real prayer. Those unto whom they pray beside Allah respond to them not at all, save as (is the response) to one [*jīm*] who stretcheth forth his hands toward water (asking) that it may come unto his mouth, and it will never reach it. The prayer of the disbelievers goeth (far) astray [13:14].

Through weakening Islam, the Muslims themselves became weak. Hence the Europeans dominated them everywhere, and the missionaries of Christianity dispersed in the Islamic countries. They slandered the Qur'an and impugned the Prophet, prayer and peace be upon him.[1] I do

1. Riḍā discussed the nature of slander (*ṭa'n*) in a fatwa published in *al-Manār*, xxv, 1924. He comments that a good Muslim can distinguish good Christian mission from that involving slander or obscenity. However, the distinction appears moot, as Riḍā clearly regards all Christian missions to Muslim lands as falling into the second category. The fatwa is especially critical of missionary schools. Umar Riyad, "Rashīd Riḍā and a Danish Missionary: Alfred Nielsen (died 1965) and Three Fatwā-s from Al-Manār," *Islamochristiana* 28 (2002): 92–94.

not fear from the missionaries that the Muslim will become a Christian. Rather, I fear that he will [be led to] doubt the fundamental essence of religion and become a libertine. Yet, however much the winds of paganism sway him, he would not ascribe divinity to other than God, as do the Christians.[2] "And unto Allah falleth prostrate whosoever is in the heavens and the earth, willingly or unwillingly, as do their shadows in the morning and the evening hours" [13:15].

These missionaries attacked the Muslims where they were weak, hitting them where they were most vulnerable. They knew that they had abandoned the Qur'an – an ugly abandonment[3] – and dispensed with it through idle talk in the books of the modern thinkers. Then they began searching for the ambiguous verses (*mutashābihāt*) in the Qur'an,[4] portraying their harmony as disharmony and representing their consistency to the people as inconsistency. And what does the feeble traditionalist do when it is said to him, "these statements are those of the dead ulama of your legal school"? Is it not frightening that, due to his ignorance, they land him in a state of shock? "Verily they have plotted their plot, and their plot is with Allah, though their plot were one whereby the mountains should be moved" [14:46].

These zealots did not stop at attacking [Islam] in books, newspapers, and religious periodicals. They even spat out the poison of their hostility in the political and academic newspapers, one alleging that Islam is the enemy of reason and religion, and another claiming that its politics harms all people. You were indeed excessive, O shooters of arrows, so much so that arrowheads broke against arrowheads. "Alike of you is he who hideth the saying and he who noiseth it abroad, he who lurketh in the night and he who goeth in the daytime" [13:10].

The sleep of the Muslims gulled you, but behold them now, there they

2. On Riḍā's comment that his concern was not Muslim conversion to Christianity, but rather a Muslim turn away from religion and towards libertinism, see also *al-Manār*, xxiii, 1922, 267; xxv, 1924, 189; xxvi, 1925, 99.
3. Ar. *hajran ghayra jamīl*, perhaps playing upon the Qur'anic *hajran jamīlan* and *sabrun jamīlan*.
4. See Riḍā's comments on *ta'wīl* and *tafwīḍ* in Article Fifteen (*Shubuhāt*, 71–72).

are, starting to awake. And perhaps the one who awakes them harms himself through that which they turn to their own advantage, since he induces them to become concerned to understand the Noble Qur'an and hold fast to its strong rope. And when they hold fast they stand erect, and when they stand erect they prevail.[5]

> Lo! Allah changeth not the condition of a folk until they (first) change that which is in their hearts; and if Allah willeth misfortune for a folk there is none that can repel it, nor have they any defender beside Him [13:11].

[*dāl*] We were making fun of what the Christian missionaries wrote attacking Islam, as we saw the Muslims paying it no attention. We had not been doing that for long before we were asked about some of their criticisms by someone familiar with their writings. He asked that we, in keeping with the requirement of the shari'ah, reply to them. According to the shari'ah we were duty-bound to respond in equal measure. Hence we responded in a civil tone, promising that we would go no further than replying to the criticisms of the critics, defending without attacking.[6]

However, the people started sending to us what they wrote, and the Muslims demanded of us that we respond. We continued clashing with them and debating with them by that which is better, combining refutation of untruth with clarification of truth. [This continued] until we placed that open section in our periodical *al-Manār al-Islāmī* (The Islamic Lighthouse), entitled *Shubuhāt al-Naṣārā wa Ḥujaj al-Islām* (The Criticisms of the Christians and the Proofs of Islam). The title signifies that the Christian religion itself does not criticize the Islamic religion, rather the Christians themselves criticize it, and that the right arguments against them are not those of those Muslims who have become an argument against their religion, but rather those of the religion of Islam itself.

Then, some earnest people suggested that we gather together the articles from this section of *al-Manār* and publish them in a separate

5. See Qur'an 3:106.
6. On Riḍā's claim that in his writings he was merely defending his own religion and not attacking that of his opponents, see also *al-Manār*, xvii, 1914,156, 189; xxxiii, 1933, 236.

book, so that they might be more easily read and studied, as needed. So we did, and here we are publishing the book in small parts, increasing its utility and as an invitation to the lazy. We will publish every four parts in a separate volume, trusting in God.

> He it is Who showeth you the lightning, a fear and a hope, and raiseth the heavy clouds [13:12]; The Thunder hymneth His praise and (so do) the angels for awe of Him. He launcheth the thunderbolts and smiteth with them who He will while they dispute (in doubt) concerning Allah, and He is mighty in wrath [13:13].

Muḥammad Rashīd Riḍā
Editor and publisher of *al-Manār*

Article One: On the Need to Respond and Clarify the Muslim View of the Torah and Gospel

[1] We have come upon a major paper written by one of those busy reading the books that the Christian missions published attacking Islam. In it, the writer asks for clarification regarding doubts that remained in his mind after reading those books. It is imperative that we address these doubts, because the defense of the religion of Islam is the most important task for which *al-Manār* was established. Yet our practice, that we have followed from the first day, concerns the matter of those who oppose us in religion, especially the Christians, and more than that, the endeavor to eliminate resentments and come to an agreement on what the success of the country entails. We desire that no one slanders the religion of the other, neither through speech nor writing. But the Christians do not agree with us about this, as do the Muslims. Hence, we see them making gatherings in order to hurt Islam verbally, publishing newspapers, such as *The Standard of Zion* (*Rāyah Ṣahyūn*), and writing books to attack its scripture. Truly, we bear this hostile action patiently and refrain from going further than addressing the doubts of the questioners among the people of our own religion, taking courtesy into account. Thus, we say:

Truly, we were astonished by this Muslim reader of the Christian books, by his being satisfied with reading them without reading the

Islamic books that confront them with their equivalent, repel their criticisms, and oppose against them that which cannot be repelled, such as *Demonstration of the Truth* (*Iẓhār al-Ḥaqq*),[7] *The Polished Sword* (*al-Sayf al-Ṣaqīl*)[8] and other such books. Our first response to the reader is that it is incumbent upon him to read those Islamic books and, after reading

7. Al-Kayrānawī's book was first translated into Arabic in 1867 at the request of the Ottoman Sultan Abdulaziz I (1861–76) and has been translated into several other Muslim languages. It is still hugely influential in the Muslim world. It was written in response to *Mizān al-Ḥaqq* (The Balance of Truth), by Karl Gottlieb Pfander, a German Protestant missionary. Pfander, like Ghibrīl, used the Qur'an to argue for the veracity of the Bible and the messianic claim of Jesus (a strategy still used by Christian missionaries in the Muslim world today). Al-Kayrānawī's book attempts to disprove those claims. Significantly, however, its argument is based in part on ideas derived from contemporary European Biblical criticism, although the author's understanding of this material was probably limited. Gaudeul suggests that it consisted primarily in his awareness of different renderings of the same verbs in different English translations of the Bible.

   Kayrānawī argues that Christianity refutes itself. He also concludes that the theories of the Christian scholars themselves indicate that the most sound gospel is not contained in the New Testament, but in the Gospel of Barnabas – Riḍā published the first Arabic edition of this gospel in 1908 under the title *al-Injīl al-Ṣaḥīḥ* (The True Gospel). On this premise, *Iẓhār al-Ḥaqq* claimed Jesus survived the crucifixion and that the gospel foretells the prophecy of Muḥammad. Riḍā was clearly influenced by Al-Kayrānawī and quotes him extensively in his *tafsīr*. An excellent analysis of the book and its importance for subsequent debates is given by Christine Schirrmacher: "The Influence of German Biblical Criticism on Muslim Apologetics in the 19 th Century," in *Muslim Perceptions of Other Religions* (New York: Oxford University Press, 1999): 270–279. See also Gaudeul, 259–61. Riḍā, *Tafsīr*, ix, 231–293.

8. Bakr b. al-Sayyid ʿUmar Tamīmī al-Dārī and Muḥammad Zakī al-Dīn Sanad, *Kitāb al-Sayf al-Ṣaqīl fī al-Radd ʿalā Risālat al-Burhān al-Jalīl* (The Polished Sword in Response to the book The Sublime Proof) (Cairo: Maṭabaʿat al-Maḥrūsah, 1895). The book refutes the claim of Qur'anic corruption set forth in *al-Burhān al-Jalīl ʿalā Siḥḥat al-Tawrah wa al-Injīl* (The Sublime Proof of the Veracity of the Torah and Gospel), a work of unknown authorship published in Jerusalem in 1893. Together with *Iẓhār al-Ḥaqq, al-Sayf al-Ṣaqīl* generated in turn another critique, *Al-Hidāyah* (The Guide) (Cairo: Maʿrifat al-Musalin al-Amirikan, 1900), subtitled "A response to the book entitled *Iẓhār al-Ḥaqq* and to the book entitled *Al-Sayf al-Ḥamīdī al-Ṣaqīl.*"

them and comparing them with the Christian books, to read and ask about what remains unclear to him. If his doubts remain, it is because the newspaper in which he wanted us to publish the answers to his questions is not, in treating the debate about the topics it addresses, sufficient for this purpose: it does not include everything that needs to be included. This is because the elimination of all of his doubts would require slander, something that our newspaper avoids, in contrast to what we read at the end of his paper.

[2] The questioner's criticisms are divided into three sections. First, contradictions between some Islamic texts and the scriptures of the Christians and the Jews. Second, the appearance of things in the Qur'an not mentioned in those books. If you are amazed by this, it is because the doubt of this Muslim is indeed amazing in the following way: silence about something is not the same as denial of its existence. How, then, can he entertain doubts about that which he believes God made clear, simply because these historians did not mention it! Third, the appearance of things in the Qur'an and hadith contradicting reality or what is established in the modern sciences by means of the claim of those from whom he got his ideas.

We respond here to the first and third criticisms. As to the second, our opinion is what we have said already, that is, there is no reason for any doubt concerning it. We begin our response with a brief discussion concerning Muslim beliefs about the Torah and Gospel. We say:

The questioner argues for the fact that the Torah and Gospel originate with God on the basis of the Qur'an. This in accordance with the wishes of the Christian missionaries whose books and words he is fond of. And I swear, by my life, there is no evidence in support of that argument except for the testimony of the Qur'an. This is because the testimony of the Qur'an is a proof that God Almighty enacted a law upon the tongue of Moses and named it the Torah. Now, this testimony is an argument against the Qur'an's veracity, because it testifies to the truthfulness of something that wisdom, knowledge and existence deem false, and moreover, something that testifies to its own falseness. As for the Torah's testimony to its own falseness, it is in what it contains in the way of inconsistency and self-contradiction. As for the testimony of reason, knowledge and existence, it contradicts those books that, in the view of the people, are named Torah. If the questioner needs to confirm this in detail, let him consult what is written about it in the *Great French Encyclopedia*, other books written by European scholars, and those of the Muslims, such as *Demonstration of the Truth* (*Iẓhār al-Ḥaqq*).[9]

As for the response to this doubt, which demonstrates the veracity of the Qur'anic testimony, it is as follows. The Torah for which the Qur'an testifies is a book of law and precepts, not a book of history borrowed from the mythology of the Assyrians, Chaldeans, and others.[10] Thus, we note the sciences of geology and archeology disproving it, or the conformity of this with some of what is related in it. Neither is it natural history. Thus, we note what has been established by experience disproving it. An example is the surety that the snake does not eat [3] earth, although it is related in the book of Genesis that the Lord said to the snake, "and dust you shall eat all the days of your life" [Gn 3:14].[11] This is to say nothing of its

9. In this collection, Riḍā refers to Tolstoy's writings on religion (Article Four). Elsewhere in *al-Manār* he refers to numerous other Western writers, several of whose works he reviews. He was familiar with the intellectual rebellion against church authority and traditional Christianity fermenting in Europe. He refers, for example, to the rejection of church teaching by philosophers such as Thomas Huxley (died 1895) and Herbert Spencer (died 1903). *Al-Manār*, viii, 1904, 139. This supports his thesis that traditional Christianity is being abandoned in Europe, rendering European mission to the Muslim world highly hypocritical. See *al-Manār*, xxviii, 1927, 144–49. On Riḍā's familiarity with Western thought in general, see Emad Eldin Shahin, "Muhammad Rashid Rida's Perspectives on the West as Reflected in *al-Manār*." *Muslim World* 79 (1989): 113–132.
10. On Riḍā's claim that the Bible was a historical book rather than a revealed scripture, see also *al-Manār*, xxv, 1924, 190.
11. Riḍā quotes from *al-Kitāb al-Muqaddas*, the so-called "Van Dyke Arabic Bible" – hereafter *VD* – translated into Arabic by the American missionaries Cornelius van Alen Van Dyke (1818–1895) and Eli Smith (died 1857). Riḍā's method of quotation is not completely consistent as he occasionally appears to put his own paraphrases between quotations marks. Where he specifies the name of the biblical book, the correspondence with *VD* is usually exact.

Dr. Van Dyke, a medical doctor, was an important presence at the Syrian Protestant College, where he supplied books on mathematics and modern science

ascription of unbefitting characteristics to God, such as His feeling of regret for creating mankind and so forth. Thus, the Torah is authentic. It is the laws and percepts that Moses, those who succeeded him among the Israelites' prophets (peace be upon them), and their rabbis, judged by. As God Almighty said: "Lo! We did reveal the Torah wherein is guidance and a light, by which the prophets who surrendered (unto Allah) judged the Jews and the rabbis and the priests (judged)" [5:44]. The Qur'an did not corroborate the numerous historical books, including those whose author and compiler was not known, and all of which were written long after Moses, author of the Torah. With this answer, the Qur'anic testimony is upheld, while the doubter's doubts about the historical difference between the Qur'an and the books of Isaiah, Ezekiel, Daniel, and others are rendered baseless, because the Qur'an does not corroborate these books.

Do not be fooled by people naming all the books of the Old Testament "Torah," as that usage is generalization. Moreover, we see the Christians

in Arabic, thereby influencing the intellectual development of Shaykh Ḥusayn al-Jisr (1845–1909), Riḍā's early mentor (see Chapter Two). Van Dyke's translation had its origins in Beirut, where the American Board of Commissioners for Foreign Missions appointed Smith to produce a new translation from the original Biblical languages (the earliest known Arabic Bible is dated 867). Smith completed most of the work, including all of the New Testament, before his death in 1857. Van Dyke was then hired to complete the project. Issa Saliba notes that Van Dyke effectively re-translated Smith's translation of the New Testament. He consciously avoided Qur'anic language, in keeping with the wishes of local Christians, but against the advice of his missionary colleagues. This decision has been reversed in more recent translations. Ford, 245. Hourani, 222–223. Riḍā, *Al-Manār wa al-Azhar* (Cairo: 1934–35), 142. Issa Saliba, "The Bible in Arabic: The 19th-Century Protestant Translation," *Muslim World* 65 (1975): 259–261. For sources on the history of Arabic Bible translation, see Ford, 367.

The translation has a reputation for being of poor quality, particularly in its use of an overly colloquial or near-colloquial style. This is significant, as both Riḍā and his Arabic-speaking opponents considerably depended on it for their interpretation of Christian doctrine. Comparison of the passages Riḍā cites with reputable English translations including the *The Jerusalem Bible* and the *New Revised Standard Version* reveals differences.

frequently naming the collected books of the two testaments, Old and New, "Torah" when they are combined.

As for the Gospel, in Muslim belief it consists of the warnings, wisdom, and precepts that God Almighty revealed to Christ, may prayer and peace be upon him, and with which he exhorted and taught the people. In the Muslim view, what exceeds that in the books that they name "gospels," is historical if a report, and that of the one who said it, if a precept or doctrine. You know that the Christians name the collected books of the New Testament "Gospel," and acknowledge that they were written after Christ at different times. Like the books of the Old Testament, these books lack the chains of transmission that the Christians adduce as evidence to vindicate them.[12]

The Qur'an testifies against the Christians that they did not preserve all of the revelation named "Gospel" with which Christ exhorted them when it states: "And with those who say: 'Lo! we are Christians,' We made a covenant, but they forgot a part of that whereof they were admonished" [5:14]. The Qur'an says likewise with regard to the Jews. The expression "the Gospel" can be applied to a portion of that revelation in the same way that the word "al-Qur'an" or "Qur'an" is applied to a portion of it. One says "so-and-so was reading [4] the Qur'an," and this usage is even attested in the Qur'an and hadith, and the Qur'an was called "Qur'an" before it was completely revealed.

Since the Torah's precepts and the Gospel's maxims were in the possession of the Jews and the Christians, the Qur'an was without doubt remonstrating them for not establishing them. Their mixing of them with historical material does not counter this remonstration. Rather, it is the reason for the Prophet's statement, may God's blessing and peace be upon him, "Neither believe nor disbelieve them," namely, when they present you with something from their scriptures.[13] This is because we do not have a criterion for distinguishing the originally revealed precepts from what was

12. Riḍā is following Kayrānawī's argument concerning the unreliability of the gospels – that they lack uninterrupted chains of transmission (*asānīd*) equivalent to those that authenticate sound hadith.

13. Bukhārī, *Tawḥīd*, 51, *I'tiṣām* 25.

added in the process of composition. Yes, in keeping with our understanding, we think it probable that all, or most, of the rulings attributed to Moses in the books of Exodus, Numbers, Deuteronomy and Leviticus are from Torah, because if they are not the Torah, then where is it? Similarly, we find more validity in Christ's "Sermon on the Mount," as in the chronicle "The Gospel of Matthew," and other sermons, as some of the European and Eastern scholars think it probable that a major portion of the true Gospel was included in the book of Isaiah. As for the reports that the people possess, we aver that whatever in them differs from the Qur'an is false, and no wonder, since God speaks truthfully, whereas historians lie. This is the meaning of the Almighty's statement: "And unto thee have We revealed the Scripture with the truth, confirming whatever Scripture was before it, and a watcher over it" [5:48]. This suffices for now, our appointment being the coming installment. If doubts about what we have written remain for the questioner, let him write to us for further explanation. We would prefer that he visit us at the offices of *al-Manār* to receive a verbal answer, as the freedom of the tongue is greater than that of the pen. And were it not that our jurists charge with unbelief one who knows that a Muslim doubts his religion, and has the ability to remove his doubt yet does not do so, we would not have written what we wrote. This is because we are preachers of harmony and agreement, and petitioners of friendship and union. But our religion imposes this in particular upon us, even though the questioner concealed his name and sought that he be answered in *al-Manār*. Thus, that was imposed upon us.[14]

Article Two: Historical Doubts about Judaism and Christianity; Comparison of the Three Prophets

[5] We wrote a brief paper with the same title as this, namely *The Criticisms of the Christians et cetera* in the fifth part,[15] mentioning in its introduction that we are petitioners of friendship and harmony, not agents of conflict and opposition, and that we do not wish that

14. Thus, Riḍā indicates his ambivalence towards this project, especially in the light of any offense that might be taken by his Christian friends and colleagues.

15. Article One in this book.

anyone among the Muslims and the Christians defames the religion of the other. This is due to our belief that, for each faction, demonstration of the good qualities of its religion suffices for the call to it, without need for defamation. Indeed, Islam implemented this principle, growing dramatically and spreading rapidly, the like of which knows no equal in history. We also mentioned that if our Muslim brothers agree with us about the agreeability of this approach, the Christians do not, because they compose books, write letters, and publish newspapers to defame our religion, sending them to us for a reply.

One of the men of letters and scholars of their religion, Niqūlā Afandī Ghibriyāl, composed a new book calling for conversion to Christianity and challenging Islam.[16] This book is distinguished from others in its objectivity and lack of profanity. He presented it to us as a gift so that we might discuss it at *al-Manār*. Then, he came to meet us, asking that we publish our opinion of it, even if it should disprove his ideas. We also met one of the missionary colleagues of the author who beseeched us to write, emphasizing the necessity of our so doing. There is no doubt that debate is the occupation of those who live by it. As the seller seeks a buyer, the debater seeks another debater. But the petition for a reply to the book was not restricted to these individuals. Some of the newspaper editors among the Christians even requested this of us, such as his excellency Ṣāḥib al-Saʿādah Salīm Bāshir al-Ḥamawī, who did so both verbally and in writing, in his honorable newspaper *al-Falāḥ*. There is no doubt that were we to respond to these authors measure for measure, we would move beyond the boundaries of defense into assault, such that they would see our hand span as a cubit and our cubit as a fathom. For if the religion of innate disposition is not established, [6] no religion may be established. And had the Muslims not concealed Islam from view, all wise Europeans would have accepted it.

That is clear to anyone who examines the three religions in terms of their holy books, in knowledge of the histories and biographies of those who brought them. We had a conversation with one of the scholars of

16. The book is *Abḥāth al-Mujtahidīn*. See Articles Five, Six, Eight and Nine.

history among the "geographical Christians," those who are not fanatical with regard to the truth of religion. The subject of the debate was, "Who is the greatest man of history?" and we imposed upon ourselves the proviso that we were not "believers" in religion. I mentioned Muḥammad, while he mentioned Moses and Jesus, may prayer and peace be upon them all. We agreed that they were the greatest of men, but disagreed as to which was greatest and most honored in terms of condition and historical influence.

I said: Moses was raised in the house of the greatest king in the world at that time, as if he was his son. Thus, he grew up in the bosom of royalty and power, was saturated with love of power and rule, witnessed the civilized way of life and the universal and magical sciences, and saw the arts of industry. He was raised in the shadow of positive and religious law, while the pride of monarchy made manifest that which shaped his temper in the way of courage and initiative. Then, when he came of age and became an enemy and an affliction to the Pharaoh and his family, he knew that he had at his disposal an oppressed and disgraced nation, in spite of what it had been granted in the way of natural intelligence, seriousness in work, and multiple offspring. Hence, he took it as his partisan support, and endeavored to establish a kingdom that his soul desired due to the royal upbringing he had received. And he opposed and fought Pharaoh, first using the power with which Pharaoh had captured souls and with whose authority he had enslaved the peoples. It is the power of the strange works in whose lap he was raised. Then, he rebelled against him using the strength of partisan support, the like of which may be seen among many peoples in many kingdoms. History informs us that among the rebels there may be one who establishes an emirate or kingdom inside the kingdom against whose authority he had rebelled. Yet Moses went out from Egypt fleeing from Pharaoh with his people. As for the crossing of the sea, the strange work that cannot be a trick, nor *legerdemain*, magic, or skill, some of the historians explained that Israelites crossed the sea at the end of the tide's ebb at a point of shallow depth. And when the Pharaoh crossed the sea with the Egyptians, the waters of the tide had begun to rise and flood, so they drowned. The like of this happened to Napoleon Bonaparte [7] as he crossed to the far shore of the Red Sea at the time of the tide's ebb. When he needed to return to the shore of Egypt, the water had begun to rise. Had he not commanded his soldiers to grasp hold of each other until the strength of the group overpowered the strength of the rising water, they would all have drowned. What exceeds this in the strange works of Moses: in its transmission are dubiosities; in its comprehension are doubts; in its evidence for his demonstration thereof and his speaking on God Almighty's behalf is speculation. If some in the past accepted it, is not possible that those today accept it. Of the law that he brought, history testifies that the greater part conforms with the Egyptians' laws. What exceeds that is not more than that of one raised with his upbringing, and granted the like of his disposition's intelligence.

As for Jesus, he was a Jewish man raised under the Mosaic Law. He judged according to the Roman codes and was acquainted with Greek philosophy. Thus, he knew the civilizations of three nations, the greatest civilizations among the nations of the earth and the most advanced in science and precept. He was not induced by any of this to legislate a new shari'ah, nor to establish a nation. Rather, he was a well-spoken teacher. His mind was penetrated by some excesses of certain Greek philosophers concerning renunciation, forsaking worldly life altogether, and humiliating the soul for the spirit's salvation and entry into the kingdoms of heaven. Thus, he began preaching this enthusiastically, and some of the poor followed him, finding consolation and solace in his message. They began enthusiastically reporting some of his miracles, as is well-known of common folk. Indeed, what is reported about him is less than a tenth of a tenth of what is reported about anyone of the Muslims' Sufi saints (*awliyā'*), such as al-Jīlī and al-Badawī.[17] As for his being born without a father, this is

17. Al-Jīlī is the popular name for 'Abd al-Qādir al-Jīlānī (1078–1166), the Sufi saint after whom the first great Sufi order, the *Qādiriyyah*, is named. Significantly, al-Jīlī propagated a distinctly "sober" form of Sufism that incorporated both orthodox law and mystical teaching. He stands in sharp contrast to antinomian Sufis, notably al-Ḥallāj, who publicly flouted Islamic orthodoxy, Al-Jīlī's career was of decisive significance in setting down several enduring and characteristic features of the Sufi brotherhood or *Ṭarīqah.*

a claim that cannot be proven except by the religion of Islam's proof, by rational proof, not by miracles. But this is not our topic here. Hence the historian, if he thinks well, would state that Jesus is the son of Joseph the carpenter, husband of Mary. This marriage is not denied by Christians.[18]

Moses, then, had a great influence, but for Jesus history does not recognize an influence worthy of mention in science, social reform, or civilization. Indeed, on the contrary, his teachings and exhortations lead to the spoliation of civilization, the destruction of culture, and the decline of humankind from its highest horizon to the lowest depth of animal existence. This is due to what they contain teaching the raising of souls in humiliation [8] and baseness, assent to abasement and oppression, and the command to forsake the flourishing and upgrading of life in the belief that the camel enters the eye of the needle, whereas the rich man does not enter the kingdoms of heaven. Furthermore, from a second angle, these are libertine teachings, because they teach that one who believes in the

Al-Jīlī also sets the precedent for the Sufi master as a paradigm of spiritual guidance living among the believers, which grew in importance after the demise of the caliphate in 1258. As Sufi master, al-Jīlī became part of a hierarchy at the top of which he stood as the perfect man (*al-insān al-kāmil*) who was the "pole" (*quṭb*) around which the world revolved. Hence, while the master himself propagated sober Sufism, Riḍā's comment refers to the al-Jīlī of legend, in whom the miraculous nature of the divine is manifest. He walks on water, floats through the air; angels, jinn and even Muḥammad appear, to express their appreciation for him. As W. Braume notes, "nothing is impossible for him" as he is "the concrete presence of the Divine." For Riḍā, such miraculous stories are to be treated with caution, while those told of Jesus, simply as such, do not corroborate Christian claims about his nature and are clearly not unique. Al-Jīlī is also believed to play a mediating role between the worshipper and the divine, another Christian-like notion of which Riḍā himself would be unlikely to approve.

Similar beliefs are popularly held about the miraculous powers of Sayyid Aḥmad al-Badawī (1199/ 1200–1276), founder of the Badawiyyah order. Sīdī Aḥmad, as he is popularly known, is also called the "pole" and is probably the most popular Sufi saint in Egypt. W. Braume, "Abd al-Qādir al-Djīlānī," in *EI*.Frederick Denny, *An Introduction to Islam* 247–252.

18. See the accounts of the slanders made against Mary in chapters four (4:156) and nineteen of the Qur'an. This issue also involves the Roman accusation that Jesus was the child of adultery.

crucifixion of Christ for the sake of his salvation is favored with the kingdoms of heaven, and has all of his sins erased. One who believed this would deem every taboo violate, following his desire.[19] From a third angle, we see that these are pagan teachings, because they command worshiping the human, extinguishing the light of the mind by commanding it to believe in the certainty of something of whose impossibility it is absolutely certain, namely three being one, and one being three. And it banishes the independence of thought and will when forcing them to be chained to the authority of the church leaders according to the following teaching: "whatever you loosen on earth will be loosened in heaven, and whatever you bind on earth will be bound in heaven."[20]

As for the claim that European civilization is Christian, it is a claim destroyed by the rudiments of thought because this is a materialistic civilization built upon love of money, power, overpowering others, glory, majesty, exaltedness and the savoring of passions, all of which is completely contradicted by Christian teaching. Also, the Europeans did not achieve what they achieved until they discarded the Christian teachings altogether. Were this civilization derived from the influence of Christian teaching, it would have ensued from it at a time close to its formation. However, it did not appear until some centuries after its appearance. The upshot is that history does not recognize for Christ an influence granting him the standing of the lawgivers and reformers of nations.

As for Muḥammad, prayer and peace be upon him, he was raised as an orphan in a nation of paganism, illiteracy, and ignorance, one lacking religious or positive law, civilization, national unity, and industry. The highest station it attained in his time was that some individuals learned to write, due to their dealings with other nations. He was not among them, nor were those who first followed him in faith. In spite of this, he founded a nation, religion, shari'ah, kingdom and civilization in a short period, the like of which knows no equivalent in history.

19. In Islamic discourse, this Christian doctrine is sometimes referred to in association with the Crusades.

20. Riḍā is paraphrasing Mt 16:19, but reverses the order of "binding" and "loosening."

He taught humanity to build its doctrines on the foundations of rational proofs, to set its cultures and dispositions on the path of moderation, to safeguard the rights of the spirit and the body, and to [9] observe the ways of God in creation and with nations. He explained the acts of worship to them in terms of their influences in purifying and cleansing the spirit, such as the salat (*ṣalāh*) preventing lewdness and the forbidden through what was stipulated in it in the way of humility*et cetera.*[21] He made good things lawful for them, forbade them abominable actions, and rendered worldly transactions focused upon the safeguarding of human welfare and the procurement of benefit. He liberated the freedom of mind and thought for them, and equalized rights among them, there being no distinction between the great king and the poor pauper, or between man and woman. He gave the woman freedom of control over her properties, set down just limits for men's control over women and for slavery, refined a system of warfare, prohibiting outrage, mutilation of those killed in battle, and the killing of non-combatants such as women, elderly men, children, and men of religion *et cetera*, as I mentioned to that historian investigator. I will elaborate the teaching about it in the coming lessons on divine oneness, if God wills.

That honored man conceded to me that Muḥammad, the best prayer and peace be upon him, is the greatest man of history, except he argued against me in terms of the Muslims' sorry condition contrasting with what had I said in my description of the religion of Islam. So I said to him: "Truly there is between Islam and the Muslims a difference like that between Christianity and the Christians or greater." Suffice to say that Islamic civilization did not exist other than through the religion of Islam (see the articles on the civilization of the Arabs in *al-Manār* volume three), receding from them whenever they innovated in the religion and strayed from its straight path, until they arrived at their present condition.[22] As for the European civilization that some people term Christian, it did not exist until the people of Europe came into contact with the

21. Compare Qur'an 24:21: "Unto whomsoever followeth the devil, he commandeth lewdness and the forbidden." Trans. author (adapted from Pickthall).

22. See *al-Manār*, iii, 289–93; 319–22; 385–91; 409–14; 529–33.

Muslims, taking their books and translating them, and they continued advancing in their civilization as they distanced themselves from Christianity.[23] He said, "this is exaggeration on both points," and the meeting ended.

It remains that the abovementioned criticisms of the prophecies of Moses and Jesus, prayer and peace be upon them both, extend to the prophecy of Muḥammad, God Almighty's blessing and peace be upon him. This is not because his religion can be rejected in the same way that what is known of their religions can be rejected. Rather, it is because he corroborated their prophecy and divine guidance. The reply is found in the summary (The Criticisms of the Christians against Islam) published in this year's fifth part.[24] Were [10] the men of religion among the Jews and Christians just, they would hold fast to this answer and agree with it, because it alone rebuts for them the objections of the scholars of history, archeology, geology, natural history, philosophy, sociology, and anthropology. As for the reply concerning the miraculous sign of Moses' parting of the waters, it is that what some historians mentioned concerning the rise and ebb of the tide is a possibility that is outweighed by the reports of revelation established by actual proof, as we explained in the lesson on divine oneness previous to this article.[25] The same may be said with regard to all of the miraculous signs and the criticisms leveled against them. We shall complete the response about what we mentioned about the historical objections to the teachings attributed to Christ.

To summarize what we are saying here: religion's affirmation is either effected through the reporting of supernatural phenomena beyond the

23. Riḍā is following 'Abduh's argument in *Islam and Christianity*. See Chapter One.
24. Article One in this book.
25. *Al-Manār*, iv, 371–79. Lesson Twenty-Nine, Discussion Sixty-Three: "The Sign or Miracle." In this dictated lesson, Riḍā goes into greater detail on the Islamic doctrine of miracles, particularly in relation to their corroboration of revelation and prophecy. He notes that the scholastic theologians differ on the exact nature of miracles, but avoids excessive speculation on this issue. Instead, he emphasizes their function in providing guidance towards the need to submit to prophetic mission and standing as a clear proof against "people of denial."

people's ken. The theory of this was given in the lesson on divine oneness, and it is also shared by all, because every nation reports about its lawgiver in that manner. Thus, what is said about the reporting of one may be said about the reporting of others. However, the reporting of the Muslims is closer to the truth than that of others for many reasons. Among them: that knowledge, composition, and oral narration have been known to them from the first century until the present day. Among them: that they were not conquered by an enemy who burned their books and destroyed the things that instill confidence in their religion and history. Among them: that they were not oppressed and forced to conceal their religion, as it is said that corruption occurs when religion is concealed. Among them: that they invented the science of biography for determining the soundness or unsoundness of a narration. The Jews and Christians lacked such advantages.

Or, religion's affirmation is effected through signs inside the self and knowledge-related signs. And this is not manifest in a prophet as manifest in connection to our prophet, God's blessing and peace be upon him, as we explained in the lesson on divine oneness published in this part. We shall elaborate our explanation in what is forthcoming, as we promised. Then, the sound proof for the prophecy of Moses and Jesus, peace be upon them, in this time is our prophet's testimony for them. God Almighty granted them miraculous signs appropriate to the conditions of the nations during their lifetimes. It is not possible that they be self-affirming now. Hence, we see whoever is educated and rational among those affiliated with Moses and Jesus discarding them completely, deeming them fabricated. Had such an individual known Islam truly, he would have accepted it, and accepted them from the perspective of rationality.

Therefore, the best service to ultimate religion is that Islam be known truly, so that Judaism and Christianity also be known [11] in an acceptable manner. That is achieved by reconciling the Torah and Gospel with the Qur'an, as we so reconciled in the fifth part. It is not achieved by seeking Qur'anic evidence for the veracity of the Torah and Gospel, and then seeking evidence from what they name "the Torah" – consisting of those numerous books, most of which were composed after the author of the

Torah – and the numerous collected books and letters they name "Gospel," for the falsehood of the Qur'an. This is because such action returns the subject to logical incompatibility, so that the evidence refutes itself. The least of what may be said on this is: "They fought with each other, both falling down." The result is the invalidation of all scriptures, namely, saying that the Qur'an constitutes evidence for the veracity of the Torah and Gospel, when, according to their claim, the Qur'an is not from God. Thus, its testimony is false and its evidence unsound. We shall return to debating the book *Researches of the Mujtahids* and the newspaper *The Glad Tidings of Peace*, uniting the religions and calling for the elimination of rancor (p. 379. vol. 4).

Article Three: Comparison between Islam and Christianity in Terms of the Three Goals of Religion

[11] In the fifth and tenth parts, we explained the Muslim view of what is intended by the "Torah and Gospel" for which the Noble Qur'an testifies.[26] We explained that, for the Christians, no proof arises for the establishment of their religion and scripture, and the prophecy of Moses and Jesus, may peace be upon them, except that of the Qur'an. The Qur'an cannot be a proof unless it is from God Almighty. Hence, it is incumbent upon them to believe in it, embrace its reform and become, like us, upholders of divine oneness. We worship Him and Him alone, not any human being, such as Christ or anyone else. We call all pagans to this faith – which represents the highest station in the elevation of human reason and in which is prosperity and salvation in the hereafter – together with the good acts that it mandates. In the lesson on divine oneness published in the previous part, we established the prophecy of our prophet, may prayer and peace be upon him, with rational evidence and that what he brought was revelation.[27] We shall elaborate on this explanation in the coming lessons, God Almighty willing.

These evangelists [12] invite us to investigate into religion. Or, they invite us to believe – it being a "matter of faith" – that one of the prophets

26. Articles One and Two in this book.

27. See Article Two.

is fully divine and fully human, and that one is truly three and three truly one, notwithstanding that reason declares this impossible. They invite us to reject one of the prophets, and to deny his prophecy completely, notwithstanding that it is supported by the strongest rational proofs. If, then, they seek to manifest the truth so as to follow it, they are making reason the foundation and appointing it the fundamental judge in weighing evidence. Otherwise, how are truth and falsehood to be distinguished? If they say, "by way of the books of religion," we say, first, "by what criteria are these books to be verified?" If they say, "by way of reason," we say, "you are forced, then, to appoint reason as fundamental judge," and it is not feasible that reason would assert the veracity of a book containing something that it deems impossible. Second, if the books of religion that you compare are in agreement, then religion is one. Otherwise, by what means are some to be preferred over others? Is it not reason that clarifies which of them are most guiding and life-giving in terms of what humankind seeks in religion?

Religion has three objectives: confirmation of the beliefs through which reason may be perfected, cultivation of the morals that perfect the soul, and the perfection of acts upon which welfare and benefit depend and that perfect the body. Were we to appoint as arbitrator a rational individual who had not previously followed the religious tradition of the Muslims or Christians, and empower him to demonstrate, on the basis of pure reason, which of the two religions truly exhausted these three objectives, on what basis would he make his determination?

He would see the Muslims agreeing on the stipulation that their doctrines' proof must be certain, as their scripture states with regard to supposition that lacks the degree of certainty: "Assuredly conjecture can by no means take the place of truth" [10:36; 53:28]. It states with regard to those who use the will of God Almighty as an excuse for their polytheism: "Have ye any knowledge that ye can adduce for us? Lo! ye follow naught but an opinion, Lo! ye do but guess" [6:148]; "Say: Bring your proof, if ye are truthful!" [27:64].[28] When mentioning the signs that it established as the

28. The complete verse reads: "They who are idolaters will say: Had Allah willed, we had not ascribed (unto Him) partners neither had our fathers, nor had we

basis of belief, it states: "Lo! herein indeed are portents for folk who understand [30:24]; Lo! herein verily are portents for men of thought [20:54]" – that is, those who have minds.

He would see the Christians agreeing that their belief is above reason, that reason decrees it impossible and unprovable.[29] There is no [13] doubt that he would determine that the Muslims' doctrines are the true truth, and would not deem worthy of consideration the statement of the author of *Researches of the Mujtahids* and others of his ilk: "That constitutes an investigation into the nature of the essence of God Almighty, whereas no one knows the nature of God save God, as Muslims and others agree." The reason is that there is a great difference between what reason proves with evidence – without knowing its deepest essence – and what it repudiates and declares unrealizable. An example of this is found in our furnishing of evidence for matter through its attributes, characteristics, and effects. And while we do not doubt its existence, we do not know the true nature of its essence. Moreover, reason does not attain knowledge of the true nature of any of the created things, but rather comprehends external appearances and attributes. But then the Torah describes God Almighty with attributes that reason rejects, such as the Lord's statement in the sixth chapter of the Book of Genesis: "And the Lord was sorry that he had made humankind on the earth, and it grieved him to his heart. So the Lord said, 'I will blot out from the earth the human beings I have created' " [Gn 6:6–7]. This indicates that He was ignorant and incapable, Exalted be He over such things.

Then, this rational individual and just judge examines the second objective, namely, cultivation of morals. He would see that the Islamic teachings concerning it stand upon the foundations of justice and moderation, without exaggeration or excess, together with preference for

forbidden aught. Thus did those who were before them give the lie (to Allah's messengers) till they tasted of the fear of Us. Say: Have ye any knowledge that ye can adduce for us? Lo! ye follow naught but an opinion, Lo! ye do but guess" (6:148).

29. Riḍā may have derived this interpretation from Biblical passages such as I Cor 1:18–2:14.

pardon, forgiveness and charity, in accordance with their Book: "Lo! Allah enjoineth justice and kindness and giving to kinsfolk, and forbiddeth lewdness and abomination and wickedness. He exhorteth you in order that you may take heed" [16: 90]. Al-Bayḍāwī interprets lewdness as excess with regard to the strength of animal desire, and abomination as excess with regard to the strength of untamed anger.[30]

> Deal justly, that is nearer to piety[5:8].[31]
> And forget not kindness among yourselves [2:238].
> And those who, when they spend, are neither prodigal nor grudging; and there is ever a firm station between the two [25:67].

– and the like, numerous verses, general and specific. He would see that the Christian teachings are built upon exaggeration and excess. Their scripture states: "Love your enemies; pray for those who persecute you," as in the gospel of Matthew 5:44. This is exaggeration in love, something of which humans are incapable, as it is beyond their control. In the Gospel of Luke 19:27: "As for these enemies of mine who did not want me to be king over them – bring them here and slaughter them in my presence."[32] In the Gospel of Luke, chapter 14:25: "and he said to them, 'Whoever comes to me and does not hate [14] his father and mother, wife and children, brothers, yes, and even life itself, cannot be my disciple.'" This exaggeration in love is excess in enmity and hatred, and its like is abundant. There is no doubt that this rational individual would adjudge the religion of moderation superior to the religion of exaggeration and excess. This is because the former elevates and strengthens human souls, as the Almighty states: "might belongeth to Allah and to His messenger,

30. Al-Bayḍāwī (died between 1286 and 1316), a Shāfiʿī jurisprudent, exegete, scholastic theologian and grammarian. He is best known for his revision of the Muʿtazilī Qur'an commentary of al-Zamakhsharī, in which he attempted to remove or refute the unorthodox views of al-Zamakhsharī contained therein, although retaining them on occasion. Al-Bayḍāwī's revision is one of the more popular commentaries. It has been published in many editions and extensively commented upon.
31. Trans. author (adapted from Pickthall).
32. The wording in this citation differs slightly from *VD*.

and the believers" [63:8]. The latter, on the other hand, lowers and debases them, as it states: "whoever strikes you on the right cheek, offer him the left," and the like with the same meaning.[33]

As for the third objective, the good acts that elevate the human species spiritually and bodily, the rational individual would see that in Islam each act of worship among these acts is joined to its benefit, such as the salat (*ṣalāh*) preventing lewdness and what is forbidden, the fast elevating piety, and worship in general being the good pleasure of God Almighty, as per His statement "seeking My good pleasure [60:1]," and other examples of acts that purify the soul and elevate the spirit.[34] He would not see the like of this in the others' scriptures. Rather, he would see in the Torah – which is the book of Christian precepts that Christians profess to believe, but do not do so in reality – that the precepts of worship are related to worldly benefit: as in chapter four of the book of Deuteronomy: "Keep his statutes . . . which I am commanding you today for your own well-being and that of your descendants after you" [Deut 4:40], and as in explaining the festivals' legitimacy through reference to harvest time, cultivation of land, and the exodus from Egypt, in chapter twenty-three of the Book of Exodus, verses fourteen through sixteen. What is this compared with the explanation of the wisdom of the feast of breaking the Ramadan fast (*'Īd al-Fiṭr*) in the Almighty's statement: "and (He desireth) that ye should complete the period, and that ye should magnify Allah for having guided you, and that peradventure ye may be thankful" [2:185]?

The rational individual would see that the Islamic precepts for worldly transactions are based upon the foundation of the maxim "preventing corruption and attaining the good," as Muslims agree, and that the general principles of these precepts are five, known as "the five general principles," namely, the protection of the religion, life, family honor, the mind, and property.[35] He would see that the Islamic shari'ah grants equal rights to those who follow it and those who do not and commands the

33. See Mt 5:39.
34. The complete verse reads: If ye have come forth to strive in My way and seeking My good pleasure (show them not friendship) (60:1).
35. In Islamic law, jihad is justifiable in defense of these five principles.

uncovering of the universe's secrets and extraction of its benefits, as per the Almighty's statement: "And hath made of service unto you whatsoever is in the heavens and whatsoever is in the earth; it is all from Him" [45:13]. He would see that the Torah and Gospel's precepts did not [15] combine these benefits. Rather, they frequently opposed them. Thus the ninth commandment states, "You shall not bear false witness against your neighbor" [Ex 20:16].[36] What is this limitation to the neighbor compared to the Qur'an's commandment in the following and other such verses?

> O ye who believe! Be ye staunch in justice, witnesses for Allah, even though it be against yourselves or (your) parents or (your) kindred, whether (the case be of) a rich man or a poor man, for Allah is nearer to both (than ye are). So follow not passion lest ye lapse (from truth) and if ye lapse or fall away, then lo! Allah is ever Informed of what ye do [4:135].

In chapter fourteen of the book of Deuteronomy, alcohol and other lusts are authorized unrestrictedly: "spend the money for whatever you wish – oxen, sheep, wine, strong drink, or whatever you desire. And you shall eat there in the presence of the Lord . . . you and your household rejoicing together" [Deut 14:26]. In chapter six of the gospel of Matthew: "Do not worry about your life, what you will eat or what you will drink, or about your body, what you will wear" [Mt 6:25]. On another matter: "Do not be uneasy for the sake of the bread which is denied."[37] It commands them thus notwithstanding that they considered bread their lifeblood. They were even commanded to seek it in their prayers, in his statement "Give us this day our daily bread" [Lk 11:3].[38] Then, what is this contradiction?

These books not only command the abandonment of acts performed for the sake of worldly life, but moreover, state that wholesome acts performed in it are of no value or benefit whatsoever. Hence, Paul states in his letter to the Romans: "Now to one who works, wages are not reckoned as a gift but as something due. But to one who without works trusts

36. The wording in this citation differs slightly from *VD*.
37. Although Riḍā indicates direct quotation, this is perhaps a loose paraphrasing of Mt 6:31. Cf. Mk 8:17; Mt 16:8.
38. The wording in this citation differs slightly from *VD*.

him who justifies the ungodly, such faith is reckoned as righteousness" [Rom 4:4–5]. This, whereas God states in the Qur'an:

> But righteous is he who believeth in Allah and the Last Day and the angels and the Scriptures and the Prophets; and giveth his wealth for love of Him, to kinsfolk and to orphans and the needy and the wayfarer and to those who ask, and to set slaves free; and observeth proper worship and payeth the poor-due. And those who keep their treaty when they make one, and the patient in tribulation and adversity and time of stress [2:177].

Then, will nations achieve success through these acts or through a faith that attributes no value to acts performed in its fulfillment?

Paul affirms this idea in chapter three of his letter to the Galatians when mentioning that the acts of God's Law are cursed, that in God's view no one is justified by the Law, and that [16] there is no need for it after Christ's coming.[39] Christ himself, however, states, "I did not come to abolish the Law, rather I came to complete it."[40] However, Christians act in accordance with Paul's doctrine, relinquishing the Torah and its precepts altogether. The messengers permitted them all prohibited things, except fornication, shed blood, what has been strangled, and what has been sacrificed to idols (Acts 15:28–29). It is as if they saw that the Torah's shari'ah was not suitable for humankind. Take for example, Ezekiel chapter twenty, which states that when He became angry with the Israelites, the Lord said:

> (23) Moreover I swore to them in the wilderness that I would scatter them among the nations and disperse them through the countries, (24) because they had not executed my ordinances, but had rejected my statutes and

39. Riḍā follows Islamic precedent in regarding Paul highly critically. In classical discourse, Paul often takes responsibility for corrupting Jesus' message, as Constantine takes responsibility for falsifying the historical position of the Christian community. Paul is specifically deemed responsible for fabricating the doctrines of Trinity and Redemption. Riḍā is perhaps referring to a passage such as Gal. 3:10–14.
40. See Mt 5:17.

> profaned my Sabbaths, and their eyes were set on their ancestors' idols. (25) Moreover I gave them statutes that were not good and ordinances by which they could not live [Ezek 20:23–25].

Ezekiel explains before this that the Israelites worshiped idols after God delivered them from Egypt. So let that Christian evangelist take a lesson from this, and also that Jew, the two who censured me for what I wrote in the tenth issue about the Israelites' desire to worship idols, whereas these two claimed that there was no report of this except that of the Qur'an (p. 411. vol. 4.).

Article Four: On Judaism and Christianity Being Derived from Paganism

[16] We mentioned in the previous summary that the beliefs of the Christians, which they have been following for a long period, are derived from pagan beliefs. We stated that the collection of books that, according to the Jews and Christians, is called "Torah" is not the Torah for which the Noble Qur'an testifies. Rather, the Qur'anic Torah consists of the precepts that Moses, peace be upon him, brought and they are – that is, some of them are – in the five books attributed to Moses, except the book of Genesis, which includes his history and mention his death. We explained that there is no means by which the People of the Book can escape from the objections that philosophers, scholars and historians make against their scriptures except by agreeing with the Muslims about this belief.

Here, we present [17] the views of one of the French philosophers who attacks Judaism and Christianity and their scriptures, quoting from the book *The Standard of Religion* by 'Alī Pāshā Mubārak, he of everlasting memory, previously the minister of education.[41] In conversation number

41. 'Alī Pāshā Mubārak (1823–1893) was an Egyptian statesman and scholar who held numerous ministerial posts between 1850 and 1891; Minister of Education (1888–91) being his last. He is known principally for his modernizing and westernizing reforms in that field. He was responsible for the foundation of Dār al-'Ulūm, the teachers' training college in Cairo based upon the European model, and the introduction of the printing of textbooks in Egypt. K. Vollers, "'Alī Pashā Mubārak," in *EI*.

ninety-four, Mubārak gives an English translator's account of the French philosopher's views.

> He states that the Torah is a compiled book and not among the heavenly books, relying on the statement of Mary Augustus "that it is not feasible that the first three chapters stand in their present form" and the statement of Eugene to the effect that what is found in the Torah pertaining to the creation of the world is legendary, on the basis that the Hebrew word *barrāh* – which is pronounced with a *fatḥah* on the *bā'*, doubling of the *rā'*, and *sukūn* on the *hā'* – means "he arranged" and "he ordered".[42] It is not possible for anyone to "arrange" and "order" something that does not exist. Thus, the application of this word to the creation of the world requires that the material substance of the world was pre-existent and eternal, and that time and space are eternal. Since they say that the matter is the essence of life, it follows that the spirit must also be eternal, since it is through the spirit that life occurs. And inasmuch as matter is light, heat, potency, movement, gravity, natural law and balance, then life and matter are as one thing that cannot be divided. All of this contradicts the Torah.
>
> He also states that the six days Moses mentions for the creation of the world are the six ages of the Hindus, the six *janbaharāt* that Zarathushtra mentions for the Magi, the paradise Adam was in was the garden of Hespirides that the dragon guarded, Adam is Adīmu mentioned in Ayzūrūyidām, and Noah and his people refers to King Deucalion and his wife Bīrā and so on.
>
> He goes far in attacking the Torah, stating that it begins with: a brother's killing of his brother, the violation of women, the marriage of close relatives and, beyond that, domestic animals, and mentioning of robbery, plunder, killing, fornication, and such matters that do not befit being attributed to those God Almighty selects and makes guardian over His divine secrets.
>
> So look at the audacity of this man against the prophet of God, Moses, may peace be upon him, and against the book of God, the Torah, although

42. This is incorrect. The *rā'* is not doubled in this Hebrew word. It is curious that the author does not refer to the Arabic *bara'a*, cognate to the Hebrew *barah*.

> the Torah is the foundation of the Gospel, thus what is said of the Torah is [18] said of the Gospel.[43]

Al-Manār: This sentence and that which follows it is the Englishman's commentary. There is no doubt that the invalidation of the Torah mandates the invalidation of the Gospel and there is no escaping that, save by Islam.

> Hence, they say that Jesus' mission was previously well-known to the Jews, on the basis of their doctrine that a *masīḥ* (an anointed one) will come to them. The word *masīḥ* is similar to the word *masāyas*, an honorable title in the Hebrew language. Indeed, Isaiah bestowed this title on Cyrus, the king of Persia, as reported in the fifty-fifth chapter of the Holy Scriptures.[44] And Ezekiel the prophet bestowed this title upon the king of the city of Tyre. In spite of this, this man paid attention to none of it, and said what he said.

> Another Christian belief is the belief that God became incarnate in the form of Jesus and that he is the God. They were not the first to speak of incarnation. Rather, it was said earlier of Jazākā and Brahma, in India's holy city, and it was said that Vishnu became incarnate five hundred times. The inhabitants of Peru in America said that that the true God became incarnate in their god Ūdīn. The birth of Jesus from the Virgin Mary through the triumph of the Holy Spirit resembles the statement of the people of China that their god Fuwah was born of a virgin girl who was impregnated with him by the rays of the sun. The ancient Egyptians believed that Osiris was born without anyone having had sexual intercourse with his mother.

> The Christians' statement that Jesus died, was buried, was resurrected and elevated to heaven alive resembles the statement of the ancient Egyptians before them about the Egyptian Osiris, and Adonis by the peoples of Phoenicia and Atis by the peoples of Frigea – except that they did not say that he was elevated to heaven. Similarly, it was said that Odin sacrificed himself, killing himself of his own choice by throwing himself in a terrible fire until he burned, and did so for the salvation of his worshippers and his

43. ʿAlī Pāshā Mubārak, *ʿAlam al-Dīn* (Egypt: Maṭbaʿat Jarīdat al-Maḥrūsah, 1882), vol. 3., 1096–1097.
44. This is incorrect. The reference is to Isa. 45, not Isa. 55. See also Isa. 44:28.

> people. Likewise, Christians believe that the incarnation of God in Jesus, his sending, and his death, were only to redeem the human race, and save it from the crime of the first sin, namely, the sin of Adam and Eve. As for the prophet Enoch, he was elevated to heaven without having been pardoned for his sin. There is no doubt that this is a legendary tale, and they have numerous others that are similar, whose explanation is lengthy and of no benefit.[45]

[19]*Al-Manār*: Due to these criticisms, and more than that, proofs against the doctrines of the Christians and the Jews, European scholars abandoned the Christian religion. Some openly announced this abandonment and moreover, so did some of their governments. Indeed, the French government made a formal announcement that it had no religion and pursued and persecuted clergy and prominent individuals who persisted in professing religious belief for a political end. For this reason, you see those philosophers and scholars who care about politics declaring disbelief in revelation, in spite of their belief that religion is necessary for humankind. Yet they found no utility in religion as they understood it, while the religion of innate disposition was concealed from them. Hence, they translated The Generous Qur'an poorly, producing a corrupt translation, not understanding the true nature of Islam from it. I give as an example an English translation of *Sūrat al-'Aṣr* (The Declining Day): "verily, by three hours after noon a man becomes bad or despicable."[46]

45. Mubārak, 1097–1098.
46. Riḍā, who is not known to have read English, re-translates an unidentified English translation back into Arabic to enable the reader to compare it with the original Arabic. Thus, the deficiency of the English translation is shown. Translations in circulation during Riḍā's time include those of J.M. Rodwell (1861, 1876), Edward H. Palmer (1880, 1900), and G. Sale (1734, 1764, 1795, 1801), which was translated into Arabic by Christian missionaries. A less likely possibility, given its chronology, is *The Alcoran of Mahomet* by Alexander Ross (died 1654). It is unclear from Riḍā's translation which, if any, of these he cites.

    Ross's translation of the above chapter reads:

    I swear by the hour of the Evening, That men are inclined to their destruction, except such as believe in God, that do good works, and have in esteem truth and perseverance. (London: Randal Taylor, 1688), 505.

Had the philosophers of Europe understood this chapter, they would have asserted that, in spite of its brevity, it dispenses with all that they know from the books of the other religions. The chapter is understood in general terms by any individual who has no more than a rudimentary knowledge of the Arabic language. The chapter is the following:

> By the declining day,
> Lo! man is in a state of loss,
> Save those who believe and do good works, and exhort one another to truth and exhort one another to endurance [103:1–3].

The individual would know, then, that the wording of the oath is used for emphasis. He would know that "man" refers to mankind in general, that "good works" are acts that improve man's condition, spiritually and bodily, individually and collectively, that "mutual exhortation to truth" is mutual assistance in taking hold of and establishing it, that "the truth" is something established and certain, while the affirmation of anything is determined on its basis, that "endurance" includes renouncing repulsive things – such as sins and harmful desires – and patience in the face of things that are hard to endure, such as defense of the truth and calamities.

Rodwell's 1861 translation (New York: Dutton, 1971) reads:
The Afternoon
I swear by the declining day!
Verily, man's lot is cast amid destruction,
Save those who believe and do the things which be right, and enjoin truth and enjoin steadfastness on each other.
Palmer's translation (Oxford: Clarendon Press, 1900) reads:
The Chapter of the Afternoon
By the afternoon! Verily man is in loss! Save those who believe and do right and bid each other be true, and bid each other to be patient.
Sale's 1734 translation (New York: A.L. Bert) reads:
The Afternoon
By the afternoon,
verily man employeth himself in that which will prove of loss:
Except those who believe, and do that which is right; and who
mutually recommend the truth, and mutually recommend perseverance unto each other.

Among the peoples of Europe, those of Russia and Spain had held most strongly to Christianity. Then recently, the Spaniards suppressed the clergy. The telegraph cable rapidly spread news of this development to every region and newspapers in every country picked up the story.[47] And when the Russian philosopher Tolstoy disproved [20] the teachings of the Orthodox Church and explained the falsity of the Christian religion, teachers of the sciences and arts – and even the students of the schools, male and female – came to his aid.[48] Thus, this is the fate of the Christian religion: as an individual grows in knowledge, he distances himself from it. Europe was Christian during the days of the darkness of ignorance and stupidity.[49] The Islamic religion, the ally of the sciences, stands opposite Christianity. Indeed, its community was at its high point of civilization and science when holding most strongly to its religion, whereas it became distanced from the religion as it distanced itself from science.

As for today, we, indeed, do not deny that some of the educated are following the path of Europeanization. Indeed, they fell victim to some of the criticisms, and some rejected the religion, following the Europeans from whom they learned. However, the reason is that these individuals had never known nor studied Islam, either before studying European thought, or after.

For this reason, we demand of our religion's ulama that they strive to grasp the reins of teaching the universal sciences,[50] because we have the most complete confidence that it is not possible for an individual who knows Islam to reject it. How can one who has lived in the light choose

47. This is probably a reference to the Spanish revolution of 1868–75 and the first Spanish republic, 1873–74.
48. Riḍā is probably referring to the famous author's rejection of Orthodox Christianity and organized religion in his essay "The Kingdom of God is Within You" (1894). The essay is the culmination of a personal spiritual crisis described in the earlier "My Confession" (1882). Tolstoy's fame sparked considerable interest in his religious ideas, leading the Church to excommunicate him in 1901.
49. See also *al-Manār*, xxv, 1924, 190.
50. Riḍā urges Islamic scholars to overcome the predicament that non-ulama – or, more generally, non-Muslims – had a monopoly on the teaching of modern and universal sciences. Riḍā clearly felt that, in the field of education, Muslims had much to learn from Christians.

darkness? This is a matter to which we shall return, God Almighty willing. (See *al-Manār*, p. 448, vol. 4.)

Article Five: On Responding to the Book **Researches of the Mujtahids'** *Qur'anic Evidence for the Veracity of the Torah and Gospel*[51]

If someone wishes to debate these Christians who compose books calling the Muslims to Christianity, and utilize objective knowledge in evaluating their literary works, so that he replies to each error that requires a reply, he would need to write a separate book about each of their dark pages, because they talk without restraint. Thus, they make errors concerning what they know and what they do not know, and resort to deluding and deceit, as they write for the common folk who do not investigate carefully.[52]

[21] In section one of investigation one, the author of the book *"Researches" of the Disputatious* – not *"the Mujtahids"*[53] – states that he establishes the veracity of the Torah and the Gospel "by incontrovertible argument and logical proof."[54] He then quotes Qur'anic verses whose meanings, in his view, are disputable rather than clear-cut. He distorts their meaning, as he and those before him distorted the Torah and Gospel.[55] We explained previously the meaning of "Torah and Gospel," the Qur'anic corroboration of them, and how this corroboration does not

51. Niqūlā Y. Ghibrīl, *Abḥāth al-Mujtahidīn fī al-Khilāf bayn al-Naṣārā wa al-Muslimīn* (The Mujtahids' Researches on the Dispute between Christians and Muslims) (Cairo: Ghibrīl, 1913). The book ran to at least four editions, the first, third and fourth being published in 1901, 1913, and 1922.
52. Ghibrīl comments in his introduction that his book is based upon his discussions with his "Muslim brothers," discussions that were conducted in a spirit of "love and sincere intention." He also states that his book is written for "rational Muslims" who "examine matters closely." Ghibrīl, 3.
53. Riḍā mocks his opponent, suggesting that his book has the wrong title.
54. Ghibrīl, 5.
55. Riḍā states that Ghibrīl deems the verses in question subject to discussion and debate and ambiguous or illogical. On the other hand, Ghibrīl himself describes the verses in question as: "clear, with the utmost clarity, to the extent that they do not require the allegorical interpretation of al-Rāzī or the exegesis of [al-Zamakhsharī's] *al-Kashshāf*." Ghibrīl, 6.

preclude the sending of another prophet with a new and more complete shari'ah. We also explained the purpose of the Islamic religion in its being more befitting for the human condition, and providing greater guidance towards humanity's prosperity. Beyond that, we explained how Paul rendered the shari'ah of the Torah and Gospel worthless, and rendered Christianity libertinism, attaching no value to good acts, but resting upon the belief that Christ came to redeem the world.

How can our friends among the Christian propagandists deem it possible that the eloquent tongue and beguiling of this Jewish man could invalidate the shari'ah of Moses and Jesus, may peace and prayer be upon them, yet not deem it possible that God would send Muḥammad, may the best prayer and peace be upon him, with logical proofs, so that he corroborate the messengers, condemn apostates, censure corruptors, clarify the truth with respect to the disputing of the disputatious, and direct his words to the Jews and Christians as Jesus directed his words to the scribes and the Pharisees: stating they did not establish the scripture, but rather embraced the outer shell and forsook the inner kernel? Indeed, had they established it, their condition would not have degenerated and their shame and punishment would not have become necessary. Yet, at the time of the mission, the Jews and Christians were under the greatest shame and punishment and at the extreme limit of willful sin and misguidance. For this reason, after a period of time, their power's prestige was diminished by the sun of Islam: "To help the unbelievers is incumbent upon us" [30:47].

The author of *Researches* relates seven verses from The Glorious Qur'an. He states that the first verse indicates that God Almighty revealed the Torah and the Gospel as guidance for mankind.[56] Yes, indeed, earlier peoples were rightly guided by both and prospered. Then, they deviated and strayed, were corrupted and became wretched, until Islam brought [22] the greatest guidance and the strongest proof. Some of them were guided by it, prospered and became masters over others. They were with its people who were uppermost, so long as they were guided by it.[57]

56. The passage cited reads: "He revealed the Torah and the Gospel: Aforetime, for a guidance to mankind" (3:3–4). Ghibrīl, 5.

57. Perhaps a reference to Qur'an 3:139: "ye will be uppermost if ye are (indeed)

He states that the second verse proves the veracity of the Torah and Gospel. The verse is: "[Say:] O People of the Scripture! Ye have naught (of guidance) till ye observe the Torah and the Gospel" [5:68].[58] And indeed it is so. However, the verse is incomplete. The author does not quote the remainder, as he is not a just man. It is: "and that which was revealed unto you from your Lord" [5:68]. Thus, it is as if he commands us to believe in part of the Book and disbelieve in part, as he and those of his ilk do with the Torah. The intended meaning of "that which was revealed unto them from their Lord" is the Qur'an, as nothing other than it was revealed after the Torah and Gospel.[59]

God Almighty commands the People of the Book to become Muslims, and believe in all the scriptures. And He makes clear that their pretext and protestation against following the Qur'an – that they possess a heavenly book and thus have no need for another – is an invalid protestation and false pretext, as they did not establish the Torah and Gospel. He made this clear in other verses declaring that they corrupted and "forgot a part of that whereof they were admonished" [5:13; 5:14] and that had they established both, shame and ignominy would not have befallen them: "If they had observed the Torah and the Gospel and that which was revealed to them from their Lord, they would surely have been nourished from above them and from beneath their feet" [5:66]. Thus is what occurred to their brothers who accepted Islam, and they indeed obtained the blessings of the sky and earth. The remainder of the verse with which we are concerned is: "That which is revealed unto thee (Muḥammad) from thy Lord

believers" – Trans. author (adapted from Pickthall) – or Qur'an 47:35: "ye (will be) the uppermost."

58. Ghibrīl, 5–6.

59. The complete verse reads: "*Say, O People of the Scripture! Ye have naught (of guidance) till ye observe the Torah and the Gospel* [cited by Ghibrīl] and that which was revealed to you from your Lord. That which is revealed unto thee (Muḥammad) from thy Lord is certain to increase the contumacy and disbelief of many of them. But grieve not for the disbelieving folk" (5:68). Interestingly, the verse immediately following, 5:69, is one of the prominent instances of Qur'anic praise of Christians.

is certain to increase the contumacy and disbelief of many of them. But grieve not for the disbelieving folk" [5:68]. This proof stands over them until the day of resurrection. Hence, these evangelists deceive the common Muslims about the necessity of following the Torah, and delude them that in fact they are following it. *Researches*' author states that Muḥammad sought the establishment of its divine statutes. And no one in Christian life establishes any of the Torah's statutes, or acts according to its precepts in worship or social life. Then, wherefore are they concerned for the Muslims, and sincerely advising them about establishing these statutes, while not sincerely advising and being concerned for themselves?

He states: the third verse makes clear that the Gospel descended from God and that Muḥammad submitted to its precepts.[60] The third verse is the Almighty's statement: "Let the People of the Gospel judge by that which Allah hath revealed therein" [5:47].[61] There is no indication here that Muḥammad, prayer and peace be upon him, submitted to its precepts. Yet [23], to confirm their desires, these people allow themselves to impute to the verses what they do not support. In this way, they have corrupted their own scriptures, and come corrupting our Book for us. But God Almighty preserved it from corruption and alteration. The verse has two readings, the first with a *kasrah* on the *lām*: *li-yaḥkum* (in order to judge), which pertains to the Almighty's statement prior to it: "and We bestowed on him the Gospel" [5:46]. Namely: We gave Jesus the Gospel in order that his people judge by it. "His people" are the Israelites, because the Qur'an informs us that he was sent to the Israelites. Hence, it is known that they were his people. Likewise, the Gospel they now have states that Christ said: "I was only sent to the lost sheep of the house of Israel" [Mt 15:24].

The second reading has an non-vowelled *lām*: *walyaḥkum*. It is an account of the preceding command with bestowal. Namely: We bestowed on him the Gospel and We commanded the one who was sent to them to act in accordance with it. And the wording permits the reading that it is an

60. Ghibrīl, 6.

61. Ghibrīl, 5.

independent command related to remonstrate the Christians for not acting in accordance with the Gospel, which confirms the Torah, and the requirement to act in accordance with the Torah, a matter whose explanation was given previously. If it is possible for the Christian evangelists today to argue against the Muslims that the Qur'an commands them to have faith in and act by the Torah and Gospel and not see that this argument mandates their faith in the Qur'an, then how can they assert that Muḥammad's command, God's blessing and peace be upon him, to them to judge by the Gospel mandates that he submit to its ordinances? (part 14, p. 536. vol. 4.)

Article Six: On the Verses on the Character of the Torah and Gospel

In the previous article, we mentioned that the author of the book *Researches* cites seven verses from the Precious Qur'an, distorting their context to corroborate the scriptures of the Jews and Christians and coerce the Muslims to believe and accept them. In discussing three of these verses, we explained the author's distortions and that the verses are a proof for the Muslims against the Jews and Christians, not vice versa. In this article, we shall discuss the remainder.

He states: "The fourth passes judgment on the error of the Muslim who does not believe in the Torah and Gospel [24] as he believes in the Qur'an."[62] We say: the fourth verse is God Almighty's statement: "O ye who believe! Believe in Allah and His messenger and the Scripture which He hath revealed unto His messenger, and the Scripture which He revealed aforetime" [4:136].[63] Muslims believe that their prophet came in truth, corroborated the messengers, and commanded that we believe in God's previous messengers and books. But he did not oblige us to act according to those books, because he dispensed with our need for them

62. Ghibrīl, 6.

63. Ghibrīl cites the complete verse: "O ye who believe! Believe in Allah and His Messenger and the Scripture which He hath revealed unto His messenger, and the Scripture which He hath revealed aforetime. Whosoever disbelieveth in Allah and His angels and His scriptures and His messengers and the Last Day, he verily hath wandered far astray" *Sūrat al-Nisā'* [4:136]. Ghibrīl, 5–6.

through a book of greater guidance. We are not perplexed as to its transmission, nor misled as to its comprehension. It includes all that is in them in the way of sound doctrine. It is preserved from corruption and error, protected from being lost and forgotten, and contains all that they lack in the way of divine knowledge, as we shall explain presently, God Almighty willing. It is free of the historical accretions and human opinions that were augmented to what remains of the heavenly books.

However, the exegetes disagree as to who is addressed by this verse. It is said that they are the hypocrites, believers outwardly, doubters or deniers inwardly. It is as if He says to them: "O you who profess faith in God, His book, His messenger and all of His books and messengers" – with their tongues and outwardly – "it is incumbent upon you to believe with your hearts, and harmonize what you profess outwardly with what you hold inwardly."

It is said that they are the believers among the People of the Book, based on what was related from Ibn Sallām and his companions. They said: "O messenger of God, we believe in you and your book, in Moses, the Torah and Ezra, while we disbelieve in everything else."[64] Hence, the verse was revealed. It is said that they are Muslims in general, and Muslims do not consider genuine the faith of a Muslim who disbelieves in the previous prophets or deems their books false. However, they do not oblige him to investigate or act in accordance with them, because God Almighty made them superfluous for us, as we stated. This is because some were lost and forgotten, as the Almighty states: "They forgot a part of that whereof they were admonished" [5:13; 5:14], while, as God states, others were corrupted by "changing words from their context" [5:41]. How can we accept a book of which a major portion has been forgotten? Perhaps the forgotten part explained and commented upon the remainder, or the remainder lacks what is essential. In that case, our acceptance of it would be wrong, or our religion would be deficient, and God's statement about the People

64. This statement is not found in any tradition in the nine collections. 'Abd Allāh ibn Sallām was a Jewish convert to Islam said to have given up his faith upon Muḥammad's demonstration of knowledge verifying his prophecy. See Bukhārī, Prophets 60, (*bāb* 1); *Tafsīr* 65, (*bāb* 6).

of the Book would apply to us: "Believe ye in part of the Scripture and disbelieve ye in part thereof?" [2:85]. Here, we suffice with obtaining evidence of the People of the Book forgetting a potion of it from the Generous Qur'an, because our debate with the opponent concerns the Qur'anic evidence for the veracity of the scriptures. We shall establish this below with an examination of those books' testimony and statements of the Christian religion's leaders.

[25] The author states: "The fifth verse makes clear that the people of Makkah (Mecca) knew the Torah and the Gospel as they knew the Qur'an."[65] We say: the verse referred to here is the following: "And those who disbelieve say: We believe not in this Qur'an nor in that which was before it" [34:31].[66] There is no evidence in the verse supporting what he states, even if it is supposed that "that which was before it" refers to the previous scriptures. This is because the reason for their refusal is faith. It is the call of the Qur'an and the one who brought it to that faith. That is, the reason is that they said: we do not believe in the book that you brought, O Muḥammad, saying it was from God, nor do we believe in the books that you said were brought from God before you. Then, where herein is the evidence that the people of the Makkah (Mecca) knew the Torah and the Gospel specifically and studied them, when they were illiterate? There were no literate individuals among them, and moreover nor were there among the Arabs generally, but for some individuals whose number did not exceed ten (it is said that they were six men). The second exegetical interpretation of the Almighty's statement "nor in that which was before it" is that it refers to the Day of Resurrection and what follows in the way of merit and punishment. This is the more likely interpretation.

The author states: "The sixth verse establishes Muḥammad's confirmation of the scripture's veracity and its equal status with the Qur'an."[67]

65. Ghibrīl, 6.
66. Ghibrīl's version is: "And those who disbelieve say: We believe not in this Qur'an nor in that which was before it (the Torah and the Gospel)" *Sūrat Saba'* [34:31], placing his own "the Torah and Gospel" between brackets at the end of the verse. Ghibrīl, 6.
67. Ghibrīl, 6.

We say: he relates the verse thus: "Say: (unto them, O Muḥammad): Then bring a Scripture that giveth clearer guidance than these two (*the Qur'an and the Gospel*) (that) I may follow it" [28:49].[68] So, reasonable people, look at these people's faithfulness in transmission and at their corruption of meaning. And these are those who are addressing themselves to the Muslims, knowing their intentness on the Glorious Qur'an. God Almighty revealed the verse thus: "Say (unto them, O Muḥammad): Then bring a Scripture from the presence of Allah that giveth clearer guidance than these two (that) I may follow it, if ye are truthful" [28:49]. That is, giving greater guidance than the Qur'an and Torah, not the Qur'an and Gospel, as the book *Researches'* author claims. The evidence for this is the Almighty's statement prior to the verse:

> Otherwise, if disaster should afflict them because of that which their own hands have sent before (them), they might say: Our Lord! Why sent Thou no messenger unto us, that we might have followed Thy revelation and been of the believers? But when there came unto them the Truth from Our presence, they said: Why is he not given the like of what was given unto Moses. Did they not disbelieve in that which was given unto Moses of old? They say: Two magics – [Riḍā:] "*sāḥrān*" and in [26] another reading "*siḥrān*" – that support each other; and they say: Lo! in both we are disbelievers [28:47–48].[69]

The wisdom of attributing unbelief in Moses to them is to demonstrate nations' dispositions and humans' behavioral similarities, even such that the present be identical to the past. Hence, philosophers say, "history repeats itself." These verses are an argument against the arrogant and a clear-cut proof for the tongues of the resisters. They contain no evidence for equivalence between the Qur'an and Torah in every respect. Indeed, the idolaters' inability to produce a book from God giving greater

68. Author's emphasis. As Riḍā indicates, Ghibrīl inserts his own "the Qur'an and the Gospel" in the middle of the verse, placing the words between brackets. Ghibrīl, 6.
69. Pickthall adds a footnote supporting Riḍā's contention, namely, that the two scriptures referred to are the Torah, and Qur'an, not the Gospel and Qur'an, as Ghibrīl claims.

guidance that that brought by Moses, and that brought by Muḥammad, does not necessitate that the scriptures that former brought is equivalent to that brought by the latter. Do you see: were it said to an individual ignorant of the science of logic, one who rejects his ulama and his scriptures, "Write me a book that is better than the book *Īsāghūjī*[70] and the book *al-Baṣā'ir al-Nāsiriyyah*,"[71] would we say that this statement demonstrates that these two books are equal in every respect?

The author states: "The seventh demonstrates the clear corroboration that the Torah is sound, uncorrupted, that it contains the ordinance of God, and that its follower has no need to appoint as judge any individual other than it."[72] We say: the seventh verse is the following: "How come they unto thee for judgment when they have the Torah, wherein Allah hath delivered judgment (for them)" [5:43]. This is what the author related of the verse. The remainder is: "Yet even after that they turn away. Such (folk) are not believers" [5:43]. The verse does not furnish evidence for that which he states about it, as we shall explain clearly here.

The verse is related to express wonder at the state of the Jews who chose the Prophet, may God's blessing and peace be upon him, as arbitrator in certain of their disputes, while disbelieving in his prophecy, such as those who sought his ruling for one among their high-born who had committed adultery. They said: "If he rules that the sentence for this crime is flogging, we shall accept his judgment. But if he rules a sentence of stoning, we will not accept his judgment" – although the sentence for adultery is stipulated for them in the Torah. But they sought to observe the easiest and lightest sentence. The sense of wonderment is that these people lack

70. An adaptation of the *Isagoge* of Pophyry (234–c. 305), founder of the Neoplatonist scholastic tradition. Pophyry's treatise on logic is commonly held to have first been translated into Arabic by Ibn al-Muqaffa' (720–756), an Arabic author of Persian origin best known for his translations into Arabic of Indian and Iranian works. "Īsāghūdjī" in *EI*.

71. I.e., *Observations (al-Baṣā'ir al-Naṣīriyyah fī 'Ilm al-Manṭiq)*, a classical work on logic by 'Umar B. Sahlān al-Sāwī (d. c. 1058), with commentary by Muḥammad 'Abduh.

72. Ghibrīl, 6.

confidence in their religion and compliance with their scripture. Hence, they appoint as judge Muḥammad, the master of a law other than their law, their law that they claim to be from God and to contain His ordinance, which is before them. It is amazing that they do not accept Muḥammad's ruling when it is consistent with their own. This is the ultimate distance from true and pure faith in their own scripture. Hence, the Almighty said after questioning their astonishing appointment of a judge: "Yet even after that they turn away. Such (folk) are not believers" [5:43]. That is, [27] their faith in their scripture was not genuine, first, because they shunned it, appealing to you for a decision, O Muḥammad. Then, second, they discarded your ruling, which was consistent with it. Or, the verse denies their faith without qualification, since the attribute of genuine faith includes that which He mentioned, and faith in the prophet Muḥammad, may prayer and peace be upon him, and that which he brought. That is, their souls were corrupted and their confidence in religion absolutely voided, to the extent that it will not ever be regained.

It is clear that a statement about God's ordinance or numerous precepts being in a book does not mandate that that book, in its entirety, is sound, free of corruption, and includes all that God Almighty revealed. I give as an example the book *Sīrat al-Ḥalabiyyah*,[73] which contains God's ordinance. But I do not believe that the book in its entirety is from God Almighty, is free from corruption, and that therefore there is no need for any other book. Rather, I believe that, in spite of this, it contains independent statements, the author's opinions and unsound transmissions. We are indeed in need of a book other than it. (p. 574, vol. 4.)

73. *Insān al-ʿuyūn fī sīrat al-Amīn al-Maʾmūn*, by ʿAlī b. Burhān al-Dīn al-Ḥalabī, which is commonly known as *al-Sīrah al-Ḥalabiyyah*. Al-Ḥalabī (died 1635) was an Egyptian Shāfiʿī scholar. The work is a biography of the prophet based primarily on two earlier biographies – Ibn Sayyid al-Nās's *ʿUyūn al-Athar* and al-Ṣāliḥī's *al-Sīrah al-Shaʾmiyyah* – but incorporating other sources. It is al-Ḥalabī's best known work. It is frequently cited as a source for early Islamic history and the origins and function of the mosque. Al-Ḥalabī is also known for his defense of the Badawiyyah Sufi order. J.W. Fück, "Al-Ḥalabī," in *EI*.

Article Seven: On Responding to the Periodical Bashā'ir al-Salām *(The Glad Tidings of Peace) – Comparison between Jews and Muslims; Muḥammad's Superiority over Moses and the Rest of the Prophets*

In the previous part, we completed refuting the criticisms in section one of the first investigation of the book *Researches of the Mujtahids*, the book whose author composed to corroborate the books called the Torah and Gospel with the testimony of the Qur'an. We had resolved to begin this part by refuting the criticisms of section two, which the author wrote for the purpose of proving those books with reason. But then we received the fifth part of the Protestant periodical entitled *Bashā'ir al-Salām* (The Glad Tidings of Peace), seeing in it a great attack against Islam and a long swim in the seas of delusion.[74] We wanted to shoot it with the truth, so that the truth refute it, and it come to nothing.[75] We will return, God Almighty willing, to critiquing that book in the forthcoming parts. (See Article 8.) The periodical's attack is divided into three sections:

The First Part: The Blessed Family Tree

[28] In this section, the author praises the Israelites and explains their virtue. He grants them more than their worth, but he does not grant God his due right.[76] He glorifies them while violating decency with regard to God Almighty. He praises the Israelite genealogical tree while defaming in the matter of the divinity. He has a discussion about that – "Whereby almost the heavens are torn, and the earth is split asunder and the mountains fall in ruins" [19:90] – such as the following (and he who relates unbelief is not himself an unbeliever):[77]

74. Compare Qur'an 73:7: "Lo! thou hast by day a chain of business" (*inna laka fī al-nahār sabḥan –ṭawīlan*).
75. Riḍā's language recalls Qur'an 17: 81: "And say: Truth hath come and falsehood hath vanished away. Lo! Falsehood is ever bound to vanish."
76. Riḍā's language recalls Qur'an 22:74: "They measure not Allah His rightful measure." Pickthall's translation might be revised. Alternatively, "They did not give God his due."
77. Referring to himself. Riḍā disclaims responsibility for the material he quotes, and which he deems completely egregious.

> Are you not amazed that the creator of the heavens and the earth is alone with the Israelites in the wilderness where He addresses them and they address Him, and He sees them and they see His majesty. Among them Moses is the one spoken to.[78] God was deep in conversation with him, exchanging various topics of discourse with him, like two people accustomed to each other and two friends very much at ease with each other.

He then shifts from this to disparaging the master of the messengers, the seal of the prophets, the one through whom God completed religion, and to denigrating all people. He says:

> So listen, O Muslim reader, and be confounded and be amazed. Is not Muḥammad for you the greatest of creation? Yet he was not worthy of addressing God directly, neither hearing His voice nor seeing His majesty, as did the general folk of the Israelites, to say nothing of their élite. Moreover, he was not worthy of addressing Gabriel (as you acknowledge). Rather, he was overcome with the feeling of fainting and moaning, straining him, so that his forehead sweated on a day of severe cold.

Thus ends his confused and haphazard discussion.

We say: paganism has become deeply ingrained in these people. Its roots have permeated the depths of their souls to such an extent that its removal has become impossible so long as they do not attach importance to action or see it as a value upheld by the religion's scriptures. The detailed explanation of their error is lengthy, and our entire periodical is not sufficient for it. For this reason, we suffice with summary, and we speak with the tongue of pure reason, not that of Islam, that being more conducive to being met with approval.

(1) Muslims report that their prophet Muḥammad, may God's blessing and peace be upon him, ascended to heaven and saw some of the greatest signs of his Lord.[79] Beyond that, most of them say – without specifying how[80] – that he saw God, be He Praised and Almighty, and spoke with Him [29] without an intermediary.

78. Ar. *kalīm Allāh*, an epithet of Moses.

79. See Qur'an 53:17–18.

80. "Without how" is an expression with a long history in Islamic discourse. It has

Moses, may peace be upon him, and those among the Israelites who were with him, however, saw lightning, heard thunder and a trumpet, were covered by smoke like the smoke of an oven, and the mountain shook by them. Hence, they trembled and stood at a distance "and said to Moses, 'You speak to us, and we will listen; but do not let God speak to us, or we will die' " [Ex 20:19]. Moreover, the Lord said: "Go down, and come up bringing Aaron with you; but do not let either the priests or the people break through to come up to the Lord; otherwise he will break out against them" [Ex 19:24]. All of this is clearly stated in chapters nineteen and twenty of the book of Exodus. It exposes the falsity of the periodical's claim that the common folk among the Israelites addressed God directly and heard His voice. So what is this falsification and deceit? The Qur'an relates: "And Moses fell down senseless" [7:143], while it states of Muḥammad: "The eye turned aside nor yet was overbold. Verily he saw one of the greater revelations of his Lord" [53:17–18].[81] Thus, is it just that you say, "we are those who are truthful because we say . . ."?

been translated as "without asking how," "in the sense in which God intended," "without further comment," and "without qualifying God in any manner applicable to His creation." "Without how" addresses the tension between the principles of utter dissociation and anthropomorphism. The latter might be supported by traditions referring to Muḥammad "speaking with" God and Qur'anic references to God's "hand," "face," and "throne." However, it was rejected by the Muslim majority, its proponents being described as "those who make God like a man." By accepting the doctrine of "without how," Muslim scholars attempted to solve the problem of anthropomorphic language by finding an appropriate midpoint between literal and metaphorical interpretation, or by asserting that such language was to be interpreted neither literally (that is, anthropomorphically) nor metaphorically. Watt notes that since 'Asharī's time, there has been a general trend away from this position and towards acceptance of metaphorical interpretation. Watt, " 'Akīda," in *EI*. Since Riḍā's time the tendency amongst educated Arab Muslims has been to play down the superhuman aspects of Muḥammad's personality. The tension between utter dissociation and anthropomorphism – *tanzīh* and *tashbīh* – is integral both to Riḍā's debates with his Christian opponents and to the issue of fundamentalist literalism.

81. This is Muḥammad's ascension, referred to above.

(2) The Israelites who were favored with this special care, and Aaron, who alone God permitted to ascend with Moses, without the priests and the youth, did not observe the most important of the commandments with which the Lord commissioned them that day. On the contrary, they abandoned the first and most important, namely: "you shall have no other gods before me. You shall not make for yourself an idol, whether in the form of anything that is . . . *et cetera*" [Ex 20:3–4]. Indeed, according to your assertion and that of your scriptures, Aaron was the one who obtained the calf for them that they then worshiped instead of God. Were these not the people who were favored with that special care and honor? Then, they committed this momentous act of disbelief, thereby deserving God's anger and hatred, the removal of His blessing from them, and its conferral upon another people, such as the Arab people, through whom God removed paganism from millions of people. It did not return to them, thanks be to Him and the completeness of His blessing.

The evidence of the Lord's anger towards the Israelites includes what we related in the third section (p. 317. part 11) about the book of Ezekiel. (See Article 3.) So, after this, is his evidence sound that God, be He Almighty and Holy, is still infatuated – far be He from such imperfection – with the Israelites and angry with the rest of His creation, and that their common folk are superior to . . . It is strange that he use verses [30] from The Mighty Qur'an as evidence of God blessing the Israelites, but does not use them as evidence of their ingratitude for blessing and affliction with punishment!

(3) In the Muslim view, the fundamental basis of faith is God Almighty's utter dissociation from resemblance to created beings. Thus, if an expression is related in revelation whose apparent meaning contradicts God's dissociation, they divert it from its apparent meaning by way of metaphorical and allegorical interpretation. It appears that the fundamental base, in the view of others, is anthropomorphism and paganism, especially those who turn a human being into a god. Thus, if a statement is related in their scriptures contradicting God's dissociation, they add to it its manifold meanings and are ingenuous in analogizing about it. For example, it is related that God Almighty spoke with Moses, so Muslims

de-anthropomorphize Him with regard to voice, direction, and place. They say: this is only a divine proclamation of an attribute worthy of God's glory that God Almighty has named speech. This is definitely not the speech of people among each other. Otherwise, the Almighty would resemble created things, which constitutes the destruction of the essence of religion and faith. As for the Christians, they say the like of that which we reported previously about the periodical *The Glad Tidings of Peace*: "and He was deep in conversation with Moses," and that the two of them were like two well-acquainted friends, and so on. This is clearly anthropomorphism. No wonder, since one who would say that Christ is a god would say that the God met privately with Moses, exchanging various topics of discourse with him: "Exalted be God Almighty above that."[82]

(4) The periodical is confused in what it says about the Prophet's state, may God's blessing and peace be upon him, at the time of the revelation. This is because it is based upon hadiths that the writer misunderstands. In the hadith "the beginning of the revelation," he interprets the statement "he enveloped me" (*ghaṭṭanī*) as referring to snoring (*ghaṭīṭ*), the sound made by one sleeping or that of the braying camel. This is incorrect. Rather, it means "he embraced me with strength and pressure."[83]

He then conflates this hadith with a hadith describing revelation and its effect.[84] The periodical's author claims that being unaffected by

82. Riḍā's language recalls Qur'an 17:43: "Glorified is He, and High Exalted above what they say."

83. Riḍā appears to have copied this definition directly from *Al-Qāmūs al-Muḥīṭ*. The reference is to hadith three in al-Bukhārī's *Kitāb Bad' Al-Waḥy*, related on 'Ā'ishah's authority: "The truth descended upon him while he was in the cave at Ḥirā. The angel came to him and asked him to read. The Prophet replied, 'I do not know how to read.' The Prophet added, 'the angel caught me forcefully (*faghaṭṭanī*) and pressed me so hard I could not bear it and more.' " In this tradition, the reference is to Muḥammad's sensation of being enveloped by Gabriel, while there is no suggestion of snoring or a sound resembling the braying camel.

84. Hadith two in al-Bukhārī's *Kitāb Bad' al-Waḥy*, related on 'Ā'ishah's authority. It describes Muḥammad as falling into a trance-like states, shivering on hot days, sweating on cold days and snoring (or making a sound like a camel).

revelation is superior and more perfect. This is a maliciously invented claim lacking supporting evidence. We say: the prophet's condition was one of the conditions of revelation. Perhaps the like of it did not occur for Moses, affecting him as Muḥammad was affected, may peace be upon them both. However, a less excellent individual may have [experiences] that a more excellent individual lacks. If we concede that Moses was superior to Muḥammad in terms of this virtue, there are numerous distinctions by which Muḥammad is superior to Moses. It is incredible that a writer such as this, who [31] did not grant God his due right, compares the virtues of God's prophets, may prayer and peace be upon them, on the basis of nothing more than his desire and poor understanding.[85]

That Periodical's Second Part: On Ishmael

The periodical's writer under-rates Ishmael, may peace be upon him, when comparing him with Isaac. If his statement, reporting and evidence about them are correct – in terms of Isaac's superiority and being the one who was sacrificed – the religion of Islam is not harmed in any respect. His statement on this matter does not necessitate any time being spent critiquing it.

The Third Part: New Testament Authors and the Call to Religion

There are two questions in the periodical's question and answer section. One is from a Muslim friend of theirs who asked them: "Are Peter, Paul, John and the other New Testament authors messengers (*rusul*) of God, and is there an Old Testament prophecy (*nubūwah*) of their sending, as there is for Christ?" The periodical's answer is that they are messengers of God. We say: a Muslim who knows Islamic doctrine would not ask this question, because a messenger in Muslim belief is a prophet through whom an independent religion is revealed, a religion that he is commanded to convey to the people.[86] Christians themselves do not claim this sense of

85. For a human being to make such a comparison contradicts Qur'anic principle: "We make no distinction between any of his messengers" (2:285). See Article Ten.
86. The issue here concerns the Islamic distinction between a legislative prophet or messenger (*rasūl*), who delivers a new shari'ah and teachings, and a teaching

mission for Peter, Paul and the other writers of the gospels and New Testament letters. [Second], Muslims do not use the word "prophecy" as it is used in the question, namely, to mean "glad tiding" (*bishārah*), whereas [Christians] argued for the apostleship of those whom the questioner mentions on the basis of miracles. And indeed, more is related about each of the Muslim *awliyā'* than about them and Christ, peace be upon him. Yet Muslims do not claim that the *awliyā'* are messengers.[87]

The second question is from another of their friends: "Why are Christians unique in their practice of dispatching missionaries and having continued to do so from the time of their first appearance until the present day?" The answer: "Verily Christianity is guidance, and whenever guidance is present in the heart, it is not possible for its possessor to restrain himself and conceal it from his people or keep it secret from them." The periodical then states that Christians are unique in guidance.

We say: First, no religion among the religions of the world arose except through mission and no individual calls others to a religion but that some follow him. However, some are propagated through their [32] inherent power, namely, the power of right guidance and dominion over souls, such as Islam. Others are propagated through coercion and compulsion, such as the Christian religion. Hence, for three centuries it remained embraced by only a few individuals. Then, some pagan kings converted to it and compelled people to embrace it with coercion, as we shall explain presently with historical testimony, God Almighty willing. Second, the Israelites, God's chosen people, who were extolled by the periodical's author, did not call others to their religion even at the time of Christ, who was one of them. So was their religion at that time one of error or right guidance? Third, the Baha'is, who speak of the

prophet (*nabī*), who delivers teachings but not shari'ah. The messengers include Noah, Abraham, Moses, Jesus and Muḥammad. Thus the question lacks a basis in Islamic doctrine.

87. For Riḍā, the *awliyā'* would include Companions as well as Sufi saints. His argument is that miracles alone do not constitute evidence of prophethood. This challenges the Christian argument that the apostleship of Peter, Paul, and John was confirmed by miracles.

Bahā'[88] – who is buried in Acre – as Christians speak of Christ, call others to their religion in every area in which they are found, almost to the extent that every Baha'i is a missionary. Would this periodical's editors maintain that they are rightly guided and that abandoning Christ's worship and worshiping the Bahā', or combining the two, is obligatory? Fourth, the answer obliges every Christian to become a missionary for his religion, as a Christian is rightly guided and the possessor of guidance is unable to conceal it. However, we see that mission is limited to those individuals among them who draw wages for it from the missionary societies. Hence, they call others to join their religion because mission is their livelihood, not because it is right guidance in their hearts, that overflows from them upon their fellow humans. Fifth, we see virtuous Christians criticizing these hired Christian missionaries, saying that they do not benefit Christianity but rather harm it, while among the newspaper editors are those who criticize them in writing. Sixth, every practitioner of a religion believes that he is rightly guided. An individual, moreover, is provoked to action by belief itself, not by the matter in which the individual believes. Otherwise, no individual would promulgate a law, nor would anyone call others to a falsehood. But obstacles prevent mission.

As for true mission, whose possessors plunge headlong into with the full force of belief, it is the mission of the disciples of Christ, prayer and peace be upon him. Few joined them in faith, while millions believed in Muslim mission for many centuries. A Muslim trader would enter one of the kingdoms of Africa or Asia, that kingdom in its entirety then embracing Islam at his hand. This mission was not cut off entirely. Rather, it became weakened through the weakening of Islam, the loss of religious education, neglect of the true Islamic sciences, the weakening of Islamic civic culture and civilization, [33] the Islamic countries' neglect of religion, and Muslims depending on their kings, emirs and governments, in violation of that which Islam imposes upon them. And the Shi'ah and Buhrā (Isma'ilis) are still calling others to embrace their religion as much

88. Bahā' Allāh (1817–1892), founder of the Bahā'ī religion. On Riḍā's attitude towards the Bahā'ī religion, see Chapter Three.

as they can.[89] These kings and emirs are the first obstacle on the path to Islam, the second obstacle being the strong European kings who assist their missionaries, protecting them after dispatching them for mission, even to the extent of waging war against a kingdom under the pretext of supporting a single priest. It is European power, then, that gave voice to these missionaries' tongues, set their pens in motion, and aimed their arrows to hit their opponents. Thus, it is clear that the true answer to the question is that the Christians evangelize because politics drives them, guineas follow them, and guns protect them (that is, defend them).[90]

As for the Muslims, in spite of their scientific, social and political weakness, they are still calling others to the religion, motivated by the motivation of faith. But they do this with a weakness that is strengthened by the power of truth, making it more successful and more liable to meet with acceptance. Christian missionaries constantly complain about Islam's progress and outstripping of Christianity in Africa, notwithstanding the intensity of the attention paid to its diffusion. They have a likely explanation for that in Islam being nearer to mankind's innate disposition and intelligence. We shall publish some of the Christian clergy's discussions on that point, God willing. (part 16., p. 619., vol. 4.)

Article Eight: On the Books of the New Testament

[33] *Researches*' author determined that the first investigation's second section would logically prove the veracity of the Torah and Gospel.[91] The proof's confirmation is that God is omnipotent and wise. Thus, there can be no doubt that He set down a constitution and wrote a law for His rational creatures, so that they would come to know their relationship to their

89. Riḍā's point concerns the distinction between Buhrā and Nizarī Isma'ilis. Although the former believe that their Imam is no longer alive, they are more engaged in da'wah or mission, due to the office of the *ma'dhūn* or *wakīl*, whose primary role is propagation of da'wah.
90. On many occasions in *al-Manār*, Riḍā asserted that his missionary opponents' motivations were more financial than religious; see *al-Manār*, xxix, 1928, 351.
91. Ghibrīl, 9–11. The section is entitled "Rational Demonstration of the Veracity of the Torah and Gospel".

Creator, their obligations towards Him and one another, the destiny of all people, the unbelievers' punishment, and obedient believers' reward. [34] Thus, they would not be lost in chaos, lacking a coercive leader and a lawgiver, being as cattle, some trampling others, or as fish, the big eating the small, some people destroying others, virtue and sin being equivalent. This would be unacceptable for God, the Omnipotent and Wise. He then asks:

> Thus, if that constitution and law were not the Torah and Gospel, then tell me, by your life, what are they? Is there an ancient holy book that achieves the intended purpose, as do the Torah and Gospel? By my life, there is not.[92]

Al-Manār: We do not respond to the author's shortcoming in establishing the fact of the law's necessity, since readers can see this by comparing it with what we wrote, and will write, explaining the need for revelation from dictated religious lessons. However, we remind him of matters that, should he contemplate them, would make his argument's invalidity plain to him:

(1) and (2) Why, before the Torah, did God leave humanity without a law for thousands of years – we do not know their number – if that would not please Him? Why was this wisdom of His not made apparent except recently, to the Israelites, when all people are his servants, and the reason given necessitates its appearance to all people? These two questions refute him and every Jew and Christian who advocates his position. But they do not refute Muslims, because the Qur'an resolves this difficulty in the Almighty's statements about messengers: "[Verily We sent messengers before thee,] among them those of whom We have told thee, and some of whom We have not told thee [40:78]; And there is not a nation but a warner hath passed among them" [35:24]. We believe that God sent messengers to all the nations that, through their high level of cultural development, had the potential for elevation to understanding His oneness, their number is not known, but by the Almighty.

92. Ghibrīl, 10.

(3) Were the people of China like cattle, some trampling others, or fish, the big eating the small, lacking a guide and a restrainer? Or were they rather in possession of civilization and virtue, both before and after the Israelites' existence? History informs us that that they were more advanced than the Israelites in science, knowledge, civilization, and order, which the law requires for its development. They were more advanced than the Christians were when they possessed nothing but the religion that their saint Paul had spread among them, and which advanced them in nothing but enmity, hatred, conflict, strife, war, and murder in the period they call "The Dark Ages," while the Chinese lived in tranquility, peace, agreement, and concord. Further, that which is said of the Chinese [35] may also be said of the Hindus. Difficulties such as this do not pertain to Muslims because, in accordance with the Qur'an's guidance, they allow that God Almighty sent prophets among the Chinese and Hindus who guided them to that which they attained in the way of happiness. Thereafter, history took its course with them, and they mingled their religion with inherited pagan tendencies until they diverted it from its true course. We believe the Christians did likewise, since there is no doubt that, in its original form, their religion was heavenly and monotheistic. Thereafter, they mingled it with the worship of human beings, such as Christ, his mother, and others.

(4) Europeans dispensed with the Torah's law, favoring positive law, and they dispensed with the ethics of the Torah and Gospel, favoring those of philosophy. They discarded asceticism, shaking the dust of humiliation off their heads. With this, they were successful, and rose from the condition in which they had been during the days when they held fast to "The Holy Book." How, then, can you state that this book alone guides mankind and refines human morality, when reality, in fact, points to the contrary? This difficulty does not pertain to Muslims, because they believe that the Jews and Christians "forgot a part of that whereof they were admonished" [5:13; 5:14] in the revelation. The remainder was corrupted and abrogated, and thus was no longer sound for human guidance. Muslims also believe that Europeans, in their good morals, are the closest people to the religion of Islam. These morals include self-dignity, high motivation, seriousness in

work, honesty, trustworthiness, being guided by universal laws, seeking guidance in the laws of innate human disposition, abiding by what can be rationally proven, and others. Muslims believe that as Europeans were guided to this through research and the broadening of knowledge, they will likewise be guided to the rest of that which Islam brought in the way of doctrine, morality, virtue, and practice.

(5) All that the author mentions in explaining the need for the law was more completely manifest among the Muslims. Such completeness was not known among the Jews and Christians. Thus, Muslims knew what God Almighty requires and what is required in terms of the servant's rights. Their condition improved through religion. In every age, their opinions converged, their morals were refined, and their civilization ascended in a degree commensurate with that of their establishment of the religion. Of this, history is an honest witness.

(6) If the Torah indeed made clear all that the author mentions in terms of the human need for the law, then why did the Gospel come into existence? If the Torah was deficient, then why did God set it down deficiently, not fulfilling this need? [36] How, on the strength of this opinion, is the evidence for the rational affirmation of the Torah and Gospel complete for him? This problem does not pertain to Muslims who believe in the veracity of the original Torah and Gospel, as they maintain that each befit its time. Thereafter, social reverses befell, sweeping away the benefit and utility, and afflicting the condition of the people affiliated with the two scriptures. Hence, God renewed the law with Islam, in a manner of general reform, every cloud lifting by its light. God preserved his book from corruption and alteration, in order that those who had lost the way could return to it.

(7) If the Torah comprises that which he mentions, as previously mentioned, then why did the Christians abandon it, neglect its law, and desert its statutes, as we explained in certain previous responses? (See Articles 3 and 5.)

(8) If the Old and New Testament books were truly divine, then why are disparity, mutual contradiction, conflicting testimony and that which clashes with reason – the sole means by which religion is understood and known – found therein? We briefly discussed its clash with reason in

certain previous sections (see Articles 1 and 4), and we shall presently explain in detail all that we allege here.

(9) If these books were divine, if they satisfied what the author mentions of the people's need for revealed laws, why is there in them what thereby violates fundamental principles and specific provisions of revealed law? Take, for example, God's resemblance to His creation, or the attribution of vile deeds to the prophets, those who are the most truthful of people and the first in being rightly guided by the religion that they received from Him, glorified and exalted be He. Other examples include that which contradicts sound morality, as we alluded to previously and will explain further. For now, we suffice with some allusions from al-Abū Ṣīrī's *Lāmiyyah*, God Almighty's blessing be upon him, who says of the Old Testament's character and of its people:[93]

It is enough for them that they likened their worshiped god
– be He glorified! – to His servants thoroughly

And that they entered a dome for his sake
When they resolved to make for Syria

And that Israel wrestled with his Lord
And threw Him down, Thanks be to Israel

And that they heard the speech of their god
While their right path would be to hear it transmitted[94]

[37] And that they played for their Lord to hear
drums and horns during the war

And that the Lord of the worlds reconsidered
In the creation of Adam, Oh what ignorance they ascribe to Him

93. Sharaf al-Dīn Abū ʿAbd Allāh Muḥammad b. Saʿīd b. Ḥammād al-Ṣandājī al-Būṣīrī (died around 1294–97), was a celebrated Egyptian poet and Qur'anic reciter. He is best known for his *Burda* ode in praise of the prophet, upon which many commentaries have been written. The title – *Lāmiyyah* – refers to its rhyming in the letter *lām* at the end of each line. "Al-Būṣīrī," in *EI*.
94. That is, speech transmitted through an angel. The Qur'an asserts that is does not befit God to speak to anyone directly, except through an angel or from behind a veil (42:51).

And that He for the sake of Adam and his son
Clapped His hands together in sorrow and astonished

And reconsidered concerning the people of Noah, and drew back
Biting His fingertips in sorrow and astonishment.[i]

And that Abraham tried to feed Him
Bread and desired to wash His feet.[ii]

And that the monies of the people were made lawful
For them through usury, breach of faith, and theft.[95]

And that they did not go out of their land
As if they reckoned exiting to be an entry

And they did not desist from calumniating David nor
Lot, and how they calumniated Reuben[iii]

And they attributed to Jacob, through his sons,
Mention of doing the terrible deed frighteningly[96]

And to Christ and his mother, and she is sufficient
As a righteous exemplar, carrying him as a virgin[97]

i. Riḍā's footnote: in this verse and that which precedes it "it occurred to Him" means that a new view appeared to Him. The book of Genesis relates that the Lord was sorry and felt sad because He had created Adam. This makes God one who changes His mind and an ignorant person [Gn 6:6]. The same point applies to Noah and his people.
ii. Riḍā's footnote: See Genesis 18.
iii. Riḍā's footnote: Here, the author is referring to the accusation that David committed adultery with the wife of Uriah (see 2 Samuel 11) and that Lot committed adultery with his daughters (see Genesis 19) and as for Rūbīl, they call him Reuben, see the story of the false accusation against him (Genesis 35).

95. Ar.*ghulūl.* This is possibly a reference to the Israelites in Egypt. Illegal stealing (*ghulūl*) is a complex technical term. See Qur'an 3:161: "It is not for any Prophet to deceive (*yaghull*) (mankind)." Alternatively, this verse may be translated: "It is not for any Prophet to take illegally a part of the booty." *Al-Ghulūl*: stealing from the war booty before its distribution.
96. This is perhaps a reference to the slaughter of the people of Shechem. See Genesis 34.
97. Cf. Qur'an 4:156, which refers to false accusations made against Mary's purity.

And by your father, did Judah not give a ring
For adultery with a married woman, and a headcloth[iv]

They untruthfully twisted tongues in what
They said of Lea and Rachael.[v]

And they alleged that Solomon the prophet was an unbeliever
And it was easy for them to inflict on him invented falsehood[vi]

And they inflicted harm on Aaron with the calf that
they accused him of fashioning in error[vii]

[38] Until he said:

God is most great, verily the religion of Muḥammad
And his book is stronger and straighter in that which it says[98]

The sun of guidance shone with it for mankind
The greatness of its perfection would not admit of its setting

And the truth shone clearly in its law that
Combined principles and provisions for guidance

Do not mention the books before it
The morning has risen and extinguished the candles

Their monuments have been effaced, would you not seek news
Of them in inscriptions, verily they are wiped out ruins

It is obvious that these invectives, which contradict that which the author and others wrote about the evidence for humanity's need for the law, and that would not befit being revealed from heaven, do not pertain to those

iv. Riḍā's footnote: In Genesis 38 it is related that Judah committed adultery with his daughter in law, thinking that she was a prostitute, and promised her a goat and gave her a ring and his headcloth and staff, as a deposit for that, and she bore twins by him.
v. Riḍā's footnote: see the story in Genesis 29–30.
vi. Riḍā's footnote: in First Kings 11 it is related that the women inclined Solomon to worship idols (may God absolve him).
vii. Riḍā's footnote: see Exodus 32.

98. This is a Qur'anic formulation.

Muslims who speak of the truth of the Torah and Gospel as we explained previously. See the fifth part (namely, part 5, volume 4[99]). (p. 654. vol. 4.)

Article Nine: Also on the Books of the Two Testaments

[38] In the eighth section, published in the seventeenth part, we explained the book *Researches*' author's opinion on the logical confirmation of the two testaments' books. We clearly demonstrated the invalidity of this opinion. Here, we discuss that which he mentions after that, namely, his attempt to argue for impossibility of the Torah and Gospel having been altered. His argument against that possibility is that the two religions, Judaism and Christianity, were spread throughout both Eastern and Western worlds: "And the scripture, especially the Gospel, was translated from the original Greek and Hebrew languages into each language of the peoples that it encountered, including Arabic, Armenian, Ethiopian, Coptic, and Latin."[100] He states:

> How, then, is it conceivable that these thousands of people, given their differences in language and doctrine, would gather together and come to an agreement on altering the scripture, especially given that the Christians were divided into factions, each debating the other? Thus, there is no question that the Muslim claim that it was altered lacks [39] supporting evidence. Otherwise, let them tell us, where are the verses that have been changed? Which verses are they? What is their origin? What purpose underlies their alteration? If they are unable to do so, and it is indisputable that they are, then say to them: how can you make this claim, when a wise scholar would not embark on a matter unless he can prove his claim.[101]

The rebuttal to this fraudulent argument is easily found in the books of the two testaments, collectively known as the Torah and Gospel, and the books of church and general history. As for the Muslim who is not conversant with them, it suffices him to state that that which contradicts the Qur'an is not from the Torah, nor from the Gospel, since the Qur'an has

99. Article One in this book.

100. Ghibrīl, 10.

101. Ibid.

been definitively proven and transmitted broadly and without interruption, orally and in writing. Those books are not like that. Furthermore, parts of God's revelation do not contradict other parts, except in the case of abrogated rulings.[102] Hence, there is no question that preference be given to the Qur'an in the event of a contradiction concerning any matter other than the abrogated rulings, because it has been definitively proven, as many Christian scholars acknowledge. Indeed, in the book *The Cutting Swords in the Teaching of Christopher Jibārah* Muḥammad Efendi Ḥabīb – who converted to Christianity and then reconverted to Islam having put the former to the test – states:

> Mr Stobart, president of La Martiniere College in Lucknow, British India, explains on page 87 of his book *Islam and its Founder*, to quote literally, "there are ample and sufficient grounds for believing that the existing Koran consists of the genuine words, and is the original composition of the prophet, as learned or transcribed under his own instruction."[103] Muir, considered among the most adept, proficient and forceful enemies of Islam today, states likewise.[104]

102. Abrogation (*naskh*): the process by which a ruling in a verse is abrogated by another in a subsequent verse. The theory of abrogation is problematic for a variety of reasons, not least of which is its dependence on an accurate determination of the chronology of the abrogating and abrogated verses, which is very difficult to establish in most cases. However, as the Qur'an upholds the practice of abrogation (2:106), it cannot be rejected as a principle.
103. James William Hampson Stobart, *Islam & Its Founder* (London: Society for Promoting Christian Knowledge, 1901), 87–88. Stobart comments: "it would seem that the religious emotions of Mahomet, and his early speculations unburdened themselves in strains of impassioned poetry; and of these, fugitive pieces many which his followers had committed to memory afterward found their way into the Koran." Ḥabīb's citation is carefully selective, if not misleading. Stobart's general views do not support his position.
104. Riḍā quotes Muḥammad Ḥabīb's *al-Suyūf al-Battarha fī Madhhab Khrīstūfūrs Jibārah*, (Egypt: Maṭba'at al-'Āṣimah, 1895 or 1896). The book discusses "the opinions of the experts in sound history on the call to belief in Christ's crucifixion" and "the European scholars' testimonies to preservation of the Qur'an and the corruption of that other than it."

As for the changing, alteration and corruption of the two testaments' books, Muslims do not assert that these books, in their entirety, were heavenly and soundly transmitted from the prophets, and that the Jews and Christians subsequently altered them after dispersing throughout the East and West, and each people embracing Judaism and Christianity had translated them into their own languages. However, investigation into their origin, original authors, and those who received them from them before that great dispersal [reveals] the problematic matter and crippling disease for which [40] the People of the Book lack a remedy or cure. This is: who wrote the five books attributed to Moses, peace be upon him? The People of the Book say that Moses wrote them, placing in them that which the Lord told him. Thus, they were a history of him and his shari'ah. But how can this answer be correct when these books speak about Moses in the third person, and the last chapter mentions his death and burial?

Some claim that that this chapter was written by Joshua. But how can this be correct when the chapter contains a report about Joshua that he was filled with the spirit and with wisdom, and that all the Israelites

Sir William Muir (1819–1905) was an influential British Islamicist who, as Ḥabīb's comment suggests, was generally regarded as hostile to Islam by Muslim intellectuals. Muir was dismissive of the Qur'an's scriptural status, deeming it a mere historical source on Muḥammad's experience. In his *The Life of Mahomet* (London: Smith, Elder, 1896), Muir commented, "tradition [that is, the Qur'an] cannot in general be received with too much caution." (quoted in Gaudeul, vol. 1., 256). Hence, the impression created by the passage Riḍā cites requires some qualification. Muir's other important works include *The Caliphate, its Rise, Decline and Fall* (London: Religious Tract Society, 1891), *The Corān: its composition and teaching and the testimony it bears to the Holy Scriptures* (London: Society for Promoting Christian Knowledge, 1878), *Extracts from the Coran in the original: with English rendering* (London: Trubner & Co., 1885).

Riḍā adopts a similar line of argument in *al-Waḥy al-Muḥammadī*. He cites certain statements in, or referring to, European works praising the Prophet's character and/or appearing to confirm the Muslim view of Qur'anic origins, in spite of the fact that he deemed their authors, like Muir, generally highly hostile towards Islam. Examples include Edouard Montange's introduction to his French translation of the Qur'an and Emile d'Armougon's *The Life of Muhammad*. Riḍā did not read French. See DeLorenzo, 18; 37.

obeyed him? This account about him, then, is from someone other than him. Moreover, how could it be that Joshua would deceive, adding something to the book of Moses without attributing it to himself? Perhaps they seek evidence for this in the fact that the book of Joshua begins with the conjunctive particle "and" (*wāw al-ʿaṭf*). Indeed, the first phrase of the book is, "*And* after the death of Moses the servant of the Lord" *et cetera* [Josh 1:1]. There is [other] evidence that the last chapter is not from Joshua that is stronger than that of the account about him and his innocence of deceit. This evidence is that the following sentence is mentioned in the chapter after the account of Moses' burial: "but no one knows his burial place to this day" [Deut 34:6]. This indicates that it was written long after Moses. Were it written by Joshua, it could not be thus. On that basis, it suffices us to say that they are in grave doubt about this. How, then, can this book be trusted and be said to have been transmitted broadly and without interruption – and from whom was it transmitted? – when its origin is in doubt?

In chapter 31 of the book of Deuteronomy is the following:

> (24) When Moses had finished writing down in a book the words of this law to the very end, (25) Moses commanded the Levites who carried the ark of the covenant of the Lord saying, (26) "Take this book of the law and put it beside the ark of the covenant of the Lord your God; let it remain there as a witness against you. (27) For I know well how rebellious and stubborn you are. If you already have been so rebellious toward the Lord while I am still alive among you, how much more after my death! (28) Assemble to me all the elders of your tribes and your officials, so that I may recite these words in their hearing and call heaven and earth to witness against them. (29) For I know that after my death you will surely act corruptly, turning aside from the way that I have commanded you. In time to come trouble will befall you, because you will do what is evil." *Et cetera.*

This, then, is the Torah that Moses wrote as a single work in a particular book. It is God's speech [41], verified by the Qur'an. So where is it? Those Moses said would act corruptly after him, deviating from the path of the truth, namely the Torah: what did they do with it? What befell the Torah due to their corruption, deviation, and stubborn errors? "The Torah" means the shari'ah, whereas these five books are historical books. In them are some of the rulings of that shari'ah, as there are for the Muslims some Qur'anic verses and rulings in the prophet's biography. The prophet's biography is not the Qur'an, nor is it the Islamic revealed law. As there is in the prophet's biography, in spite of the careful attention paid to its transmission, both that which is sound and that which is unsound, it is more befitting that there be in the histories of Moses and other Israelite prophets that which is sound and that which is unsound. Their author did not examine them with even a portion of the Muslim narrators' care in their examination of their prophet's biography. Moreover, we stated that the authors of those histories are unknown.

The author of the book *Summary of the High Proofs for the Veracity of the Fundamentals of the Christian Religion* (*Khulāṣat al-Adillah al-Saniyyah 'alā Ṣidq Uṣūl al-Diyānah al-Masīḥiyyah*)[105] acknowledges that the original copy of Moses' book

> was once removed from its place and fell into danger when idol worship prevailed in the kingdom of Menesa and Amon, as true worship of God was cut off among the Israelites. At that time, it was discarded along with the old things,[106] whence it was rediscovered in the kingdom of Hosea the Pious.[107]

He then states:

> It is impossible that the original copy of Moses' book survived until the present day. We do not know what happened to it. The more likely possibility is that it was lost along with the ark when Nebuchadnezzar destroyed the Temple. This might be the reason for a tradition that was in circulation among the Jews, stating that the holy books had been lost and that Ezra the Scribe, who was a prophet, gathered together the scattered copies of the holy books and corrected their mistakes. Thus, they regained their original status.

105. This is an abridgement of the book *Al-Adillah al-Saniyyah 'alā Ṣidq Uṣūl al-Diyānah al-Masīḥiyyah.*
106. Ar. *al-rithath.* Riḍā's footnote: *rithath* is the plural of *riththah,* which refers to garbage and old things, such as worn clothes and other things that are discarded in the most base place and no longer given any consideration.
107. See 2 Kings.

Would the reader of these and similar statements be deceived by the book *Researches*' author's [42] statement that the scripture was preserved among thousands of people in numerous languages?[108] The scholars of theology in his school acknowledge that the worship of God was lost among the Jews after the worship of idols had prevailed, that the only transcript of the Torah was lost and that its existence is therefore impossible. They acknowledge that the Jews confessed that all of their books were lost, because they were in the Temple that the pagans destroyed, taking the books and destroying them. Hence, they lacked an authoritative record of their religion's fundamental basis, except for Josephus' assertion that every Israelite tribe had a copy of the Torah. But where are these copies? If his assertion is correct – and it is the report of a solitary authority[109] with which he supports his religion – then those would be the copies that Nebuchadnezzar destroyed.

Thus, there remains a sole point for us to investigate. This is the claim that Ezra the Scribe wrote all of the Jewish scriptures as they were originally and, moreover, corrected their original mistakes, thereby improving them. On this point, Muslims enquire about the evidence for this and about the reason for the occurrence of mistakes in the copies, such that they required Ezra's emendations. They also enquire about the copy of the Torah that was, as Moses wrote it, an independent shari'ah, and about its uninterrupted successive transmission to Ezra. They then ask: if it were possible that Ezra the Priest corrected the errors in the Holy Books, then why is it not also possible that Muḥammad, the Messenger of God and the seal of the prophets, would do likewise? By God, prejudice is indeed a disease of the heart that intervenes between it and truth's reception. O God, inspire these people to seek the truth with sincerity and devotion, and judge between them and us in truth. And You are the best arbiter.

Is it related in their holy books that Ezra wrote the Torah and the rest of the holy books as they were? Indeed it is not. It is related in chapter seven of the Book of Ezra that during the reign of Artaxerxes, King of

108. Ghibrīl, 10.

109. In hadith studies, such a report is referred to as *akhbār al-Āḥād* and is considered of weak authority.

Persia, Ezra went up (and his relationship with Aaron is mentioned, he being related to him through fifteen fathers) from Babylon, was a skillful writer in the shari'ah of Moses – the shari'ah bestowed by the Lord, the God of Israel – and that he went to Jerusalem in the fifth month of the seventh year of Artaxerxes' reign. It states:

> (10) For Ezra had set his heart to study the law of the Lord, and to do it, and to teach the statutes and ordinances in Israel. (11) This is a copy of the letter that Artaxerxes gave to the priest Ezra [43], the scribe, a scholar of the text of the commandments of the Lord and his statutes for Israel: (12) Artaxerxes, king of kings, to the priest Ezra, the scribe of the law of the God of heaven . . . etc. [Ezra 7:10–12].

This is their evidence from their holy scriptures that Ezra was inspired to write the Torah and the holy scriptures after they had been lost. As you see, it does not prove that. Rather, the utmost that may be said of him is that he was among the scribes of the religion or the revealed law, in the way that you might say a certain Companion was a "scribe of revelation." Thus, were we to assume that the Qur'an was lost to the Muslims and had not been persevered in the heart, and then allege that Mu'āwiyah was inspired to write it – because he is described in some books of religious history as having been a scribe of revelation – would the People of the Book accept this argument from us?

Furthermore, the historicity of King Artaxerxes – who gave this testimony for Ezra, the reason for which we do not know – is uncertain. It is inconsistent with the confused Old Testament reports in the books of Nehemiah and Ezra. Hence, it is not known whether he is Artaxerxes the First, namely Ardashir, who is known to the Persians as Zarathushtra, or whether he is Artaxerxes the Second.[110] Ezra mentioning him after Darius would suggest that he is Artaxerxes the First, but history contradicts this. We will not explain this contradiction at length. Whoever is interested may consult the books of history and the encyclopedia's summary of it. The contradiction renders the report untrustworthy. Muslims would not

110. Riḍā appears to be incorrect here. Ardashir and Zarathushtra are not the same individual.

accept a report about their prophet, one with an uninterrupted chain of transmission close [to the prophet], were it to contain such a blatant contradiction as this. (p. 743. vol. 4.)

Article Ten: The Sinlessness of the Prophets and Salvation

> It will not be in accordance with your desires, nor the desires of the People of the Scripture. He who doeth wrong will have the recompense thereof, and will not find against Allah any protecting friend or helper. And whoso doeth good works, whether of male or female, and he (or she) is a believer such will enter Paradise and they will not be wronged the dint in a datestone [4:123–124].

[44] In the previous section, we mentioned that we seek friendship and harmony, and that debates among the religions and legal schools are of little utility and are perhaps harmful, producing no benefit. This is because most people are blind followers of tradition – and how traditionalists neglect logical proof! We said that these Evangelical missionaries compelled us to reply to their misrepresentations by sending us books and newspapers attacking Muslim beliefs and importuning us to reply to them. Their importuning was combined with the requests of many Muslims who said that, other than *al-Manār*, no Islamic periodical in the region was published to serve the religion with sound knowledge. Hence, it was incumbent upon us to reply to the criticisms facing Islam. According to the decree of our religion, this importuning and requesting made replying to these books and newspapers an incumbent duty for us. In view of the law, we would sin were we not to reply.

"Whenever I treat a wound, another wound opens." Indeed, we had been replying to their last book, which had gathered together the substance of their criticisms.[111] Then behold: we received the periodical *The Glad Tidings of Peace* unsolicited and without prior correspondence. Then, in recent days, the Evangelical newspaper *The Standard of Zion* was sent to us. Upon it was written: "I request a reading of the article about the prophets' sinning and a reply to it."

111. *Researches of the Mujtahids.*

> The Gazelles so outnumber Khirāsh; that Khirāsh does not know what to hunt.[112]

[45] However, a few signs of truth suffice to destroy the majority of falsehood. Hence, we say (beginning with this article):

> Muslims say that God sent many prophets to the world and the greatest of them are six. These are Adam, Noah, Abraham, Moses, Jesus – namely Christ – and Muḥammad. Many state that all of these prophets were sinless and hence were capable of granting salvation to their followers. But had they been sinners that would not have been easy for them, since it is not possible for sinners to bestow salvation from sin on others.[113]

This is literally what he stated. He then follows this with the claim that, Christ apart, these prophets were disobedient sinners, drawing evidence from their stories in the Old Testament.

As for Adam's disobedience, it is well known. As for Noah, it is mentioned that he drank wine. The author acknowledges that no other sin of his is mentioned in the Torah. But he asserts that there is no doubt that he was a sinner. As for Abraham: "Indeed, it is related of him that he sinned twice, due to his fear of the people." As for Moses' sinning, the author states:

> When God commanded him to go to Pharaoh he betrayed great fear and increasing cowardice, inducing God to become angry with him. And when the Israelites were in the wilderness after their exodus from the land of Egypt, Moses spoke incoherently once. Hence, due to this sin, God did not grant him the possibility of entering the land of Canaan, but caused him to die in the desert.

The author also seeks evidence for their sinning in the Glorious Qur'an, in that which is related in the verses concerning their seeking of forgiveness, except Christ, as this is not related about him. He concludes the article – after a long discussion praising Christ, prayer and peace be upon him – with the Muslim claim to have faith in him (whereas they are the

112. An allusion to a proverbial story.

113. With the exception of Adam, incorrectly included here, these are messengers (*rusul*), as distinct from other prophets (*anbiyā'*). See Article Seven.

true believers in him) and their reliance on him for their salvation (whereas they rely on none save God alone). By "faith in him," he means the Protestant understanding of faith, as in a section on the first page of this edition he wrote that the other sects "are Christians in appearance, but not in truth," and that God will hurl them into the eternal fire. As for the rebuttal to the article, it may be made from several angles.

[46] One: the greatest of the prophets in the Muslim view are Noah, Abraham, Moses, Jesus, and Muḥammad, prayer and peace be upon them, and they name them "prophets of resolve."[114] Adam is not among them, as per the Almighty's statement, "and we found no resolve in him" [20:115].[115] Among the ulama, some forbid declaring some prophets more virtuous than others, as this can only be known by revelation.[116]

Two: Muslims do not believe that it is the prophets who, because of their sinlessness, save the people from God's punishment and admit them to their standing in God's blessing. They rely but on God alone for that. They believe that salvation depends on true faith and sound action, and that the prophets were sent but as preachers and warners who teach the people the sound faith that is acceptable in God Almighty's view and the good action that pleases Him. Hence, whoever believes and acts soundly, salvation would be hoped for him through the bounty of God Almighty, who brings him success and guides him. Whoever disbelieves after the call to God and its stipulations reaches them, their disbelief increases for the sinners naught but loss.[117]

114. Ar. *ūlū al-ʿazm*. Compare Qur'an 46:35: "Then have patience (O Muḥammad) even as the stout of heart (*ūlū al-ʿazm*) among the messengers (of old) had patience."
115. Trans. author (adapted from Pickthall). Hence, in the Qur'anic view Adam is not among those known as *ūlū al-ʿazm*.
116. Compare Qur'an 2:285: "We make no distinction between any of His messengers," where "we" probably refers to the Prophet and the believers, and Qur'an 2:253: "Of those messengers, some of whom We have caused to excel others, and of whom there are some unto whom Allah spake while some of them He exalted (above others) in degree," where "We" refers to God.
117. Riḍā paraphrases Qur'an 35:39: "Their disbelief increaseth for the disbelievers naught save loss."

Three: these opponents were not cognizant of the meaning of the prophets' sinlessness, in the view of the Muslims, for they presumed that they state that so as to establish that the prophets save the people because they are sinless. We respond to them that in the Muslim view there arises a rational proof for that: God Almighty placed the prophets as guides and leaders so that they be emulated. Were He to tempt them with disobedience – which would violate the law that they bring – they would not have been worthy of being exemplars of guidance. This is because God set guidance by actions above guidance by speech in the human disposition. Indeed, the prophets informed us that God Almighty commanded that they be emulated. So had they violated His command, there would have been inconsistency and a command to commit evil in His command, which is impossible. The meaning of their sinlessness is not that that they differ from mankind in every degree, such that they not fear that which frightens in life, not feel pain from that which causes pain, and not be wary of evil (and we shall presently clarify the issue in dictated religious lessons).

Four: Nothing in the way of sin was reported about Noah in the Old Testament, except drinking wine, and it is reported in these gospels that Christ also drank wine. Thus, were we to state that whoever has not been reported to have disobeyed [47] is fit to be the people's savior, then that would befit Noah as it befits Christ. Moreover, there are among the virtuous in this Muhammadan nation many of whom no disobedience was observed.

Five: That which the author reports about Abraham makes clear that he needed and desired salvation from an evil and a sin greater than telling apparent lies that may be interpreted allegorically. Take, for example, Abraham saying of his wife, "This is my sister." This means "sister" in religion. In terms of rational and legal principle, if the two harms are contrasted, the sin of lying is necessarily the lesser of the two. If a sinner tried to rape your woman, to enslave or commit adultery with her, and you could save her from him by lying, doing so would be incumbent upon you. Then, you would be the lying and disobedient one in the picture, but in truth the obedient one following your obligation.

Six: That which the author mentions about Moses' fear does not involve disobeying God or violating His law. This is but a permissible human quality. It is the fear of reverence and veneration for the high office to which he was commanded.

Seven: If the rational evidence for the prophets' sinlessness was not correct, the absence of a report of Christ's disobedience does not preclude its occurrence, since the absence of something's existence does not, in itself, necessarily follow from an absence of knowledge about it.

Eight: That prophets seek God Almighty's forgiveness does not prove that they rebelled and violated God Almighty's religion after the call to prophethood. Rather, it proves that, due to their elevated knowledge of God and that which is mandatory in the way of His praise and glorification, they deem neglecting that which is best – should they do so on occasion – a sin and a deficiency.[118] Did you not observe among those closest to the kings and sultans those who committed sins – without violating the positive law – for which they sought forgiveness from the kings? "And Allah's is the Sublime Similitude" [16:60].[119] Further clarification of this is forthcoming in dictated religious lessons.

Nine: If we were to postulate that the Muslims' evidence for the prophets' sinlessness was unsound, then the Christians would have no argument against them. But that would cast doubt on ultimate religion. (p. 816. vol. 4.)

Article Eleven: The Muslim View of Fear and Hope; Defamation of the Companions and Successors on the Basis of this View

[48] In its fourth issue the evangelical periodical *The Glad Tidings of Peace* published a section attacking Muslims in general and the great noble Companions in particular. It faults them and their religion for their hope for God's blessing and fear of Him. This is the extent of these people's knowledge of God and God's religion. The periodical asserts: "Many

118. In Shi'i and Sufi teaching, prophets are generally considered sinless both before and after the call to prophethood. In Muḥammad's case, sinlessness would be extended to his ancestors back to Adam.

119. Compare N.J. Dawood's translation, "But the most sublime are the ways of God." N.J. Dawood, *The Koran* (trans.), 191.

Muslims die on the carpet of hope in entering the garden and enjoying its blessings, based upon the magnanimous promises they have in their Qur'an." It then states: "What causes that but their ignorance of their true selves and the Almighty Creator's perfections?" Then, for clarification, it states that Muslims of knowledge and intelligence became extreme in devotion, worship, prayer and supplication to God Almighty. The periodical found the cause of this worship in their not having found that which would relieve their souls of the heavy burden of carrying their sins. It cited the result but not the cause when discussing fear of God on the part of Abū Bakr the Truthful,[120] 'Alī ibn Abī Ṭālib and Sufyān al-Thawrī. And it counted Sufyān among the Companions when he is not among them.[121] But knowledge is not a prerequisite for speech in these agitators' view. There is also distortion in the statement, but honesty is not a condition of reporting for these evangelists.

It is not for us to investigate its reporting, explaining corruptions and weaknesses of weak reports.[122] In forgiveness we ignore that and the statements with which the writer offended decency in relation to these Imams, of whom mankind is proud. Were Muslims to believe the books known as the Bible, and were their religion to permit them to elevate anyone above the prophets, then history would provide for them that which would elevate these Imams over the Biblical prophets. This is because the like of that which people report about their prophets' cruelty, sinning, drunkenness, adultery and shedding of blood – God absolve them from what they say – was not reported of them. [49] We pass this over and explain their purpose in condemning fear and hope – the two bases of every sound religion – to

120. A Qur'anic epithet applied by Muḥammad to Abū Bakr (died 632), the first rightly-guided caliph, in numerous classical sources. A. Rippen "al-Ṣiddīk" in *EI.*

121. Sufyān al-Thawrī (716–78) of Kūfah was a notable early exegete, jurisprudent and was particularly prominent as a *muḥaddith* or hadith scholar. Although he was a vital link in many important chains of hadith transmission, Riḍā is quite correct in observing that he was not a Companion but belonged to a later generation, as his dates indicate. Muḥammad Ṣiddīqī, *Hadith Literature: Its Origin, Development and Special Features* (Cambridge: Islamic Texts Society, 1993), 7.

122. Riḍā is perhaps referring to his opponents' citations of hadith rated as weak (*ḍa'īf*).

our readers. Their purpose is to establish a doctrinal principle that would sanction sins and evils – which are the primary object of their preaching – and attract people to their religion. This principle is that salvation from sin in the afterlife, and eternal life in the heavens, are only obtainable through the belief that God found no way to save mankind from the sin of his father Adam except by becoming incarnate in a human body, empowering over Himself a group that was the most superior of peoples, their crucifixion of Him, and His becoming cursed by the ruling of the divine law and shari'ah! Whoever extinguishes the light of his mind, ruins the natural disposition of his soul, and accepts this principle, is one saved, one who inherits the highest heavens, even if he kills, commits adultery, drinks alcohol, obtains the property of the people through deceit, treats worshippers unjustly, and is the bane of civilization. For this reason, the writer, who I can only characterize as a propagandist for this doctrine, explains that the reason for the fear of God of Abū Bakr, 'Alī and Sufyān is their ignorance of the principle of redemption. This means that had they known and believed it, they would have lived safe from God's stratagem and punishment, unrestrained and exulting in their desires and pleasures. The gist is that the Muslim who is subdued by hope for God's blessing and His promise to those who do good is ignorant and in error. The Muslim who fears God in awe and glorification – or because he suspects that he is deficient in performing the sound acts that benefit mankind, and in the knowledge and qualities that purify the soul – is ignorant and in error. The gist is that faith in God and His Angels, books and messengers – without making distinctions among them – disciplining of moral character and reform of actions: none of this benefits the truthful Muslim, nor avails him anything. What, then, is the condition of the miserable Muslim? As God Almighty afflicted him with purity of innate disposition and integrity of the light of the mind, he did not accept that principle, from which those raised under it freed themselves, following what they reasoned and discerned. Yet the scriptures of the people are not devoid of texts indicating that their messengers and saints feared God Almighty and hoped for His blessing. This is because they were not libertines, but an upright people.

The Wise Qur'an informs us that God Almighty's religion is one in essence and that all the prophets and the upright believers in them followed it. It is:

- The absolute unicity of God Almighty.
- His utter dissociation from the characteristics of [temporal] events.
- His assigning of worship as an obligation.
- Fear of the obstacle of sin and evils.
- The hope that leads to goodness and righteousness.

We see all wise Christians agreeing with us about this principle, and desiring that the missionaries and leaders of each religion be guided to it, so that religion be as God decreed it: a source of human happiness, not a curse and source of unhappiness, nor a stimulant of dispute, enmity and hatred among them.

Imam al-Ghazālī mentions many types of fear: fear of death before repentance, fear of revoking repentance and breaking commitment, fear of incapacity to fulfill obligations, fear of the disappearance of the heart's tenderness or that cruelty be substituted for it, fear of deviating from the straight path, fear of the overpowering force of custom in intensifying well-known desires, fear of being conceited with good deeds, fear of arrogance when blessed with many bounties, fear of being distracted from God by something other than God, fear of becoming careless through the ongoing of bounties, fear of uncovering negative consequences of acts of obedience through the appearance to a person of that which is unexpected, fear of his being burdened with others' sins through backbiting, fraudulent acts, deceit or the holding of grudges, fear of that which might suddenly befall him in the future, fear of calamity befalling, fear of being deceived by the ornaments of this world, fear of God uncovering the innermost thoughts in a moment of heedlessness[123] and fear of a bad ending. Other types of fear may be enumerated, while the most elevated fear is the fear of awe and veneration for God, to Him belong glory and power. All of this is sinning in the view of these evangelists. (p. 98. vol. 5.)

123. See Qur'an 86:9: "On the day when hidden thoughts (*sarā'ir*) shall be searched out."

Article Twelve: Muslim Faith and Practice

[51] In the eighth issue of the periodical *The Glad Tidings of Peace* is a section with this title. It may be summarized as follows: in the Sunni school it is possible "that somebody has true faith in Islam while persisting in his evil actions." The writer makes two objections to this. The first:

> That faith which does not instill repentance and sound practice in the believer, but abandons him when his evil tendencies outweigh his good tendencies and his losses surpass his gains . . . is a false faith devoid of benefit. It diminishes the Creator's generosity while intensifying the created creature's misery.

The second objection: "the incapacity of Muhammadan faith for complete salvation." Indeed, after the first objection the author cites verses from the Two Testaments, indicating that he desires perfection in the human being. But the verses cited do not demonstrate that the believer is immune from sin. After the second objection, he cites some verses proving that faith in Christ suffices for salvation. But he did not impose sound practice as a requirement of faith.

If these disputants believed that which they say, then their right guidance would be close at hand and their being convinced even nearer. But they express themselves awkwardly, twisting their tongues with the scripture in order to tempt the ignorant common Muslims with it, unconcerned should the statement be a proof against themselves. Their New Testament states that righteousness and acting by the divine law do not benefit an individual in any respect, but that faith in Christ alone suffices him, as thereby he is saved and inherits the kingdoms [of heaven], even if he be the most evil evildoer and shameless of libertines. The Qur'an barely mentions faith except when coupled with sound action, while it is related in the sound hadith that faith is speech with the tongue, belief in the heart, and action through the pillars.[124] This hadith is confirmed by

124. The hadith is: Abū Sa'īd's Hadith, may Allah be pleased with him. Ṭariq bin Shihāb reported: It was Marwān who initiated (the practice) of delivering the sermon before the Prayer on the 'Īd Day. A man stood up and said: the Prayer

seventy-five Qur'anic verses, without counting the verses in which sound action is mentioned without faith.

[52] The Almighty states, "And lo! verily I am Forgiving toward him who repenteth and believeth and doth good, and afterward walketh aright" [20:82]. He to whom glory and power belong states:

> It will not be in accordance with your desires nor the desires of the People of the Scripture. He who doth wrong will have the recompense thereof, and will not find against Allah any protecting friend or helper. And whoso doth good works, whether male or female, and he (or she) is a believer such will enter Paradise and they will not be wronged the dint in a date-stone [4:123–124].[125]

He whose praise is sublime states:

> They only are the (true) believers whose hearts feel fear when Allah is mentioned, and when the revelations of Allah are recited unto them they increase their faith, and who trust in their Lord; Who establish worship and spend of that We have bestowed on them. Those are they who are in truth believers [8:2–4].

He whose names are blessed states:

> By the declining day,
> Lo! man is in a state of loss,
> Save those who believe and do good works, and exhort one another to truth and exhort one another to endurance [103:1–3]. (See Article 4)

should precede the sermon. He remarked: this (practice) has been done away with. Upon this Abū Saʿīd remarked: this man has performed the duty prescribed on him. I heard Allah's Messenger (may peace be upon him) say: Whoever, among you, sees something abominable should rectify it with his hand; and if he has not strength enough to do it, then he should do it with his tongue; and if he has not strength enough to do it, (even) then he should (abhor it) from his heart, and that is the least of Faith.

The tradition is found in all of the nine collections, except those of Dāramī and Mālik. See Muslim, Faith (*Īmān*), 70.

125. "Desires" (*amānī*) might be translated "dogmas," elevating practice above doctrine.

This short chapter is more inclusive of virtue and deeper in guidance than all the books in the world, heavenly or unheavenly, and suffices for an independent religion for people of understanding.

The net with which the writer and those like him trap the ignorant into accepting Christianity is that human salvation is limited to believing – that is, to state, even without understanding:

- That God is composed of three elements, each identical to the other two, so that the three are one.
- That one of the three, the son, became incarnate in a human body by means of another, the holy spirit. Thus, this human being became God, the son of God, a human being, and the son of a human being who became God.
- That He empowered His enemies over Himself, so that they could crucify Him. And He bore pain and the divine curse in order to save the people from the sin of their father Adam, and also their own sins, because He found no other way to bestow salvation upon His servants.

This writer, and those like him, do not require from those they call to their religion anything except this irrational statement, which does not motivate the soul to sound action, but rather encourages it towards every sin. The ignorant one would love that sins be permitted him and that he be saved by a spoken profession. If the Christian propagandists had seen fit to stipulate the relinquishment of sin and sound action as a condition of this profession that they call "faith," then what, apart from this irrational and incomprehensible profession, distinguishes their religion? Does he not realize that were he to call a Muslim to his religion, demanding of him relinquishment of sin and performance of good acts, he would be unable to entrap him, [53] however ignorant he may be? This is because he would say: "This imposes upon me the like of that which my religion imposes upon me, and places another burden upon me. This is belief in that which I find irrational and incomprehensible: namely, that one is three and three is one, and that God is incapable of saving the people without debasing

His high nature through being incarnate in one of them, feeling pain and cursing Himself."

Muslims believe that faith refines and reforms dispositions through acts. Yet it is nevertheless possible that the believer's lust or desire take hold of him so that he commit evil, especially if he were not raised under the acts of faith from childhood. But he would quickly return and repent. The Almighty states, "Lo! those who ward off (evil), when a glamour from the devil troubleth them, they do but remember (Allah's guidance) and behold them seers!" [7:201]. The Lord states, "Forgiveness is only incumbent on Allah toward those who do evil in ignorance (and) then turn quickly (in repentance) to Allah. These are they toward whom Allah relenteth" [4:17]. On repentance, He states that he who performs good works thereby erases his sins: "Lo! good deeds annul ill deeds" [11:114]. Thus, if he falls short, he is under God's will.

From what we have summarized, then, it is clear that in the Muslim view faith produces sound action, while acts are of no value in Christian faith. As for *The Glad Tidings of Peace*'s statement on the upshot of the first objection, it is:

> On the basis of that stated above, every faith that does not have perfection as its objective and piety as its benefit is either a false faith in the true God, as that of Christians and Jews in name only, or it is a true faith, but in a false and imaginary god based on delusion.

Which is that of the Muslim. The periodical was correct in that which it wrote about Christian faith, and that was not its standard practice, as their faith is nothing but professed names and statements going no further than the mouth, as reason renders them false and is unable to conceive of them. As for its subsequent statement, which is:

> I assume that you did not forget to mention the people who are recognized as Muslims by agreement, in spite of being disobedient and sinful people, such that it is decreed that they be imprisoned in the fire for a period not less than nine hundred years and not more than seven thousand years, *et cetera.*

The specification is incorrect. It has no basis in the Qur'an or hadith and is unimportant in the Muslim view, although it is mentioned in some books: how many books of fabricated hadiths and false statements![126] We have no proof beyond that which is related in the Generous Qur'an and sound hadith. [54] As for the writers' discussion on matters of the afterlife, that which was not reported in the Qur'an and *mutawātir* hadith – which are very few in number – is not required for faith in what concerns the hidden world.[127] This is what we have stated. It is the principle Muslims rely upon.

As for the Almighty's statement, "There is not one of you but shall approach it [i.e., the hellfire]" [19:71], it is not, as the author claims, addressed to Muslims. This is because all of the verses prior to it concern unbelievers.[128] Hence, it is said it is addressed specifically to them. It is also said that it is addressed to the people in general. The intended meaning is that the believers arrive at that time, and pass alongside and kneel in front of the hellfire before entering the garden. Thereby, in entering the garden, they appreciate the degree of God Almighty's blessing upon them.

Two statements: I conclude this response with two statements. The first is for those Muslims who send us these newspapers, seeking our response to them. Do not be saddened by this aggression to which you are unaccustomed, O Muslims. Do not consider it among the evils of the freedom of the

126. On Riḍā's critique of weak (*ḍaʿīf*) and fabricated (*mawḍūʿ*) traditions, see *Tafsīr*, vii, 31. The authority of such traditions is to be contested even when they are supported by citation by such an eminent scholar as al-Ghazālī. Riḍā comments, "we state that these hadiths lack attribution to the prophet," and lists several examples.
127. There are various traditions on the number of *mutawātir* hadiths. According to one account, they number as few as three, although a higher number is generally given. Riḍā provides more detail on the terms *mutawātir* and *tawātur* in Article Thirteen. On his use of *mutawātir* in *Debates of the Reformer and the Traditionalist*, see Chapter Four.
128. Qur'an 19:68–71 reads: "And, by thy Lord, verily We shall assemble them and the devils, then We shall bring them, crouching, around hell. Then We shall pluck out from every sect whichever of them was most stubborn in rebellion to the Beneficent. And surely We are best aware of those most worthy to be burned therein. *There is not one of you but shall approach it.* That is a fixed ordinance of thy Lord." Author's emphasis.

press. It is among its benefits. This is because this aggression, through attacking your religion, awakens you from your sleep. It instills in you the desire to research and seek evidence, and enlivens the spirit of group pride and competition among peoples. Thus, you may come to know your religion's truths through logical proof and evidence. And research does not add to the truth, other than in making it more apparent.

The second statement is for the Christian opponents who call themselves evangelists: we believe that you attack the religion of Islam – if not for which no religion would be proven in this enlightened age – for payment, not out of belief in the truth of that which you say and write. Hence, one of you forsook evangelism when he was fired from the [missionary] society and his salary was withheld. Were you to believe in the religion, you would know that God's religion is one: the Creator's dissociation; His divine oneness; sincerity in His worship; relinquishment of evil; righteous acts; and bringing benefit to His servants. You would see that Islam served humanity with this corrective reform, that it is the religion of all the prophets – manifest in the most fully developed form – that released the People of the Book from disputation and difficulties. But desire diverted you from this. So "act according to your power. Lo! We (too) are acting. And wait! Lo! we (too) are waiting" [11:121–122].[129] (p. 436. vol. 5.)

Article Thirteen: **The Glad Tidings of Peace's** *Absurd Treatment of Islam and the* **Jāhiliyyah**

[55] In its ninth issue, *The Glad Tidings of Peace* published a section on Islam and the *jāhiliyyah* claiming that, in doctrine and practice, Islam is inferior to pagan Arab society. Indeed, it discusses this at great length in a discussion of Islam's greatest pillar of faith, God Almighty's oneness. It claims that Islam increased the paganism of pagan Arab society! It argues that case in six points:

129. Riḍā quotes Qur'anic verses addressing the disbelievers: "And say unto those who believe not: Act according to your power. Lo! we (too) are acting. And wait! Lo! we (too) are waiting" (11:121–122).

(1) The fact that faith in Muḥammad is imposed after faith in God Almighty. It deems this polytheism, when it is nothing but faith in revelation and God's messengers. In the Muslim view, whoever denies the prophecy of Moses or Jesus is an unbeliever, as is one who denies the prophecy of Muḥammad, prayer and peace be upon them. So it is apparent that in the view of the evangelist author faith in revelation is polytheism and paganism. His assertion about the joining of the two names in the two testimonies does not add weight to the criticism, as the form of the testimony related in *The Two Sound Collections*[130] is: "I testify that there is no God but God alone; He has no partner. I testify that Muḥammad is His servant and messenger." Is, then, the servant a Lord and god? As for joining the names in the spoken or written testimony, this is not prohibited, except when mentioning God Almighty is withheld and withdrawn entirely. Does the writer not say "God bless so-and-so" and such things? The writer finds intolerable a statement in certain Muslim books: the two testimonies of the confession of faith were inscribed on the throne before the creation of the heavens and earth. In this form, the statement is not Islamic doctrine. Thus, for whoever lives and dies without hearing it, or hears it but does not believe that it is related in the hadith at all, neither the former nor the latter would be considered a destruction or diminution of his faith. And if we stated that this inscription was proven and sound, then where is the paganism therein? God is God and the servant is the servant. Yes, this does indeed indicate honoring [Muḥammad]. Would the writer assert that all God's servants are equal in knowledge, worship of God, and bringing benefit to His creation, and that honoring one of them and deeming him superior to another constitutes polytheism? Would he assert that pure monotheism be that the evangelist believe that Moses is like Pharaoh and Abraham is like Nimrod, there being no

130. The collections of al-Bukhārī and Muslim. The statement "I testify that there is no God but God and I testify that Muḥammad is his servant and messengers" occurs in numerous traditions in the major collections, including at least four traditions in those of al-Bukhārī and Muslim (see for example Bukhārī, Prayer, 442). There are also numerous other traditions containing the same testimony in similar wording.

difference between them? This is the Christian missionaries' understanding of religion and this is that which they detest in the Muslims. Praise be to God, Lord of the worlds.

(2) [56] The author asserts that Muslims grant the hadith the status of the Qur'an, deeming them equivalent for deriving rulings, in spite of their belief that the Qur'an is God's speech while the hadith is Muḥammad's speech. He asserts that the Shi'ah abandoned the hadith, thus angering the Sunnis. Both claims are false. Sunnis do not state that the Qur'an and hadith are equivalent, while the Shi'ah did not reject the hadith. The Qur'an is the fundamental basis of the religion, while the sunnah elaborates it. The Almighty states, "We have revealed unto thee the Remembrance that thou mayest explain to mankind that which hath been revealed for them" [16:44]. The Qur'an has special characteristics and advantages that the sunnah lacks, such as the necessity of belief in all of that which is in it and worship being performed through its recitation.

As for the hadith, faith is not harmed by the rejection of any particular hadith (and whoever is of the view that something has been transmitted broadly and without interruption is not permitted to reject it, even if it is not a hadith, but the *mutawātir* hadith does not apply here).[131] The hadith is divided into sections, and the acceptance of that in it pertaining to matters of temporal life is not mandatory – it is possible that it be

131. In Islamic law, all four legal schools deem the rejection of a *mutawātir* hadith damaging to faith. In contrast, the rejection of an *aḥādī* hadith is not so considered. Riḍā's statement appears liberalizing and modernizing: that *any* tradition, as such, may be rejected contradicts established legal teaching (and would be particularly objectionable from a Ḥanbalī perspective). Riḍā recedes from such a general proposition and qualifies his statement by commenting that an individual cannot reject *anything* that he deems consecutively attested (*tawātur*) and cites the *mutawātir* hadith as a specific example of this general principle.

Riḍā's critical stance towards *fiqh* materials does not entail a similarly critical attitude towards the hadith. While rejecting traditions he deemed *ḍa'īf* and *mawḍū'* (*Tafsīr*, vii, 31), he staunchly upheld those rated *ṣaḥīḥ* and *mutawātir*. Overall, he was more accepting of the tradition than 'Abduh, and made greater use of it than his mentor in his *tafsīr*. Riḍā held Ibn Kathīr's commentary, which used the hadith extensively, in high regard (*Tafsīr*, xii, 173).

erroneous, as seen in the sound hadith on the pollination of date palms. In it the Prophet, God's blessing and peace be upon him, states, "You are more knowledgeable in the affairs of your lives."[132] As for that which pertains to the matter of religion, it derives either from independent reasoning or from revelation. As for the prophets' independent reasoning, the Sunni ulama allowed that there be error in it, but not that they would remain upon an error. Rather, they receive revelation explaining the truth concerning it, as happened in the case of the captives at Badr. As for that which the prophets state from God's revelation, this must be accepted. Muslims distinguish between the Qur'an and revelation that the prophet expressed in his own words, which Muslims call a report and hadith of what happened. Hence, if there is irreconcilable contradiction between the two, the Qur'an is to be acted upon, not the hadith.[133]

It is impossible, therefore, that the sound hadith, being second in rank,

132. This is a well-known hadith: "From 'Ā'ishah from Thābit from Anas: the Prophet, God's prayer and peace be upon him, went past a group of people who were pollinating [dates] and he said, 'If you didn't do that it be would be good.' Thus it came out without formed dates. He passed by them and said 'what's the matter with your dates?' and they said 'You said such-and-such.' And he said, 'you are more knowledgeable about the affairs of the world [i.e. the affairs of your lives].' " Among the nine collections, this tradition is found in those of Muslim (Virtues) and Ibn Mājah (*Aḥkām*, 2462). It is also found with different wording in the *Musnad* of Aḥmad ibn Ḥanbal, where the chain of transmission is rated *ḥasan*. Riḍā's comment concerning the non-binding nature of material in the hadith pertaining to temporal matters represents a liberal position.

133. Riḍā's comment refers to the Muslim belief that the hadith, like the Qur'an, is revealed, hence his description of it as "revelation" (*waḥy*). But all four Sunni legal schools place limits on the concept that the hadith is revelation. The prophet's actions, including his speech, are inspired by revelation but the actual wording is the prophet's, not God's. Thus, the hadith has a lesser status than the Qur'an. Although the hadith, as Riḍā notes, is a form of revelation, it is twice removed from God. First, the wording is the prophet's. Second, the same tradition is frequently reported in various different wordings (although this does not apply to traditions deemed *mutawātir bi al-lafẓ* or *mutawātir* in actual wording as well as in meaning). The tradition on the pollination of dates Riḍā cites is such a case: such traditions, which are not *mutawātir* in wording, are of probable but not absolute certainty.

is equivalent to the Qur'an. Thus, the prophet, God's blessing and peace be upon him, asked of Ma'ādh [ibn Jabal] when sending him to Yemen, "by what will you judge?" Ma'ādh replied, "By the book of God and if [the ruling] is not found [therein], by the sunnah."[134] The prophet approved of his answer. The same is related of Abū Bakr, 'Umar and other Imams of the religion, namely, that they first examined the Qur'an, and applied the ruling they sought if they found it therein. Otherwise, they investigated the sunnah, acting upon it. So let the Muslims see how the Christians invent the religion's fundamentals (*uṣūl*) for them, building upon them their accusation of clear polytheism. So this is their bigotry, while this is our tolerance. Thanks be to God, Lord of the worlds.

(3) [57] He states: "The third point is the mentioning of Muḥammad's name together with God's name in numerous places in the Qur'an, which is equivalent to assigning Him a partner in commanding and forbidding, loosening and tying[135] and the requirement of obeying and loving Him." *Et cetera.* The writer states that he provides evidence solely from chapter [nine] of the Qur'an, entitled "Repentance" (*Sūrat al-Taubah*). However, he cites three verses: two from "Repentance" and one from [chapter thirty three], "The Parties" (*al-Aḥzāb*). Indeed, he corrupts the two verses, while putting them between brackets to indicate direct quotation.

He writes: "Allah is free from that which they associate, and so is His messenger." In contrast, God Almighty states: "Allah is free from obligation to the associators, and (so is) His messenger" [9:3].[136] He writes:

134. This is a *mursal* tradition (the Successor is missing from the chain of transmission). Among the nine collections, it is found those of Abū Dawūd (*Aqḍiyyah*), Tirmidhī (*Aḥkām*), Aḥmad ibn Ḥanbal (in three places), and Dāramī. It is notable that Riḍā does not quote the tradition in full but has omitted the third part. This reads: "and if it is not found therein I will judge by my opinion."

135. Ar. *al-ḥall wa al-rabṭ*. Alternatively, "loosening and binding," a function of those in authority. In classical Arabic, this expression is more commonly rendered *al-ḥall wa al-'aqd.*

136. Trans. author (adapted from Pickthall). Riḍā's opponent writes "*inna Allāha barī'un mimmā yushrikūna wa rasūluhu.*" This contrasts with the Qur'anic "*inna Allāha barī'un min al-mushrikīn wa rasūluhu.*" Riḍā's opponent's corruption here is replacing "from the associators" with "from that which they associate."

"And it becometh not a believing man or (*aw*) a believing woman" etc., while God Almighty states, "And it becometh not a believing man or (*wa lā*) a believing woman, when Allah and His messenger have decided an affair" [33:36].[137]

As for the response to the criticism, it is clear: God Almighty's rulings were acquired from His messenger. Thus, in the matter of religion, all that the messenger ruled reached him from God Almighty. Its attribution to Him is [therefore] sound, as the attribution of natural events to their causes is sound, since God Almighty linked them together. In this, there is nothing that may be called polytheism. It is as if the writer states that his religion charges with polytheism he who would say, "It befits mankind to be ashamed before God and people," or some such statement, as he combines the name of the people with the name of God in a single precept.

So let the Muslims see the Christian missionaries' "honesty" in reporting and contrast what the author wrote – corrupting Qur'anic verses and making erroneous ascription to the chapter – with what happened to us with one of the great ulama. He alerted us to the obligation of calling attention to an error that occurred when the Gospel was quoted in *al-Manār*: *lam tujarribūnanī* (you did not test me) was published as *lam tujarribūnī*, the "protecting *nūn*" being omitted from the verb.[138] Let those

This verse is often cited to emphasize the importance of the declension of the noun, "His messenger" (*rasūluhu*) being in the nominative case; otherwise, the verse would read: "Allah is free from obligation to the associators and to His messenger," which is significantly different.

137. The complete verse reads: "And it becometh not a believing man or (*wa lā*) a believing woman, when Allah and His messenger have decided an affair (for them), that they should (after that) claim any say in their affair; and whoso is rebellious to Allah and His messenger, he verily goeth astray in error manifest" (33:36). The corruption Riḍā notes here is his opponent's replacement of "*wa lā*" with "*aw*" (or).

138. *Nūn al-wiqāyah.* This technical term refers to the *nūn* of the pronominal suffix for the first person singular, which is "*nī*" instead of "*ī*." It is referred to as "protecting" because it protects the inflection of the preceding verb, which would otherwise be "swallowed" by the *yā*'.

who are just reflect on our reporting from the people and their reporting from us, to distinguish the truthful from those who lie and separate the tolerant from the zealots. Thanks be to God, Lord of the worlds.

(4) He states: "The fourth point is Muslims taking Muḥammad as their master." He then derives from this that Muslims believe that they are Muḥammad's servants and states that this is the polytheism with which he is concerned. The rebuttal to this point is that Muslims did not mandate that anyone say "our master" when mentioning the prophet. This characterization of him, prayer and peace be upon him, is not related in Qur'an or sunnah. Indeed, [58] some ulama considered adding the words "our master" to the salat (*ṣalāh*) – appending the statement "there is no God but God" – reprehensible. Some said it was recommended, as this is one of the titles of reverence people are accustomed to using for eminent individuals and equals.[139] It is peculiar that the writer finds evidence for this form of address – which, in his view, entails polytheism – in the verse: "Lo! Allah and His angels *make salat* (*ṣalāh*) *over* the Prophet" [33:56].[140] This is because prayer (*ṣalāh*) from God is blessing, while prayer from other than God is supplication (*du'ā'*), as the ulama have made clear.[141] Thus, were every individual for whom we seek blessing a god of ours, and every individual we address as "master" a god of ours, then we and the writer would have innumerable gods! Yes, indeed, Muslims believe that Muḥammad is the most superior of the prophets and messengers. They give voice to that through the honorific title, as the prophets are the most superior of

139. This refers to the practice of those Muslims who add the words "our master" (*sayyidunā*) at four points in the salat (*ṣalāh*). The debate as to the legitimacy of this appending resulted in a considerable amount of legal commentary. In keeping with his general reformist approach, Riḍā disapproves of this addition, while rejecting his opponent's interpretation of its implications.

140. Author's translation and emphasis. Pickthall's translation reads: "Lo! Allah and His angels shower blessings on the Prophet."

141. Salat (*ṣalāh*) is a technical term referring to the regulated and formalized communal Muslim ritual prayer. It may also refer to a beneficent act of God, as in verse 33:56. *Du'ā'*, in contrast, refers to a more personal, spontaneous and individualized form of prayer that has much in common with the Christian understanding of prayer.

Adam's children. Hence, he is the most superior and the master of Adam's children. But they are not his servants. As for the reason for his being held in high estimation, it is clear from his influence. Indeed, we have written on this, and will write on this, God willing. So let those who reflect reflect on the artifice of these Christian evangelists and their fabrications, which amuse the sad. Thanks be to God, Lord of the worlds.

(5) He states, "The fifth point is Muslim extremeness concerning Muḥammad's pre-existence, to the point that they state that he is the eternal light, pre-existing humanity" *et cetera*. We say: this extremeness is not in any way derived from the religion. Thus, it is not found in the Qur'an, books of sound hadith, or books of doctrine. It is only found in the books of stories and births that deserve no respect, and the religion forbids speaking without knowledge. However, the common folk, among whom this exaggeration circulates, do not dispute the temporal existence of their and other prophets. Thus, it would be unsound to label one who professes that as somehow a polytheist.[142] So let those who perceive, perceive the extent of these people's knowledge of the religions that they declare false and in need of their people's rejection. Let them produce for us a Muslim who speaks as they do, without knowledge and attacks them through making claims and then judgments. It suffices us to be among the Muslims. Thanks be to God, Lord of the worlds.

(6) He states, "The sixth and final point is Muslims taking Muḥammad as an intercessor." He then states, "Taking a created being as an intercessor with God is identical to pre-Islamic Arab polytheism, not more, not less." He then states that the pre-Islamic adoption of numerous intercessors is less polytheistic than the Muslim limitation of intercession to [59] a

142. This refers to the belief that God exists alone at the beginning of creation. He then creates everything, the first created thing being the Muhammadan light (*al-nūr al-muḥammadī*). Hence Muḥammad predates Adam. This notion is intimately connected with that of Muḥammad as the Perfect Man (*al-insān al-kāmil*). It is a Sufistic and Shiʿi doctrine (where it is also applied to the Imams) with some parallels in Jewish, Gnostic and neo-Platonic thought. After being subject to some dispute, it had become generally incorporated into Islamic orthodoxy by the nineteenth century. Riḍā, however, clearly deems it unsound, considering it another un-Islamic accretion or innovation.

single intercessor – although the Muslims did not limit it. The response: in the Muslim view, intercession is supplication. Hence, Muslims say in the prayer over a dead person: "We come to You as intercessors for him. O God, if he were a doer of good acts, then increase his goodness"[143] *et cetera.* Hence, every Muslim is an intercessor and, moreover, every believer in God who calls on God Almighty for himself and others. Supplication for others is called intercession. It is as though the evangelist writer states that his religion charges with polytheism anyone who mentions one who has died, such as his father or someone else, saying, "God Almighty have mercy upon him." So, thus does "the religion of tolerance" proceed: its people pronouncing fatwas upon opponents. If they should respond with the truth, they call them fanatics. But this need not dislodge us from the tolerance of the Muslims. Thanks be to God, Lord of the worlds.

If you are amazed, the statement of those who take their prophet as a god is indeed amazing, namely that those who state that their prophet is God's servant, but that he is the most superior of His servants because he grants His created beings the most superior benefits and guides them, if He wills, with the most complete guidance, are those who associate God with another. This is because they recognize their prophet's virtue, ask for God Almighty's mercy upon him and obey him in that which he brings from God Almighty!

After setting forth the above, the author states:

> Against that is rebutted our adoption – we, the Christians – of Christ as the sole intercessor between God and people, based upon that which is related in the gospel. I answer: if we had believed that Christ was created (thus) and took him as the sole intercessor, or he and others with him, we would without doubt be polytheists. But if Christ was in truth the eternal word of God – "He is the Creator and not the created. All things came into being through Him and without Him not one thing came into being["][144] – then we are not polytheists. Rather, we worship the one God, His name be blessed!

143. This is an abridgement of a Companion tradition related by Abū Hurayrah. Among the nine collections, it is found only in that of Mālik (Funerals, 479), where it is rated *ṣaḥīḥ*.
144. Riḍā's opponent indicates direct quotation. The wording differs slightly from *VD*.

This means that polytheism is the [Muslim] people's belief that their prophet is God's servant and that his intercession is supplication to God. It means that pure monotheism is the people's belief that their prophet, who was born 1902 years ago, is God, the Pre-existent, the Eternal, the Creator of all things before and after him, that he is the intercessor, namely that he is an intermediary between the people and himself, they crucifying and cursing him for their salvation! Excellent! How good is this monotheism! These are the Christian reformers' criticisms. To God be thanks and blessing that He made us Muslims and peace be upon the messengers. Thanks be to God, Lord of the worlds. (p. 517. vol. 5.)

Article Fourteen: Response to the Periodical **al-Jāmi'ah***'s*[145] *Attacks on Islam*

> [Some of those who are Jews] change words from their context and they say: "We hear and disobey; hear thou as one who heareth not" and "Listen to us!" distorting with their tongues and slandering religion. If they had said "We hear and we obey; hear thou, and look at us" it had been better for them, and more upright. [But Allah hath cursed them for their disbelief, so they believe not, save a few] [4:46].

145. The humanist journal published by Faraḥ Anṭūn in Alexandria (1901–1904), New York (1906–1908), and Cairo (1909–1910). It was primarily dedicated to promoting secularism, particularly, as advocated in the article Riḍā cites here, through a separation of religious and civil authority. Anṭūn grew up in Tripoli where he became friends with Riḍā. In 1897 they traveled to Egypt together, though thereafter they saw little of each other, Riḍā settling in Cairo and Anṭūn in Alexandria. A noteworthy episode in Anṭūn's career was his high-profile public debate with Muḥammad 'Abduh. It was occasioned by Anṭūn's 1902 article on Ibn Rushd, in which he argued that Islamic theology discouraged scientific and philosophical investigation into the origins of the universe. Anṭūn's biographer relates that as Riḍā read through the article, he began to feel confirmed in his misgivings about his friend's religious convictions. He quickly drew it to his mentor's attention and the result was the Anṭūn-'Abduh debate carried out in the pages of *al-Manār*, v, 1902–03, and *al-Jāmi'ah*. Donald M. Reid, *The Odyssey of Faraḥ Anṭūn* (Minneapolis: Biblioteca Islamica, 1975).

[60] Verily, *al-Manār*'s readers know that we did not open this door to attack the religion of Christianity, or any other, in the first instance. We opened it only to respond to their criticisms, criticisms that might lead one ignorant of Islam to doubt the religion absolutely and ruin his moral character. That would be a disaster for him and for the people. The attacks of those who attack Islam have no purpose but this planting of doubt, which loosens the Islamic ties and weakens the Muslims. This is because it dispossesses them of their character as an ummah, so that they become divided individuals, lacking group solidarity and religion. Were they aiming at converting the Muslims to Christianity, we could to some extent excuse them. But experience informs history that millions of Christians became Muslims, while not one Muslim convert to Christianity stands facing each of these millions, except individuals for whom Islam was merely the name inherited from their forefathers.

The famous sage Master Jamāl al-Dīn al-Afghānī (God Almighty have mercy upon him) was asked: what underlies the call to the Dahrī school in India? Why is mission not limited to Christian mission? He replied: it is impossible that a Muslim would convert to Christianity, as Islam is Christianity and more. It commands belief in Jesus' prophecy and the truth of his mission, while rejecting the myths and innovations that the Christian groups added to his religion. So, when those who aimed at loosening the Islamic ties tried Christian mission and did not succeed in that, they shifted their strategy to sowing doubts about the fundamental basis of ultimate religion through calling people to the Dahriyyah.[146]

146. See *al-Manār*, xii, 1909, 20. The Dahriyyah are defined as holders of various materialistic beliefs in Islam, although the definition appears vague. The term derives from the singular *dahrī*, the adjectival form of *dahr* (time), which is a Qur'anic term (45:24) referring to those who believe in "naught save time."

Goldziher delineates several subsequent meanings attached to the term in classical discourse. These include those denying bodily resurrection and the afterlife, those deviating from true faith, those believing only in what is accessible to the senses and those believing in the eternity of time or the cosmos, thereby denying (or perceived to deny) a cause or a creator, all of which contradicts the orthodox affirmation of the sole eternity of God and his attribute as creator. Among the major classical thinkers, Ibn Ḥazm identifies the Dahriyyah as

[61] Likewise, when the like of *al-Jāmi'ah*'s editor saw that the evangelists' planting of doubts through Christianity did not succeed with the Muslims with the religious method, he, like them, embarked upon planting doubts with the scientific method. He exerted his effort to convince them: (1) that their religion, like other religions, is the enemy of reason and knowledge, (2) that their Imams in doctrine (the scholastic theologians) denied causes and (3) that combining religious and civil political authority in the office of the caliph harms Muslims, causing their social retardation. In the opinion of *al-Jāmi'ah*'s editor, if the Muslims wish to become sophisticated and successful, they must listen to his advice. That is, they must:

(1) Set their religion apart from reason and knowledge, as these would complete its destruction, as they completed the destruction of Christianity. So, if they attempt to combine religion and knowledge – as some of their Imams have advised them in *al-Manār* and other publications – they would

"those who profess the *dahr.*" Al-Ghazālī and al-Shahrastānī include Ibn Sīnā and al-Fārābī among the Dahriyyah, while Ibn Rushd does not name them, mentioning them only in connection with al-Ghazālī's critique of their positions.

The modern period brought greater definition to the term, the influence of European natural science having led to the growth of a variety of materialistic doctrines in the Islamic world. This was particularly the case in India and hence al-Afghānī's reference to events there. Sayyid Aḥmad Khān, for example, was influenced by the notion of taking natural laws as criteria for religious values. This concept spread to the extent that it became known as a new religion, officially listed as *Necari* in the *Census of India.* In 1878, when in Hydarabad (living under the close scrutiny of the colonial authorities), al-Afghānī wrote a refutation of its doctrines in Persian that was translated into Arabic by 'Abduh in 1885, under the title *Refutation of the Teachings of the Dahriyyah and Explanation of their Depravity and Proof that Religion is the Foundation of Civilization while Unbelief is the Ruination of Culture* (Risālah fī ibṭāl madhhab al-dahriyyīn wa bayān mafāsidihim wa ithbāt anna al-dīn asās al madaniyyah wa al-kufr fasād al-'umrān). A second edition was published in 1902 under the title *Refutation of the Dahriyyah* (Radd 'alā al-Dahriyyah). Al-Afghānī argues that only religion can guarantee the stability of society, contrasting it with the destructive effects of materialistic atheism. He traces the evolution of his opponents' beliefs from ancient Greece through Voltaire and Rousseau to Darwin. I. Goldziher, "Dahriyya" in *EI.*

only be attempting the impossible and, moreover, destroying their religion, such that they be left without both knowledge and religion.

(2) Believe that God Almighty's ways with causes and effects flow uninterruptedly as a matter of fact, in contrast to that which religion and the scholars of theology determine. Hence, if they believe in reality it is incumbent upon them to disbelieve their Imams and vice versa.

(3) Install their caliph as a secular ruler who devises laws and precepts, relinquishing that legislated by God for that legislated by the sultan, rendering their religion exclusively a matter of worshiping God Almighty.

That is, in the opinion of *al-Jāmi'ah*'s editor Muslims must abandon half of their religion, the precepts of worldly transactions, and make the other half accord with the wishes of one who desires that reason, knowledge and causes be relinquished for the sake of worship.

This is the substance of the periodical *al-Jāmi'ah*'s editor's advice to the Muslims. In order to make it acceptable, he cites for them statements from certain of their Imams, distorting their meaning to deceive the simple-minded.

We explain these issues, and clarify the truth about them, that there be an argument against these aggressors who "would put out the light of Allah with their mouths, but Allah will perfect His light, however much the disbelievers are averse" [61:8].

Causes or God Almighty's Ways in Creation (and Imam al-Ghazālī's Proof of them)

[62] In a text he fabricated, *al-Jāmi'ah*'s editor states that we cited the Almighty's statement, "thou wilt not find for the way of Allah aught of power to change" [33:62; 48:23], to prove that natural laws neither change nor are altered. He then states:

> Although, were *Ḥujjat al-Islām* Imam al-Ghazālī to be raised from his grave and hear this statement, he would break the pen of that periodical's editor and laugh at his simple-mindedness and unfamiliarity with the matters he investigates, as he cites that verse for the purpose he mentions, notwithstanding that it was not in any respect related in the Qur'an in relation to this matter.

This editor of *al-Jāmiʿah* speaks in preparation for deceiving the Muslims that that in which he arbitrarily proceeds – making judgments through interpreting God's book with his poor opinion – is acquired from Imam al-Ghazālī. He distorts the context of al-Ghazālī's words, not understanding their intent.

If al-Ghazālī would be amused at the "simplemindedness" of one who derived most of his knowledge of religion from his book *Revival of the Religious Sciences* (*Iḥyā' al-ʿUlūm al-Dīn*), in belief and action, studying it time after time from his early youth – as he studied all that he examined of his books – with concentration and sincerity, then would he laugh or cry at the composition of the stubborn infidel who searches his discourse for a statement that he can distort contextually, so as to deceive the Muslims with something that contradicts their religion, something "vindicated" by the discourse of one of their Imams, when the argument lacks a supporting passage? We leave the like of this behind and present al-Ghazālī's teaching on causes and God Almighty's ways. We explain the truth concerning the matter of these two points, the understanding of which is obscure to many people, such that planting doubts about it among the common Muslims became easy for the like of *al-Jāmiʿah*'s editor. This is because among them there remain those who read what he writes, in keeping with the Islamic principle of open-mindedness.

The teaching of al-Ghazālī: *Ḥujjat al-Islām* states in the third chapter of *The Book on Trusting in God* (*Kitāb al-Tawakkul*):[147]

> [On obtaining what is beneficial for single persons]
>
> We say that there are three degrees of means by which one obtains what is beneficial: [a] those that are always reliable, [b] those that are presumed to

147. Book thirty five in al-Ghazālī's *Iḥyā' ʿUlūm al-Dīn* (*Revival of the Religious Sciences*). *Tawakkul* is a verbal noun deriving from *wakala*, meaning "to entrust in," "to have confidence in," or "to depend on God." It is a subject to which al-Ghazālī devotes some forty pages in *Iḥyā'*. He defines it thus: "*tawakkul* expresses the heart's confidence in the One Trustee (*al-wakīl al-wāḥid*)." *Iḥyā'*, (Cairo: 1933), iv, 223, (quoted in L. Lewishon, "Tawakkul" in *EI*.).

The term, whose cognates occur sixty times in the Qur'an, is prominent in the

work, with a presumption in which one is confident, and [c] those which one imagines might work, but a fantasy in which the soul is cannot confide itself with complete confidence nor can be at peace with it. The first degree [63]: means that are always reliable. These are those in which other means following after them are arranged according to the planning of God and His will in an uninterrupted and invariant order. This is like having a meal put before you when you are hungry and need it, yet you did not lift a finger to prepare it, so you say: "I am one who trusts in God, and the condition of such trust is renouncing effort. Lifting a hand to do it would be effort and action, like chewing it with the teeth and swallowing it, in accordance with the palate being higher than the digestive organs." But this is pure idiocy and has nothing to do with trust in divine providence. If you were to wait for God most high to create satiety in you without bread, or to create in bread a motion towards you, or you enjoin an angel to chew it for you and send it to your stomach – that would simply display your ignorance of the practice [*sunna*] of God Most High. As would your not sowing seed in the ground yet hoping that God Most High would create plants without seeds, or thinking that your wives would give birth without intercourse, as Mary – praise be to her – gave birth. All of that is idiocy, yet stories of this sort abound to the point that it would be impossible to count them.[148]

After determining that trust in God is not achieved in this degree through the relinquishment of action, he discusses the second degree, namely that

hadith and Qur'anic exegesis, and by al-Ghazālī's time was considered one of the pillars of faith. *Tawakkul* is a foundational concept in Sufi discourse, where it is expressed as a religion of "absolute dependence," as an attitude of inner spiritual orientation rather than external practice, as one of the degrees of *tawhīd* revealed through the science of mystical unveiling, and as reliance solely on God's providence for sustenance. The doctrine was sometimes taken to extremes, as exemplified by the reputed case of Abū Ḥamza al-Khurāsānī, who fell into a pit and refused to be rescued by a party of travelers; "relying upon God alone." Al-Ghazālī, as in the excerpts Riḍā quotes here, rejected such literalistic interpretations as naïve. In this respect, he was followed by the Sufi majority. For a detailed discussion of *tawakkul* in Islamic discourse, see L. Lewisohn, "*Tawakkul*" in *EI*. For analysis of al-Ghazālī's interpretation, see David Burrell, translation *On Faith in Divine Unity and Trust in Divine Providence: Kitab at-tawhid wa tawakkul*, (Louisville, KY: Fons Vitae, 2001).

148. Burrell, 73–74.

in which a cause is presumed. He explains that trust in God is not achieved in this degree either:

> So the renunciation of all means is contrary to His wisdom, and amounts to ignorance with respect to God Most High, whereas acting according to the necessities of the practice [*sunna*] of God Most High, while placing one's trust in God – Great and Glorious – and not in means, is not inconsistent with trusting in divine providence.[149]

This detailing concerns the procurement of benefits, and he cites its equivalent for their preclusion and for the avoidance of harmful things whose causes are definite or presumed. He explains that trust in God, however, is the avoidance of things of imaginary benefit, such as incantations, omens, and cauterizing, which are discussed in the hadith. Among that which he explains here through reference to the divine sunnah is the following:

> Similarly for means employed to protect one's property: it does not diminish trust in God to secure the door to one's home when one goes out, or to hobble a camel, for these means are known to be part of the *sunna* of God Most High, whether they be effective or probable means.[150]

He then cites proofs of this from the Qur'an and sunnah. These are well known.

In the discussion on medicine, which falls under the avoidance of harms, he gives the following beautiful statement: "It can hardly belong to trusting in God to dispense with the *sunna* of the One in whom we trust!"[151] He states, of the prophet's use of medicine, God's blessing and peace be upon him: "he would not forego having recourse to treatment in accordance with the *sunna* of God Most High, thereby letting his community feel their need."[152]

149. Burrell, 77.
150. Burrell, 113–114. I have substituted "probable" for Burrell's "probably."
151. Burrell, 127.
152. Burrell, 145. In Burrell's translation the complete sentence reads: "In the same way, using means or renouncing them was indifferent to him, given his spiritual vision, so *he would not forego having recourse to treatment in accordance with the*

[64] Clearer than this is the following statement, after a long explanation of causes:

> In this way it is made clear that the One who makes causes to be causes carries out His *sunna* by linking whatever is caused to their direct causes as a demonstration of divine wisdom. So it is that treatments are causes subservient to the authority of God Most High, like all other means. Just as bread is a treatment for hunger and water for thirst, so oxymel is a treatment for jaundice and scammony for diarrhea – yet with two qualifications. First, the remedy for hunger and thirst by bread and water is clear and manifest in and perceived by everyone, while the remedy for jaundice by oxymel is known only to a few specialists, yet whoever becomes aware of the second kind [of connection] by experience links it, so far as he is concerned, with the first. Second, the fact that treatments purge – that oxymel can suppress jaundice – is a function of other conditions in the body and causes in conjunction, and it is often difficult to be apprised of all such conditions. It may be that one or other missing condition will keep the treatment from purging. With regard to quenching thirst, however, that does not require many conditions other than water, though there could be certain obstacles whose presence assured the malady of thirst no matter how much water one drank – but that is rare. In any case, the failure of causes can be restricted to these two factors. What is caused follows the cause without exception once the conditions of the cause have been fulfilled.[153]

What text on the inseparability of causes and effects is stronger than this last statement? [Yet] *al-Jāmi'ah*'s editor deceives the [common] Muslims that this Imam al-Ghazālī denied causes, and denied that the meaning of God's sunnah – that neither changes nor is transformed – is causes and their linkage to effects. After this, then, is confidence in the statements of *al-Jāmi'ah*'s editor or the goodness of his intentions possible? Is it permissible for someone other than a firmly established scholar to examine the

sunna of God Most High, thereby letting his community feel their need – especially since there is no harm in having recourse to treatment, by contrast with storing up possessions, which is very harmful." Author's emphasis.

153. Burrell, 128–129.

writings of this planter of doubts, who seeks to alienate the common Muslims from their doctrines?

Reconciling this with what al-Ghazālī States in The Incoherence of the Philosophers

The explanation of causes given by Imam al-Ghazālī in *The Book on Divine Oneness and Trusting in God* is that believed by Muslims. He wrote it in this book to explain for Muslims the station of trust in God, which is the highest station of faith, while he has another discussion on this matter, with the philosophers, not the Muslims. It is necessary that his discussion there be spoken in language differing from that with which he addresses the Muslims, but not contradicting it. This is because here he explains the reality that is proven by existence and with which the revealed law is in explicit agreement, while there [65] he discusses causes and true effects with regard to creation and destruction. That which he states in the two passages is the unavoidable truth, as we explain.

Before delving into the second part, a statement preparing the subject is necessary: those among the early philosophers who were mistaken took apparent common causes for definite logical causes. They attributed effects to them, asserting the existence of an uninterrupted and essential linkage – the severing of which is impossible – between the two. Had a strong proof of that arisen for them, Muslims would not have opposed them, as the agreed upon principle in the view of the scholastic theologians, is that God Almighty's power and will do not concern what is impossible, but only what is possible. Yet for that they had no proof, only fallacious arguments from which al-Ghazālī and others removed the veil. Those causes – of which the opinion concerning their uninterrupted linkage was given – are [not necessary, but] possible, and linked [with effects] through God Almighty's action.

Had people accepted the opinion of those philosophers, the development of knowledge would have stopped at those apparent [causes], whose alteration they had considered logically impossible. There is, however, only one logical impossibility: the agreement of two opposites, or two contrasts equivalent to two opposites, or their mutual elimination. Had the marvels unveiled by science in our time been mentioned to those incapable philosophers, they would have deemed them impossible, relating speculative specious arguments about that, such as what they related on the doctrine of bodily resurrection, whereas examples of bodily resurrection are clearly and completely apparent today to the scientists of chemistry.

Imam al-Ghazālī states in *The Incoherence of the Philosophers* [The Natural Sciences: Introduction]:

> This is what we wished to mention on the science, which, in their view, is called "theological." [1] Regarding what are called "the natural sciences," these consist of many sciences whose divisions we will [now] mention so that it would be known that the religious law does not require disputing (*munāzaʿ*) them nor denying (*inkār*) them, except in places [we will mention].[154]

I draw the reader's attention to his linking of "denying" with "disputing" in order to contrast them. "Denying" something is to deem it absolutely false, while "disputing" it is to discuss its evidence, to thereby manifest the truth, deriving from two individuals "disputing" over a garment. Then, after enumerating the types of natural science known in his time, the Imam states:

> [18 There is no necessity to oppose them in terms of the revealed law in any of these sciences. 19] We only oppose them in these sciences with respect to four questions. The first is their judgment that [66] this connection between causes and effects that one observes in existence is a connection of necessary concomitance, so that it is with neither [the realm of] power nor within [that of] possibility to bring about the cause without the effect or the effect without a cause.[155]

154. Michael E. Marmura, translation, *The Incoherence of the Philosophers = Tahāfut al-Falāsifah: A Parallel English-Arabic Text* (Provo, Utah: Brigham University Press, 1997), 164. The passage quoted is the introduction to Part Two of the *Tahāfut*. In Marmura's edition, the first sentence in this passage – "This is what we wished to mention on the science, which, in their view, is called 'theological' – is missing." Author's translation of this sentence.
155. Mamura, 166. Marmura comments that this statement "clearly suggests that al-Ghazālī has the philosophers' theory of necessary causal connection in mind."

The effect of this dispute is apparent in all the natural sciences. He then states:

> [23] The contention[156] over the first [theory] is necessary inasmuch as [on its refutation] rests the affirmation of miracles that disrupt [the] habitual [course of nature], such as changing the staff into a serpent, revival of the dead, and the splitting of the moon. Whoever renders the habitual courses [of nature] a necessary constant makes all these [miracles] impossible. [The philosophers] have thus interpreted what is said in the Qur'an about the revivification of the dead metaphorically, saying that what is meant by it is the removal of the death of ignorance through the life of knowledge. *They interpreted [metaphorically] the staff devouring the magic of the magicians, [thereby] negating the divine proof manifest at the hand of Moses – [this] being the doubts of those who deny.*[157] As regards the splitting of the moon, they often deny the existence [of its occurrence] and claim that there has been no soundly transmitted, indubitable reporting of it.[158]

Al-Ghazālī critiques this theory and then discusses another that "allows natural things to cause each other, while at the same time allowing the occurrence of miracles rejected by the philosophers." In Marmura's view, the second theory is introduced "simply for the sake of argument." Marmura, 241. See M.E. Marmura, "Al-Ghazālī on Bodily Resurrection and Causality in the *Tahāfut* and the *Iqtiṣād*," *Aligarh Journal of Islamic Thought* 2 (1989): 46–75, esp. 59 onwards, and Marmura's introduction to his translation of the *Tahāfut.*

156. Ar. *nizā'*, contention or dispute.
157. Marmura offers the italicized passage as a possible translation that is supported by "al-Ghazālī's insistence that the miracle is created on behalf of the prophet as a proof for the authenticity of his prophethood." However his preferred reading is based upon the alternative *'alā ibṭāl.* In that case, the sentence would read: "And they interpreted the staff devouring the magic of the magicians as the refutation by the divine proof, manifest at the hand of Moses, of the doubts of those who deny [the one God]." Overall, the text appears unclear. Marmura, 241.
158. Marmura comments: "The term used is *yatawātar*, the reference being to *tawātur*, the innumerable corroborative individual reports of a historical event of a geographical place that yield knowledge that is certain. *Tawātur* is included by the Islamic philosophers and logicians as yielding premises usable in strict demonstrative proofs." Marmura, 241. Riḍā also stresses the importance of knowledge established as *tawātur* or *mutawātir.* See Article Fifteen (*Shubuhāt*, 78, 79).

So may seekers of truth see the distortion of the Christian *al-Jāmiʿah*'s editor as they are. The Imam states: "The dispute over the first [theory] is necessary inasmuch as [on its refutation] rests the affirmation of miracles that disrupt [the] habitual [course of nature]." This means that the object of the dispute in the first theory is the denial of the affirmation of miracles through their inclusion in the category of logical impossibilities, whose existence is impossible and with which God's power is not concerned. *Al-Jāmiʿah*'s editor states the following from this Imam's tongue: "Then he states, 'denial of this opinion is incumbent upon us, as it denies the affirmation of miracles.' " Thus, he substitutes "denial" for "dispute" (*nizāʿ*), adding to it that his substitution is necessary. We explained the difference between denial and dispute previously. If the editor of *al-Jāmiʿah*'s reporting from Ranān and others is of this nature in terms of its comprehension and honesty, then we "congratulate" whoever reads [and believes] that which he wrote for his knowledge being identical to ignorance and his right guidance the same error.

Then, in explaining the truth about the issue in terms of the knowledge that supports that which Muslims believe, Imam al-Ghazālī states:

> [Seventeenth] Discussion: [On Causality and Miracles]: The connection between what is habitually believed to be a cause and what is habitually believed to be an effect is not necessary, according to us. But [with] any two things, where "this" is not "that" and "that" is not "this,"[159] and where neither the affirmation of the one entails the affirmation of the other nor the negation of one entails the negation of the other,[160] it is not a necessity of the existence of the one that the other should exist, and it is not a necessity

159. Marmura comments: "The sentence starting from 'where' in the translation is a relative clause, and so is the one that follows it. The issue is not that two are not identical. Avicenna [Ibn Sīnā], for example, is very specific in maintaining that cause and effect are two separate things. What is at stake is whether the connection between them is necessary." Marmura, 242.
160. Marmura comments: "Now there are relations existing between two separate things that entail each other – if A is to the left of B, then B is necessarily to the right of A, and so on. But this, according to Al-Ghazālī in this passage (and elsewhere as well), is not the case with causal relations." Marmura, 242.

> of the nonexistence of the one that the other should not exist – for example, the quenching of thirst and drinking, [67] satiety and eating, burning and contact with fire, light and the appearance of the sun, death and decapitation, healing and the drinking of medicine, the purging of the bowels and the using of a purgative, and so on to [include] all [that is] observable among connected things in medicine, astronomy, arts, and crafts. Their connection is due to the prior decree of God, who creates them side by side,[161] not to its being necessary in itself, incapable of separation. On the contrary, it is within [divine] power to create satiety without eating, to create death without decapitation, to continue life after decapitation, and so on to all connected things. The philosophers denied the possibility of [this] and claimed it to be impossible.[162]

He then gives a clear example of this that does not need mention.

That which Imam al-Ghazālī states here is agreed upon by the philosophers of this age, as they do not assert that any of these connections, generally known as causes and effects, are absolute logical necessities, whose severing is an impossibility of which the mind cannot conceive. On the contrary, in their view all of these things are [merely] possible, while the severing of the "inseparability" occurs often. They call that lacking a known cause "supernatural phenomena," while some severings were effected through the scientific unveiling of secrets of the universe. And, on the basis of these discoveries, they anticipate that which has yet to occur, such as the revival of dead persons, whereas they would not anticipate it were it impossible in their view. But *al-Jāmi'ah*'s editor does not distinguish the necessary from the possible. Thus, he confuses certain matters with others. Al-Ghazālī explains in that stated above that two logically inseparable things – inseparable in the one being affirmed by the other's affirmation and denied by its denial – are two things whose

161. Marmura comments: " *'Alā al-tasāwuq*: 'Side by side' or 'one alongside the other,' but not 'one following the other' and not 'in a successive order.' What al-Ghazālī is talking about is concomitance, where the priority is not temporal. His critique is of the Avicennan concept of essential cause, where cause and effect are simultaneous." Marmura, 242.

162. Marmura, 170.

inseparability cannot possibly be severed, for God Almighty's power does not concern what is impossible.

Agreement of al-Ghazālī's Two Statements with Bacon's Teaching[163]

As stated previously, al-Ghazālī states in *The Book on Trusting in God*: that God's sunnah in ordering the universe is the tying in it of causes to effects in an absolute and uninterrupted link that is not disrupted, except when the conditions through which causes materialize are not fulfilled. Hence, he states that cause follows effect when there is no obstacle: "it is inevitable." He explains the like of the Almighty's statement, "Thou wilt not find for Allah's way of treatment any substitute, nor wilt thou find for Allah's way of treatment aught of power to change" [35:43], in terms of this ordering of the uninterrupted linkage of causes and effects. This is the correct interpretation.

In [68] the book *The Incoherence of the Philosophers* he states: this linkage between common causes and effects is not, in spite of its continuity, logically necessary. Its absence is not impossible. It is only constant in daily experience and, in fact, through the wisdom of the universe's Creator and Arranger. If God, in His wisdom, decreed links between the universe's events, then people would need to search for them and be guided by them in their affairs and interests. For this to provide guidance would not depend on the logical impossibility of something's severing from everything ordinarily appearing to be its cause.

163. Roger Bacon (died 1292) was an English philosopher, a pioneer in the development of the scientific method. He is known as the founder of experimental science – an attribution Riḍā revises in Article Fourteen (*Shubuhāt*, 69). Bacon advocated reform of the church's approach to education and sought to develop a system for all knowledge. His writings were strongly criticized by the church and led to his imprisonment. Shortly before his death, he denounced the church in his *Compendium of Theological Studies.*

While Bacon is primarily known for his work on science, his achievements in philosophy and theology are also significant. Among Muslim thinkers, Ibn Sīnā was probably the most important influence on his thought in these latter subjects. Bacon advocated the deployment of mathematics and Greek and Arabic scientific knowledge in the service of theology. He also urged the study of the Hebrew, Greek and Arabic languages to facilitate Biblical exegesis.

One who contemplates [the teachings of] the early philosophers recognizes that they depended on theoretical evidence in order to determine something's logical impossibility, possibility, or necessity. Al-Ghazālī and other Imams of scholastic theology explained that what is meant by a "logical impossibility" is the agreement of two opposites, their mutual elimination, or the agreement of two contrasts, which means two opposites. They state: God Almighty's power does not concern what, in view of reason, is impossible and necessary imperative. Rather, God Almighty's power only concerns what is possible. Thus, the application of the scholastic theologians' opinion concerns two important matters, which are the basis of human progress. The first is that which is proven to be imperative (necessary) or impossible is not desired by the desirer – neither in terms of acquisition, nor in terms of reliance upon God Almighty – because it does not change. The second is that things that are possible obey regular rules that it befits a person to discover and benefit from. However, it is not befitting that he bring to a stop the development of his preparation upon the appearance of the initial perception that it does not change. Rather, it is incumbent upon him to search, that perhaps he may find another divine sunnah, the sunnah whose continuity appears to him conditioned by it. Then he may combine together the two sunnahs' benefits. An example of that is the apparent divine sunnah concerning the fire that burns that which is susceptible to burning. It is not desirable that the individual assert that the prevention of burning is impossible because burning is necessary. Rather, it is incumbent upon him to investigate, because burning is possible [but not necessary]. Perhaps its occurrence is conditional upon the absence of one of the substances that, were they known, would prevent burning. Indeed, that which generally prevents burning has been discovered and is now used to protect public offices.

Thus, with this determination *Ḥujjat al-Islām* refuted those speculative philosophers doctrinally (although Ibn Rushd misunderstood some of what he said and contested some of it) and demonstrated the Islamic religion's ruling in liberating the human mind from those speculative bonds, such that it swim in God's kingdom, rightly guided by God's ways [69] therein. Bacon adopted this proposition. Hence, he determined that speculative evidence cannot be relied upon to prove scientific matters unless it is supported by experience and experimentation. Bacon stated this maxim, which they consider the basis of the new scientific arising in Europe, while before him it was known to the Muslims (as mentioned previously in [Imam 'Abduh's] articles on *Islam and Christianity*). It would have been clearer and more apparent to him had he not believed in things contradicting it, such as sorcery, alchemy, and the philosophers' stone, which are imaginary matters not reaching the level of a considered hypothesis. However, Europe was prepared – in order to advance science – to adopt that which he stated on the need to depend on experience and experimentation. Hence, they acted upon it and science advanced thereby. Bacon is considered the Imam of this path, which the Muslims determined and implemented before him.

The upshot is that *al-Jāmi'ah*'s editor is wrong in [the following] claims: that Imam al-Ghazālī denied causes, that al-Ghazālī's teaching on divine sunnah contradicts that which we have stated – and persist in maintaining – in *al-Manār*, that between it and Bacon's maxim stands a high fence, and that if the inseparability of causes and effects or laws was not necessary (that is, a logical imperative whose nonexistence is impossible), positive law would degenerate into chaos. If He were wise, the Creator of the universe and Author of its laws would not proceed with anything except in accordance with an ordered system, as His mighty book demonstrates and as existence demonstrates. Thus, whence chaos? Who would state that the universe's ordered system is contingent upon God Almighty being incapable and unwise? This is not stated by anyone except the Christian *al-Jāmi'ah*'s editor, [who does so] to prove that the Muslim scholastic theologian's teaching is inherently false and leads to the denial of God Almighty's wisdom and omnipotence. Among those who reject the religion and attack Islam and its well-known Imams, we have not seen anyone more incoherent in his attacks than the like of this "honorable" writer, who sought fame and success without following their [true] path, as did the imbecile who defecated on that great church's altar to bring fame to his name. Shameful is the fame gained by disdaining the truth and corrupting the Imams' words for a few coins that flow from an enemy of Islam. He desires to vent his anger on its people, even with fallacious discourse. Yet Islam is above being hobbled by delusions.

Article Fifteen: Response to al-Jāmi'ah*'s Denial that Islam is the Religion of Reason*

[70] We have been explaining, and continue to explain, that the religion of Islam is the religion of reason. Our proof is the Book, the sunnah and the Imams' words. However, we were tested by those who planted doubts about the religion among the Muslims and among those who call to it, by deluding them: that that which we state is not of the religion and harms it, since it is incumbent upon Islam to become reason's enemy, like other traditional religions; that basing it on reason would foreshadow its destruction, as the other religion was destroyed; and that were it rational, it would be a science, not a religion. In addition, other doubts were planted. But we take our religion from the rational, transmitted evidence in our Lord's Book, not from the disputers who plant doubts.

> In the name of God, the Compassionate, the Merciful
> *ḥā' mīm*
> The revelation of the Scripture is from Allah, the Mighty, the Wise.
> Lo! in the heavens and the earth are portents for believers.
> And in your creation, and all the beasts that He scattereth in the earth, are portents for a folk whose faith is sure.[164]
> And the difference of night and day and the provision that Allah sendeth down from the sky and thereby quickeneth the earth after her death, and the ordering of the winds, are portents for people who have sense [45:1–5].
> Woe unto each sinful liar!
> Who heareth the revelations of Allah recited unto him, and then continueth in pride as though he heard them not. Give him tidings of a painful doom [45:7–8].

This is the book of God. It furnishes evidences and rational proofs through which it demands certainty in faith from people of reason.

164. Riḍā quotes incorrectly: *li al-mūqinīn* should read *li al-mu'minīn.*

Certainty is but by rational proof, while knowledge of something obtained through its proof is the highest and surest knowledge. Hence, after the verses mentioning the People of the Book, the Almighty states, "And now have We set thee (O Muḥammad) on a clear road of (Our) commandment; so follow it, and follow not the whims of those who know not" [45:18]. This is followed by "This is a clear indication (*baṣā'ir*) for mankind, and a guidance and a mercy for a folk whose faith is certain" [45:20].[165] *Baṣā'ir* is the plural of *baṣīrah* (sure knowledge), which is proof leading to certainty.[166] He then states of the deniers, imitating them: "And they say: There is naught but our life of the world; we die and we live, and naught destroyeth us save time;[167] when they have no knowledge whatsoever of (all) that; they do but guess" [45:24]. Thus, He denies that they have knowledge, making clear that supposition is of no benefit in religion, as that sought in it is the knowledge of certainty, as He states [71] in "The Star" (*Sūrat al-Najm*): "And they have no knowledge thereof. They follow but a guess, and lo! A guess can never take the place of the truth" [53:28].

Those short verses demonstrate that Islam is the religion of reason, that it is a science, and that certainty is sought through it. They demonstrate that supposition does not suffice for faith in its fundamental principles (*uṣūl*). These include God Almighty's oneness, knowledge, omnipotence, sending of prophets, and the mission of the seal of the prophets, prayer and peace be upon him and upon them. Verily, the verb "to reason" occurs approximately fifty times in the Qur'an, which also mentions reason and "those who have reason in speech." The signs of faith are [also] established without the root '-Q-L, as, for example, in the words "mind" and "intellect." The word "intellects" occurs in ten to twenty verses. Thus, knowledge of the universe is the way of faith and Islam. Him to whom glory and power belong states:

165. Author's translation (adapted from Pickthall).

166. Compare the Qur'anic "I call on God with sure knowledge (*'alā baṣīratin*)" (12:108).

167. *Dahr*, from which *dahrī* and *dahriyyah* derive. See Article Fourteen (*Shubuhāt*, 60).

> Hast thou not seen that Allah causeth water to fall from the sky, and We produce therewith fruit of divers hues; and among the hills are streaks white and red, of divers hues, and (others) raven-black; And of men and beasts and cattle, in like manner, divers hues? The erudite among His bondmen fear Allah alone. Lo! Allah is Mighty, Forgiving [35:27–28].

Thus our religion, and God be praised, is knowledge, while all of our knowledge is religion, as it increases our faith and knowledge of God, be He glorified. In the hadith is related, "This knowledge is religion, so examine the one from whom you take your religion."[168] As for the statement of those who plant doubts declaring that knowledge is limited to things that are perceived: in the philosophers' opinion all that you perceive is not said to be known [with certainty], as it may be a case of deception or ignorance. No science safeguards certainty as does the science of mathematics, and its proofs are rational, not perceived.

Contradictions between Rational Evidence and Transmitted Evidence

We have mentioned more than once in *al-Manār* that that which Sunni Muslims and others whose Islam is untrustworthy agree upon is that if there is related in the apparent revealed law that which contradicts clear-cut rational evidence, then acting in accordance with the rational evidence is the imposed duty. For transmitted texts, we have the science of allegorical interpretation or delegation.[169] This matter is discussed in the

168. An abridgement of a *mursal* tradition (the Companion is not listed in the chain of transmission). Among the nine collections, it is included in those of Muslim and al-Dārimī.
169. *Tafwīḍ*. The notion of *tafwīḍ* arises in connection with the Qur'anic distinction between clear and decisive verses and ambiguous verses (see Qur'an 3:7). Riḍā mentions the distinction in his introduction, where he claims that missionaries have used it to misrepresent the Qur'an (*Shubuhāt, jīm*). Decisive verses are unproblematic, as they present no problems of understanding or interpretation. Ambiguous verses are problematic either because their meaning is unclear, or because their apparently clear meaning contradicts Islamic doctrine or another verse. In such cases, in Riḍā's view, the revelation must be accepted literally, while acknowledging that the truth it contains transcends the verse's literal or linguistic meaning. The tension inherent in the literal acceptance of a

books on doctrine studied at al-Azhar and other Islamic schools in all areas. Take *al-Jawharah*'s statement:[170]

> [72] Every text instills the delusion of anthropomorphism. Interpret it allegorically or by delegation and seek dissociation.

Interpreting God Almighty's statement, "Allah tasketh not a soul beyond its scope" [2:286], Imam al-Rāzī states of its allegorical interpretation:

> Verily, it has been established that when a contradiction occurs between the rationally determined and the apparent and transmitted, either both are believed, which is impossible, as it entails combining two opposites, or the rationally determined is deemed false and the apparent and received preferred. That would necessitate resorting to contesting rational evidence, and when it is thus, divine oneness, prophecy, and the Qur'an are deemed false. Giving preference to the transmitted evidence would necessitate degrading rational evidence and received evidence simultaneously. Thus, it remains only to affirm the veracity of the rational evidence and correlate the transmitted evidence with it through allegorical interpretation.

Then, in this manner, he furnishes the evidence against the Mu'tazilah concerning the issue of God's commandment, they agree with the Sunnis about it.

This issue is well known to the Muslim ulama and there is no need for us to confirm it with reports. However, at this time the publications of those who plant doubts about the religion are widespread among us. If a Muslim reports an expression among his religion's fundamental principles, they state that it is from him. It is not far-fetched that among the

non-literal truth is resolved by "delegating" or "deferring" the matter to God, hence *tafwīḍ*, which in this context is synonymous with *taslīm* ("handing over"). This principle is stressed on numerous occasions by both Riḍā and 'Abduh in their *tafsīr*. For example, in explanation of the ambiguous verses, 'Abduh comments, "I follow the path of the *salaf* concerning necessity of *taslīm* and *tafwīḍ* concerning that which relates to God Almighty, His attributes, and the unseen." Riḍā affirms his mentor's sentiment (*Tafsīr*, i, 252).

170. Riḍā quotes verse forty-four of Ibrāhīm b. Ibrāhīm al-Laqānī's *al-Jawharah* or *Jawharat al-Tawḥīd*, a creed in verse by that produced many commentaries. Al-Laqānī (died 1631 or 32) was an al-Azhar professor. Watt, 140.

ignorant there be those misled by their words. It was mentioned previously – in [Imam 'Abduh's] articles on *Islam and Christianity* – that Islam's second fundamental is the priority of reason over a report in the event of a contradiction. The proof of this is taken from the Qur'an and from some of the Imams' teachings. Had we desired to present in detail the reports pertaining to opinions and meanings, and the rest of the books of scholastic theology and exegesis, and those of the modern thinkers – such as *Ḥawāshī al-Bājūrī*[171] and *al-Risālah al-Ḥamīdiyyah*[172] – we would have greatly extended the discourse in the same vein.

Doubts about the Issue

Were it said: after demonstrating the philosophers' incoherence in their theoretical evidence for knowledge of God Almighty, Imam al-Ghazālī stated:

> Hence, no party among them is free from shame as regards [Ibn Sīnā's] doctrine. That is what God does with those who stray from His path, thinking that the inner nature of divine matters is grasped by their reflection and imagination.[173]

Would this statement demonstrate that the religion is irrational or not?

[73] The answer: understanding the Creator's (*al-Khāliq*) essence and true nature, and the essence and true nature of the Creator's (*al-Bārī*) attributes, is not among the requirements of religion, nor among those of philosophy. If the wise and the ulama are unable to comprehend the essence of observed forms, how can those who aspire aspire to knowledge of the essence of the observed forms' Creator through theoretical evidence and poetic fancy? This is something with which the religion does not burden us. Al-Ghazālī's statement in his critique of the philosophers

171. *Jawharat al-Tawḥīd*, Ibrāhīm b. Muḥammad Bājūrī's commentary on Laqānī's text of the same name. Bājūrī (1783–1860) was a popular and prolific Egyptian Shāfi'ī scholar. Watt, 140.
172. A work by Shaykh Ḥusayn al-Jisr, Riḍā's early mentor. See Chapter Two.
173. Marmura, 105.

demonstrates that Islam does not burden the people with the irrational, as the planter of doubts claims.

Similar is his statement in *The Investigation into Divine Knowledge (Baḥth al- 'Ilm al-Ilāhī)*, addressing the philosophers after demonstrating their incapacity and incoherence [Sixth Discussion: On the divine attributes]:

> What is intended is to show your impotence in your claim of knowing the true nature of things through conclusive demonstrations, and to shed doubt on your claims. Once your impotence becomes manifest, then [one must point out] that there are among the people those who hold that the realities of divine matters are not attained through rational reflection – indeed, that it is not within human power to know them. For this reason, the giver of the law has said: "Think on God's creation and do not think on God's essence."[174]

This statement from al-Ghazālī, then, like the previous statement, is made specifically to demonstrate the human incapacity to know the true nature of the Creator (*al-Bārī*) and the true nature of His attributes. Indeed, centuries and epochs have passed and other centuries and epochs will pass, until the end of the human age, and humans [will] not attain knowledge of the true nature of God and the true nature of His knowledge and other attributes. The same point is made by [Imam 'Abduh], author of the articles *Islam and Christianity between Science and Civilization.* He states (*al-Manār*, p. 544.):

> It is necessary that the matter of the world winds up with the fraternization of knowledge and religion, in accordance with the sunnah of the Qur'an and the Wise Remainder [an epithet of the Qu'ran: 3:58] and that human beings adhere to the meaning of the sound hadith, "Think on God's creation and do not think on God's essence." Thereupon, God completed His religion, although the unbelievers be hateful and followed by those inflexible and despairing.

The statements of Imam al-Ghazālī and this Imam are one. There is no difference between them. Had Islam imposed upon us that we comprehend the nature (*kunh*) of God Almighty's essence (*dhāt*), and the essence

174. Marmura, 107. The tradition cited is not found in any of the nine collections. It is rated *mawqūf.*

of His attributes, it would have been imposing upon us that which cannot be conceived or attained. But God states, "Allah tasketh not a soul beyond its scope" [2:286].

[74] We might add to this that in *The Incoherence of the Philosophers* – the book from which we cited these two statements – Imam al-Ghazālī did not intend to explain the Islamic principles. He only intended to explain the weakness of the philosophers' speculations on matters of the divine – and verily, the false is eliminated by the false. Hence, he states in the lines preceding the second statement (p. 45.):

> [39] We did not plunge into this book in the manner of those who introduce [what is constructive], but in the manner of those who are destroyers and objectors. For this reason we have named the book *The Incoherence of the Philosophers*, not *The Introduction to the Truth.*[175]

Thus, it is unsound to derive his teaching on doctrine or anything else from this book, as we highlighted in the article on causes and effects (Article Fourteen). Rather, his teaching [should] be derived from his books on doctrine and fundamental principle. Therein he concurs with the rest of Sunni Imams that reason is the fundamental basis of Islam and that its clear-cut proofs cannot be opposed. Thus, if, in its apparent meaning, that related in the revealed law contradicts these proofs, the ruling is that stated above.

Were it said: verily, we know that the Muslim Imams of doctrine and fundamental principle were not in disagreement as to Islam being the religion of reason, would you [thereby] know that the Islamic philosophers departed from this principle, separating reason and religion?

The answer: "indeed no." The philosophers were more desirous of reconciling reason and the revealed law than others. The philosopher of Islam in the West, Abū al-Walīd ibn Rushd, God Almighty have mercy upon him, composed a book on this issue, affirming therein that which the Sunnis had previously affirmed. That book is entitled *The Book of the Decisive Treatise Determining the Connection Between the Law and Wisdom*

175. Marmura, 107.

(*Faṣl al-Maqāl fīmā bayn al-Sharī'ah wa al-Ḥikmah min al-Ittiṣāl*). In this book, he affirms that the revealed Islamic law mandates rational reflection and makes reason the basis of doctrine. He then states (p. 8.):

[*Demonstrative truth and scriptural truth cannot conflict*]

Now since this religion is true and summons to the study which leads to knowledge of the Truth, we the Muslim community know definitely that demonstrative study does not lead to [conclusions] conflicting with what Scripture has given us; for truth does not oppose truth but accords with it and bears witness to it.

[*If the apparent meaning of Scripture conflicts with demonstrative conclusions it must be interpreted allegorically, i.e., metaphorically.*]

This being so, whenever demonstrative study leads to any manner of knowledge about any being, that being (*dhālik al-mawjūd*) is inevitably either unmentioned or mentioned in Scripture. If it is unmentioned there is no contradiction, and it is in the same case [75] as an act whose category is unmentioned, so that the lawyer has to infer it by reasoning from Scripture. If Scripture speaks about it, the apparent meaning of the words inevitably either accords or conflicts with the conclusions of demonstration about it. If this [apparent meaning] accords there is no argument. If it conflicts there is a call for allegorical interpretation of it. The meaning of "allegorical interpretation" is: extension of the significance of an expression from real to metaphorical significance, without forsaking therein the standard metaphorical practices of Arabic, such as calling a thing the name of something resembling it or a cause or consequence or accompaniment of it, or other things such as are enumerated in accounts of the kinds of metaphorical speech.

[*If the lawyer can do this, the religious thinker certainly can. Indeed these allegorical interpretations always receive confirmation from the apparent meaning of other passages of Scripture.*]

Now if the lawyer does this in many decisions of religious law, with how much more right is it done by the possessor of demonstrative knowledge! For the lawyer has at his disposition only reasoning based on opinion, while he who would know [God] [has at his disposition] reasoning based

> on certainty. So we affirm definitely that whenever the conclusion of a demonstration is in conflict with the apparent meaning of Scripture, that apparent meaning admits of allegorical interpretation according to the rules for such interpretation in Arabic. This proposition is questioned by no Muslim and doubted by no believer. But its certainty is increased for those who have had close dealings with this idea and put it to the test, and made it their aim to reconcile the assertions of intellect and tradition. Indeed we must say that whenever a statement in Scripture conflicts in its apparent meaning with a conclusion of demonstration, if Scripture is considered carefully, and the rest of its contents searched page by page, there will invariably be found among the expressions of Scripture something which in its apparent meaning bears witness to that allegorical interpretation or comes close to bearing witness.
>
> [*All Muslims accept the principle of allegorical interpretation; they only disagree about the extent of its application.*]
>
> In the light of this idea the Muslims are unanimous in holding that it is not obligatory either to take all the expressions of Scripture in their apparent meaning or to extend them all from their apparent meaning by allegorical interpretation.[176]

This is the substance of it.

You say: God is most great, the truth shines and glitters. It is apparent that the Muslim scholars – the theologians, philosophers, exegetes and jurists – do not differ on Islam being the religion of reason and its law being based on reason, and addressing reason (not the heart alone). It is apparent that that which the Master Imam ['Abduh] states in the articles entitled *Islam and Christianity between Science and Civilization* on the contradiction between the rational and reported evidence is that agreed upon in the pure community. It is this to which *al-Manār* has been loudly calling. It grew too great for Islam's enemies. Hence, they deceived with great deception. Yet they will find no helpers beside God.[177]

176. G.F. Hourani, *Averroes on the Harmony of Religion and Philosophy* (London: Luzac Oriental, 1961), 50–51.

177. Riḍā paraphrases Qur'an 71:25: "And they found they had no helpers in place of Allah."

[76] Were it said: In *The Incoherence of the Incoherence*, Ibn Rushd has another discussion that appears to contradict his statement here. Take for example his statement:

> Philosophy investigates everything related in the revealed law. If it comprehends it, the two comprehensions are equivalent, which is the most complete knowledge. If it does not comprehend it, it indicates the deficiency of human reason, the law alone comprehending it.

And his statement:

> The ancient philosophers did not discuss the problem of miracles, since according to them such things must not be examined and questioned; for they are the principles of the religions, and the man who inquires into them and doubts them merits punishment, like the man who examines the other general religious principles, such as whether God exists or blessedness or the virtues. For the existence of all these cannot be doubted, and the mode of their existence is something divine which human apprehension cannot attain. The reason for this is that these are the principles of the acts through which man becomes virtuous, and that one can only attain knowledge after the attainment of virtue.[178] One must not investigate the principles which cause virtue before the attainment of virtue, and since the theoretical sciences can only be perfected through assumptions and axioms which the learner[179] accepts in the first place, this must still more be the case with the practical sciences.[180]

The answer: this discussion does not negate that discussion, nor does it contradict it. Rather, it supports the first statement and the statements of all the Muslim Imams before and after him, up to [Imam ʿAbduh], author of the articles entitled *Islam and Christianity between Science and Civilization.* Were we to hypothesize a contradiction between the two

178. Simon Van den Bergh, trans., *Averroës' Tahāfut at-Tahāfut* (The Incoherence of the Incoherence) (London: Luzac, 1954). Van den Bergh comments that the philosophical implication of virtue is a Stoic idea.

179. *Mutaʿallim.* On the variant readings of this word – *mutaʿallim, muʿallim, muʿlim* – see Van den Bergh, 372.

180. Van den Bergh, 315.

statements, then the viewpoint of the first would be the obligatory precept, as it definitively explains his teaching and belief, his and that of other Muslims. As for his statement here, it is a report about the early philosophers. Their opposition to us does not harm us, so long as we are confident that we are on the path of the truth confirmed by logical proof. Yet Ibn Rushd states here that the early philosophers do not oppose us in these issues, that is to say, that was a requirement of their school. Else, he explains that they had no discourse on the issues that he mentions. Thus, the dispute between him and al-Ghazālī on this occasion is limited to the reporting of the philosophers' disputing the matter of miracles [77] and virtues' foundations with the sects. Al-Ghazālī attributes it to them in general, while Ibn Rushd states that there was no investigation into that except for that of Ibn Sīnā. And the matter is straightforward.

As for the harmony, you see him in the beginning discussing the philosophers' view of the religions and their bases, not Islam, which is the most elevated of them. And together with that, he acknowledges matters that do not place the ultimate religion above reason, meaning that there be in it something that reason deems impossible and devoid of soundness. Among them:

[1] That which philosophy does not comprehend through theoretical speculation demonstrates that human reason is incapable of independently attaining it. Hence, it stands in need of the revealed law's guidance with regard to it. There is no doubt that, to this day, human reason is incapable of comprehending all that is before it. It uses and benefits from electricity, while it does not positively comprehend its true nature. In that case, how can it positively comprehend matters of the afterlife or resurrection? Our statement that the religion of Islam is rational does not mean that all of its issues may be comprehended by way of independent reason. Rather, it means that there is nothing therein that reason declares impossible, such as three being one, one being three, and God being united with a man. Were this not the intention, reason would independently set down the religion, with no need for revelation.

[2] His opinion that the religion's bases, such as miracles, are existing matters whose existence is beyond doubt. That which exists cannot be

impossible, as an impossibility cannot exist. His statement about them – that the mode of their existence is a divine matter beyond the reach of human understanding – does not mandate the religion's irrationality or its incorporation of something rationally impossible. This is because our reason is incapable of comprehending the mode of the generation of these existing things, which we perceive and do not doubt. Hence, all the more reason for human reason's incapacity to comprehend the mode of the existence of miracles. It is easy for every rational individual to distinguish that which is impossible, and whose existence is inconceivable, from that whose existence is beyond doubt, even though comprehension of the mode of this existing thing's origination is not attained.

[3] These established existing religious foundations are to be adopted through accepting and following the revealed law (not the opinions of people), without empowering philosophical theory to investigate their feasibility and the mode of their existence. This is because such investigation is foolish and harmful. And what foolishness [78] and harm is greater than planting doubts through valueless speculation about an existing thing that benefits people in order to dissuade them from benefiting from it? What foolishness is greater than the foolishness of one who disputes that established to exist through observation or successive testimony (such as miracles), or demands of the individual that he not follow the virtuous path until he investigates its feasibility and the mode of its actualization with speculative intellectual evidence, while he sees and perceives that [virtues] are obtained through action, and that the way to obtaining them is action, not intellectual speculations?

How excellent is that which the philosopher [Ibn Rushd] also related on this issue (p. 129):

> As to the objection which Ghazali ascribes to the philosophers over the miracle of Abraham, such things are only asserted by heretical Muslims. The learned among the philosophers do not permit discussion or disputation about the principles of religion, and he who does such a thing needs, according to them, a severe lesson. For whereas every science has its principles, and every student of this science must concede its principles and may not interfere with them by denying them, this is still more

> obligatory in the practical science of religion, for to walk on the path of religious virtues is necessary for man's existence, according to them, not in so far as he is man, but in so far as he has knowledge; and therefore it is necessary for every man to concede the principles of religion and invest with authority the man who lays them down. The denial and discussion of these principles denies human existence, and therefore heretics must be killed. Of religious principles it must be said that they are divine things which surpass human understanding, but must be acknowledged although their causes are unknown.
>
> Therefore, we do not find that any of the ancient philosophers discusses miracles, although they were known and had appeared all over the world, for they are the principles on which religion is based and religion is the principle of the virtues; nor did they discuss any of the things which are said to happen after death. For if a man grows up according to religious virtues he becomes absolutely virtuous, and if time and felicity are granted to him, so that he becomes one of the deeply learned thinkers and it happens that he can explain one of the principles of religion, it is enjoined upon him that he should not divulge the explanation, and should say "all these are the terms of religion and the wise," conforming himself to the Divine Words, "but those who are deeply versed in knowledge say we believe in it, it is all from our Lord" [3:5]. These are the limits of the law and the limits imposed upon the scholars.[181]

[79] Truly I say: this is that which may be correctly attributed to those who are wise and rational. We illustrate it with another example that we often mentioned in our discussion with the Ikhwān. This is that medicine is a science whose benefits have been proven to people through experience and observation. Hence, it would be a stupid and foolish notion to say to someone who is ill: it is incumbent upon you not to accept the doctor's treatment before you first investigate the principles of medicine and prove

181. Van den Bergh, 322–323. Riḍā cites p. 129, which corresponds to pp. 527–528 in van den Bergh. Van den Bergh comments: "It is hardly necessary, I think, to draw attention to the ambiguity of Averroës's religious views." The final sentence in the cited passage – *hādhihi ḥudūd al-sharā'i' wa ḥudūd al-'ulamā'* – is not included van den Bergh's text: author's translation.

with theoretical evidence that it is beneficial and useful, so that you would then know [the answers to the following]: What is the cure prescribed for you by the doctor? How are its parts related to each other? How is it effective in fighting the disease? What is the rational evidence for its effectiveness? And such things.

Likewise, it is a foolish notion to say to the people: before believing in the proven miracle that you have perceived – or that was transmitted to you broadly and without interruption – it is incumbent upon you to investigate its causes, until it be as though you were in its presence [perceiving] how God Almighty created it. Then, you should also investigate everything related in the revealed law, so that through theoretical evidence you learn [answers to the following]: Why is it as it is? How was it? After all of that, if you understood all the issues in terms of theoretical evidence, believe. If you did not understand them, disbelieve.

The sick person is extirpated through the sickness of the body, until he becomes disordered in mind or is dying and unable to comprehend the details of medicine through reflection and investigation. And that is entirely acquired. Reflection and experience produced examples of its operation among the people. Likewise, vices and false doctrines extirpate the soul, rendering it its own affliction and the people's affliction. And the soul does not reach these states through reflection. Thus, it remains that that which is correct is that which Islam has determined: namely, reflection is enjoined concerning the fundamental principles (*uṣūl*) through which knowledge of God Almighty and the veracity of prophethood are established. When we believe in God's omnipotence, will, and knowledge, and believe that He bestowed revelation upon some of his servants and inspired them to guide the people to that which brings them happiness in their lives after death, then it is easy for us to utterly accept all that those to whom revelation is revealed say (the prophets, peace be upon them). If we find therein something whose apparent meaning contradicts rational clear-cut evidence, we reconcile it with the rational clear-cut evidence through allegorical interpretation, or we entrust the matter to God, together with accepting the rational evidence. This is that upon which the Muslim Imams are in consensus, as stated previously. That suffices in regard to [80] Islam's character as the religion of reason, as Muslims do not neglect clear-cut rational evidence under any circumstance.

Ibn Rushd was eloquent in his opinion that allegorical interpretations apparent to those firmly rooted in knowledge are not to be widely distributed. Rather, they are to remain specifically for their [specialist] people. Thus, they do not become a cause for the common folk to open the door to disputation of that which they did not understand among the universal sciences' truths. Disputation is the cause of doubt. Thus, it is enjoined to educate the doubters, while ignoring the disputatious.

The Development of Religions and their Culmination in Islam

Quoted from *The Theology of Unity*, by the Master Imam ['Abduh]

> When religions first began, men understood their well-being, whether general or particular, only in a most rudimentary way, rather like infants lately born, who know only what comes within their senses and distinguish only with difficulty between the present and the past. Only what they can manually touch do they really cognize, and they have no inner awareness by which to "sympathize" with family or fellow, being concerned simply with self-preservation and too pre-occupied for the implications of their relationships with others, unless it be a hand to feed them or to steady them on their feet. Religions in that sort of context could not intelligibly relate themselves to men on subtle aspects of consciousness or "extend" them with rational proofs. On the contrary, the great grace of God is seen in their handling the peoples as children, in just the way that a parent treats his child – with the utmost simplicity and within the senses of hearing and sight. Though the meaning and purpose were there to be known, obedience was irrespective of actual comprehension and intelligent knowledge. Religions came with astonishing and impressive miracles [81] and laid upon men the forms of worship consonant with their condition.[182]

182. Kenneth Cragg and Ishaq Musa'ad, trans. *The Theology of Unity* (London: George Allen Unwin, 1966), 132.

(*Al-Manār*: until now, that which has been known among these religions is that of the Jews. It will be clear to one who reads their holy books – that collectively they call "The Torah" – that the description of them therein is appropriate. This includes the Lord calling the Israelite people "the thick necked," meaning broad necked, indicating brutish stupidity. He demonstrated miracles and horrors to them, and the Israelites were humbled. Then, they returned to their rebellion. He explained the precepts to them through special occurrences, such as their deliverance from the Egyptians. He punished them with the strongest of punishments for relinquishing any ruling, such that, for example, whoever works on the Sabbath be killed.)

> During the centuries that followed peoples flourished and declined, waxed and waned. They quarreled and agreed. The times brought sufferings and there were endless vicissitudes of prosperity and adversity, through which they were prompted to finer sensitivity and deeper self-awareness, which may not unworthily be compared to what goes on in women's hearts or belongs with growing youth. A religion came which spoke to these feelings and, tenderly confiding to these compassions, made its appeal to the gentle arts of the heart. It laid down for men sacred laws of asceticism, drawing them away from the world altogether and turning them towards the higher life. It taught men not to press even their undoubted rights and barred the doors of heaven to the rich. Similar attitudes characterizing it are well enough known. It ordained patterns of Divine worship consistent with its understanding of man and in line with its message, and had a deep effect in breaking the ills and retrieving the evils of the souls that hearkened to it. But in the course of a few generations the resolve of men grew weak and wary of it. Men lapsed from its provisions and precepts as being more than they could sustain. They took to assuming that there was an inherent impracticability in its commands. Its very custodians themselves began to rival kings for their authority and to vie in wealth with the idle rich. The great mass of people declined sadly from its noble quality through "reinterpretation" and in their wan fancies imported all kinds of false accretions. So things went, in respect of actions and disposition. Purity was forgotten and integrity bartered. As for dogmas, these were compromised by schism and heresy. [82] The custodians

abandoned all its principles, except one they mistakenly supposed to be its strongest pillar and chief ground, namely the veto on intellectual inquiry into the faith, or indeed into the details of the universe and on the pursuit of secret things of the mind. They promulgated the principle that reason and religion had nothing in common, but that rather religion was the inveterate enemy of science. It was not simply that this view could be taken by anyone for himself: rather they strenuously imposed it as the proper thing for all. They pressed the doctrine with such force as to provoke the most shameful of all conflicts in human history, namely civil war within the household of religion for the imposition of religious decrees. And thus the very foundations were broken up and communal relationships destroyed. Concord, cooperation and peace were ousted: schism, contention and strife reigned in their place. And so men continued until the advent of Islam.[183]

(*Al-Manār*: The reader observes that the master attributes all that was innovated in Christianity, and was an evil upon humanity, to the leaders who forsook Christ's asceticism – while claiming that they were his deputies – for vying with the kings and seeking to be better than them. So let no one imagine that Muslims believe that in Christ's religion itself there is something that, in its essence, is harmful to the one addressed by it.)

At length, human society reached a point at which man came to his full stature, helped by the moral of the earlier vicissitudes. Islam supervened, to present its case to reason, to call on mind (*fahm*) and intelligence (*lubb*) for action, to take emotion and feeling into partnership for man's guidance to both earthly and heavenly blessedness. It clarified the things that provoked human discords and demonstrated that religion with God was one in all generations, that there was a single Divine purpose for their reform without and their cleansing within. Islam taught that the sole aim of outward forms of worship was to renew the inward recollection (*dhikrā*) of God and that God looks not on the form but on the heart. It required the devotee to care as well for his body as for the soul, enjoining outward as well as inward integrity, both of which it made mandatory. Sincerity was made the very heart of worship and [83] rites were only laid

183. Cragg, 132–33.

> down in so far as they conduced to the hallowing of moral character. "Verily prayer preserves men from foul and evil things." (Surah 29.45.) "Man is created restless. When evil befalls him he despairs, but touched with good fortune he becomes niggardly – though not those who pray." (Surah 79.19–22.) The rich man who remembers to be grateful is raised by Islam to the same level as the poor man who endures patiently. Perhaps Islam even esteems him higher. Islam dealt with man in its exhortations as a wise and sober counselor would deal with a mature person summoning him to the full harnessing of his powers, both outward and inward, and affirmed this quite unequivocally to be the way of pleasing God and showing thankfulness for His grace. This world is the seed plot of the world to come. Men will not come by ultimate good save as they endeavor a present well-doing.[184]

Then he states:

> Islam dispelled the clouds of illusion which obscured from the mind the realities of the macrocosm of this world and the microcosm of man. It affirmed that the great signs of God in the making of the world hinge on Divine laws, laid down in the eternal knowledge of God and ever abiding unchanged. Yet God's part in them must never be overlooked. On the contrary, the remembrance of Him must be alive in every act of cognizance we make. In the Prophet's words: "The sun and the moon are signs of God: they do not suffer eclipse of any one's death, nor for his birth. If you see an eclipse let it remind you of God and wait for the re-appearance of the light."[185]

(*Al-Manār*: The sun was eclipsed on the day of the death of Abraham, son of the Prophet, prayer and peace be upon him. Some of the people thought it was eclipsed due to his death – hence the prophet's statement, which was related by al-Bukhārī and others.)[186]

184. Cragg, 133–34.
185. Cragg, 136.
186. The tradition referred to is: "Al-Mughirah bin Shu'bah, may Allah be pleased with him, related: The sun eclipsed during the lifetime of the Messenger of Allah (may peace be upon him) on the day when Abraham, the Prophet's son, died. Upon this the Messenger of Allah (may peace be upon him) said: 'Verily the sun and the moon are two signs among the signs of Allah. They do not eclipse on

> This confirms that all earthly phenomena follow one pattern, within the age-long care of God for the laws on which He established the universe. Islam also drew back the curtain that obscured the conditions of human well being, whether of persons or peoples, and of the trials with which men are beset. It made the issue unmistakably clear in both respects.[187]

After discussing the condition of individuals and [stating] that that which afflicts them occurs by dint of their own deeds and other than that, the master states:

> It was not this way, however, in respect of nations. There is a spirit from which the life of nations takes its rise, illuminating their true well-being in this world here and now, before the other world is reached. It is the spirit God has implanted in His Divine laws for the right ordering of thought and reflection, the discipline of desire and the curbing of ambition and luck. [84] It is the spirit which bids us assess every question on its proper merits and pursue all objectives soundly, keeping faith, holding brotherly affection and co-operating in right dealing, with mutual loyalty through thick and thin. "He who wishes his reward in the world, We will give him thereof." (Surah 3.145.) God will never deprive a nation of His favor as long as this spirit animates them. Rather He will multiply their blessings in proportion to its strength and diminish them when it is weak. Should the spirit no longer be found in the nation, happiness also takes its leave and peace with it. God then turns its strength into decline and its wealth to poverty. Well-being then gives way to wretchedness and peace to trouble. While they slumber in neglect, they will be overpowered by others, either by tyrants or by just masters. "If We desire to bring a nation to destruction, We first warn those of them who live in comfort. But if they go on in sin, they bring down upon themselves a righteous judgment and We utterly destroy them." (Surah 17.16.) God has commanded righteousness, but they have perverted it to evil. In that event, wailing and

account of the death of anyone or on account of the birth of anyone. So when you see them (in a state of eclipse), supplicate Allah and observe the Prayer till it is over.' " Among the nine collections, it is found in those of al-Bukhārī (Friday Prayer, 985, 1000; Etiquette, 5731), Muslim (Eclipse, 1522) and Ibn Ḥanbal (in several places).

187. Cragg, 137.

> weeping will bring them no help at all, nor will intercession, nor the surviving appearances of activity. Their only hope of staying the rot is to repair again to that gracious spirit and seek its renewed descent from the heaven of mercy upon their affairs, through the promptings of thought and recollection, of patience and thanksgiving. "Truly God does not change a people's condition until inwardly they change themselves." (Surah 13.11.) "This was the pattern of God's relationship to those who passed away before you: you will never find the way of God to vary." (Surah 33.62.) There is no finer word than that spoken by 'Abbās ibn 'Abd al-Muṭṭalib when he prayed for rain: "O God, there is no distress that comes upon us without our having transgressed: and none is lifted off us save by repentance."
>
> The earliest of the Islamic peoples lived by these laws. While the Muslim spirit was exalted by these noble beliefs and worked them out in worthy actions, other peoples supposed that by their prayers they could shake the earth and rend the heavens with their lamentations, while they wallowed in their passions and persisted in their extravagant ways, so that their idle hopes of intercession profited them nothing.[188]

This is the substance of *The Theology of Unity.*

The Similarity of Religious Education and Education in Schools

This is that stated by the master in *The Theology of Unity,* originally published in 1315 A.H. [1897]. The al-Azhar board of administration decided to teach it officially at al-Azhar Mosque, and it is known that the chairman of this board is the shaykh of the mosque. He is among the other ulama on the board. Moreover, the rest of the [85] al-Azhar ulama agree with that which is in this book. And the meaning of the religion of Islam's nature as the religion of reason may be discerned from the above statement from it. The Qur'an testifies to this in scores and hundreds of verses. It is also known that Muslims believe in the true nature of the Christian religion, and its character in bringing reform to the people, but for a limited period that passed when it was dispensed with by means of the last religion.

188. Cragg, 137–39.

It was stated previously that God's religion is one – "We make no distinction between any of His Messengers" [2:285] – and that the revelation's message differed in accordance with the people's readiness to receive it. Hence, the Mosaic law, and that resembling it prior to it, was studied in the manner of primary school [studies]. The Christian religion resembles secondary school, while the Islamic religion resembles the highest school, which is the final education. This does not imply a diminution of Judaism and Christianity, as the existence of high schools does not diminish primary and secondary school, as both are necessary for it. The goal of all is one. Do not forget that the similarity relates to humanity in general. It is not said that it is necessary for each individual to become a Jew, then a Christian and then a Muslim. This is what we stated in support of that which sound knowledge guides towards concerning the laws of human development. The people adopted that through the rulings of those laws. Thus, millions of Jews and Christians converted to Islam in groups. In that, they were as one who moves from a school to a higher one. Had not it not been for the [Muslim] leaders who rendered the religion tradition-bound and erected a fence of sensory and illusory power around it, and had it not been for the incidents that befell Islam's path through the intercession of the leaders among the kings and emirs and their enticement of the ulama and jurists, the early religions would not have been left with the body of followers with which they founded large nations. (p. 807. *et cetera* vol. 5.)

Article Sixteen: Civil and Religious Authority – In Response to **al-Jāmi'ah**'*s Denial of Civil Authority and the Shari'ah in Islam*

[86] We Muslims believe:

- That God Almighty's religion is one in essence.
- That the explanations and guidance it contains differ only in accordance with the [conditions of] the ages.
- That people in every age take from religion's guidance that which accords with the capacity of their readiness.
- That the social conditions of the preceding nations led to the loss of

their religion's scriptures, completely or partially, when a long period passed after those who brought them.

- That the religious communities appearing closest to Islam were not safeguarded from this loss.
- That Islam is the only religion whose scripture was preserved in its entirety.
- That Islam appeared during a time in which the social conditions had improved to such a point that we can determine that none of the mind's gains vanished after it, nor will vanish, as it is the beginning of a new era in human history.

We stated: the religious communities closest to Islam in time were not safeguarded from loss. It is clear that we mean Judaism and Christianity, as each of these factions lost the uninterrupted transmitted support for its holy books. This no longer exists verbally or in written form. This is the object of the Almighty's characterization of them as "those unto whom a portion of the Scripture hath been given" [3:23; 4:44; 4:51] and His statement – to Him belongs glory and power – "they forgot a part (*ḥaẓẓ*) of that whereof they were admonished" [5:13; 5:14]. "Part" means "portion" (*naṣīb*), namely, meaning that they preserved part of that which they were given and forgot part. When part of the religion is lost, the remainder becomes untrustworthy, even if it were safeguarded from corruption and addition. How much more so, then, if it were not safeguarded? Verily, God Almighty sent down the Qur'an "confirming whatever Scripture was before it, and [as] a controller (*muhaymin*) over it" [5:48].[189] The word "Scripture" is used here in the generic sense, while the "controller" is the "watcher" (*murāqib*) that has information about that which it is watching over. Thus, that which the Qur'an verifies of those scriptures is of the portion they were given, while that which it reports and is not present therein is of the part they forgot, and that which it declares false is of [the part] that they added and augmented. And the Qur'an is the just judge: "Lo! this (Qur'an) is a conclusive word, It is no pleasantry" [86:13–14].

189. Author's translation (adapted from Pickthall).

[87] The enjoined duty is that they appoint it as arbitrator in that which unfolds, refrain from that which it forbids, and implement that which it commands. Those who conform acted thus, while the others blocked the path to it. The cause of blocking is religious authority, whose holders, serving their own interests, rendered the religion purely traditionalist, its doctrines tethered to the hands of leaders, such as monks and bishops, who force them upon the people, while forbidding them other doctrines, and raise minors, male and female, to believe in the necessity of accepting and deferring to them in every matter of religion. The effect of such an upbringing remains apparent in one raised in the schools of the priests. Hence, you find him debating you on the matter. If your proof is brought against him, he would state: this that you say is clear and rational in itself. But it concerns the matter of religion and the priest states the opposite. No statement may be made on religion but that of the priest, and it is not required that his statement be rational or comprehensible!

Hence, if a Christian states: religious authority is the agitator of reprehensible fanaticism, the birthplace of hatred and enmity between neighbors and friends, the obstacle preventing equality of rights between people of the same nationality, the shackles through which will and power are suppressed and the fetters through which reason and thought are restrained, the Muslim would agree to it and not dispute it. He would agree to it thanking God Almighty that his own religion lacks a faction to whom Islam granted the right of controlling minds and spirits, setting down for them what it wills and forbidding them what it wills and dealing with the Muslims – in the name of religion – as it wills.

Then, he would turn around and see that those Muslims who imitated the spiritual leaders of the Christians did not reach the point of attaining a truly regular authority through which they could hold thought accountable for its inclinations and minds accountable for their knowledge. Rather, these were those who permitted along with thought and imagination that which those other than them did not permit. They considered every piece of knowledge an approach to God Almighty, because they state: for to God the paths number the breaths in creation.

Then, he would turn and look from another angle. He would see that the authority of these imitators in spiritual authority is not great but when religious knowledge is diminished, their influence was not strong but when Islamic rule's influence is attenuated. Their authority did not grow in an area but that it was a disaster for the Muslims and for Islam. If you have forgotten the events surrounding the Mahdī of Sudan, you have in front of you the incident of the rebels of Marakesh.

[88] It is the right of the scholars, rational individuals, writers and speakers to state what they wish of Christian spiritual authority. They have the right to separate and distance it from civil authority as much as they are able to, because it is an authority that was and is harmful, wherever it existed and exists, most of its harm occurring in the days when it was joined to civil authority. They have the right to call it "authority," because in every kingdom it has a general leader who appoints the rest of the leaders in the kingdom. These leaders – who are the pillars of the general leader's authority – are dispersed in each city and village, whereas not all villages and farms have civil leaders, as they have these spiritual leaders. They have the right to wrestle with and oppose this government. They have the right to curb its power and weaken its tyranny. They have the right to say that were it not separated from civil authority, we would not have smelled the breath of freedom. They have the right to excuse the French nation, since it attempted to uproot this authority entirely. The Muslim excuses them in all of this, as it is the practice that Islam brought, as we stated at the beginning of this article. Thus, whoever did not derive it from Islam directly may derive it from the order of innate disposition, should knowledge guide him toward it. Islam is nothing but the religion of innate disposition, the guide to its order and God's laws for it.

It would be a clear wrongdoing to blame Islam itself for the establishment of religious authority as it is known to the Christians. It is Islam that invalidated every authority that would enable a faction to become a sovereign over another faction's spirit and a controller of its freedom in anything beyond that which the revealed law sanctions for every leader and follower. Those who followed the laws of those who preceded them and imitated them in matters such as this did not imitate well. The spirit of

Islam prevented them from affecting it in all that they desired. But Islam was not safe from enemies who attributed all of their faults to it, and knowingly lied about it. Yes, they fabricated falsity against it, because they read what we and certain Imams wrote in explanation of the denial of this authority. Thereafter, they did not desist from finding fault with Islam in relation to it. Behind planting doubts in Muslim minds about their own religion and estranging them from it, they have a goal at which they aim. We referred to it in a previous article[190] and we promised to explain the truth about it, as we explained other matters among their doubts and criticisms.

A Testimony on the Subject from al-Manār*'s First Year*

[89] In issue 22 of *al-Manār*'s first year, we published an article on "The Spiritual Authority of the Sheikhdom of the Spiritual Path,"[191] stating at the beginning:

> In the development of his society, man passed through stages. Periods and ages passed over him, while he was restrained in will and shackled in senses by two great strong powers whose possessors had complete influence and free disposition over individuals. These powers are those of religion and politics or, as named by the people of this age, spiritual and temporal power.[192]

Then, after discussing the condition of these two powers, their influence, and the condition of the nation governed by them, we stated:

> In general, a nation in this condition is always agitated, like the rider's arrow that neither rests firmly nor is stable. All that befalls nations in the way of development and poverty, knowledge and ignorance, happiness and unhappiness, may be attributed to the free disposition of emirs, rulers, and spiritual leaders. Evil befell nations more than good, and misery was more prevalent than happiness, because the just and wise ruler

190. See Introduction, *jīm*.

191. Ar.*Sulṭat Mashyakhat al-Ṭarīq al-Rūḥiyyah. Al-Manār*, i, 404–410. Originally published August 15, 1898.

192. *Al-Manār*, i, 404.

is not immune from stumbling. If he stumbles, the nation stumbles with him, and falls. Verily, the erring ignorant ruler destroys in a short period what the wise built over long periods.

For this reason, the attainment or completion of people's happiness is dependent upon the establishment of positive codes and revealed laws, spiritual and temporal (i.e. civil), and the rendering of the people [living] under them as equals (namely, with no distinctions among them), the leader having no privileges over the follower beyond that which distinguishes some followers over others and that without which there could be no leadership, such as the necessity of obeying the ruler. And no one is required to obey anyone in that which exceeds the shari'ah and positive law. However, no heavenly shari'ah was brought and no positive human code was instituted with this specification and [establishment] of equality until the coming of the Islamic religion. It established the two laws (civil and spiritual) simultaneously, rendering people equals, making no distinction between one individual and another, except in terms of knowledge and practice. It pulled out [90] the roots of blind obedience. It demonstrated that the call to truth is but through proof and logical demonstration, in the manner of the Almighty's statement, "Say: This is my Way: I call on Allah with sure knowledge, I and whosoever followeth me" [12:108] – the ulama explain that "sure knowledge" is clear proof – and the Almighty's statement, "Say: Bring your proof (of what ye state) if ye are truthful" [2:105].

Based upon this, the Companions would consult the Prophet, God's blessing and peace be upon him, about an opinion saying, "Is this your own, O messenger of God, or was it revealed as revelation?" If he said, "It is my own," they would offer their own opinion. Perhaps the prophet would defer to their opinion, as happened in some of the [early Muslim] battles (such as Badr and Uḥud). The Commander of the Faithful 'Umar ibn al-Khaṭṭāb halted Imam 'Alī and a Jewish man to interrogate them. 'Alī scolded 'Umar after the interrogation, as he had not been equal in his treatment of him and his opponent, because he addressed him with his surname, while addressing his opponent with his common name. Addressing someone with his surname is a form of exaltation, and exalting someone over his opponent – even in such a manner as this – violates the principles of justice and equality. And a woman challenged 'Umar on the issue of withholding of the dowry when he was on the pulpit, arguing against him with the verse: "and ye have given unto one of them a sum of money (however great), take nothing from it" [4:20].[193] So he said, "A woman was correct and 'Umar was incorrect."

More telling than this is that in order to straighten the line [of soldiers] on the day of Badr, the prophet, prayer and peace be upon him, poked Sawād ibn Ghizyah in the stomach with a *qidḥ* (an arrow without feathers or blade) while he was uncovered. So he said, "You have hurt me, allow me then to retaliate." So he exposed his stomach for him that he return like for like. Then he began hugging him, that plea having been made in order to receive that great honor. Before his death, the prophet permitted whoever among the people to whom he owed a debt to demand it from him, and that retaliation be taken upon him if the debt be the like of hitting. And when a man claimed that the Prophet had once hit him, he granted him permission to hit him. The man said, "I was naked of the shoulder or back" (the narration is unclear). So he removed the garment from his noble shoulder for the man, who responded as did Sawād ibn Ghizyah.

The upshot is that Islam established worship of God alone, freedom within the framework of the shari'ah, equality among people in rights and obligations, and liberation of will and thought from every [91] communal headman's authority and every spiritual leader's control. Accordingly, the Muslim is completely God's slave, completely free in relation to anything other than Him.[194]

This is some of that which we stated on the issue approximately five years ago. It was followed by a discussion of the authority of the sheikhdom of the spiritual path, how it appeared and what followed.

Summary of the Evidence for Denying Religious Authority in Islam

(1) The strongest evidence that there is no religious authority in Islam as there is in Christianity is the establishment of the messenger's role in the

193. The complete verse reads, "And if ye wish to exchange one wife for another and ye have given unto one of them a sum of money (however great), take nothing from it. Would ye take it by the way of calumny and open wrong?" [4:20].

194. *Al-Manār*, i, 405–407.

Qur'an as that of a conveyer (*muballigh*), rather than a controller, steward, or enforcer over the people. The Almighty states, "Thine is only to convey (the message)" [42:49]. Him to whom glory and power belong states, "The guiding of them is not thy duty (O Muḥammad), but Allah guideth whom He will" [2:272]. He whose nature is blessed states, "Lo! thou (O Muḥammad) guidest not whom thou lovest, but Allah guideth whom He will" [28:56]. He whose name is mighty states, "and thou (O Muḥammad) art in no wise a compeller over them" [50:45]. He whose strength is Almighty states "Remind them, for thou art but a remembrancer, Thou art not at all a warder over them" [88:21–22]. He whose splendor is sublime states, "nor art thou responsible for them" [6:107; 39:41]. How can this be compared to a religious community whose leaders claim they are God's agents on earth? Can an opposite be compared to an opposite?

(2) The prophet's conduct, prayer and peace be upon him: you heard previously that he checked himself, drawing back from his own opinion and deferring to that of his Companions. More remarkable than this is that he deferred to the opinion of consensus over his own opinion in the matter of the captives of Badr, when the latter was the more correct. Hence, God harshly scolded him until he cried, prayer and peace be upon him.

(3) The rightly-guided caliphs' conduct – as you heard previously of 'Umar and applying in the same manner to the rest of them: their conduct in implementing the principle of equality and appointing the ummah as arbitrator over themselves was not derived from their individual merits. Rather, this was something that they derived from the Qur'an and the prophet's conduct, as you learned. Their merit was only that they understood Islam in its entirety and were more rigorous than others in jealously guarding it and acting in accordance with it.

(4) [92] Had Islam legislated or permitted this authority which is known in the religious communities that preceded it, including the Buddhists, [Hindu] brahmins, Israelites, and Christians, then a system of regulations and leaders for it would have existed among the Muslims, as there were for other religious communities. However, nothing of this nature existed. There only existed a party that took upon itself the task of pedagogy and providing guidance. Then, it became divided into parties and groups that

lacked authority over any individual, being followed only by those who wished to do so of their own volition. With that, those of this party were not immune from the jurists' accusation that they had deviated from the religion and sundered the rulers' unity. Hence, they did not appear except where knowledge of the religion and its legislation was weak, as we stated previously. As for the title "Shaykh al-Islam," it is among the inventions of the kings and emirs who were far removed from religious bearing. Hence, they enlisted one who had such a bearing, thereby to influence the souls of the common traditionalist folk.[195]

Yes, religious authority existed in its true form among the Bāṭiniyyah. Furthermore, this party had a civil government in the form of the 'Abīdiyyūn (the Fāṭimids). However, Bāṭinī teaching was not Islamic in any way and therefore the 'Abīdiyyūn were not able to endorse it openly.[196]

195. "Shaykh al-Islam" is an honorific dating from the tenth century, when it was applied to ulama and Sufi mystics, but it does not appear to have been clearly defined. From the fifteenth century, it was primarily associated with the Ottoman office of the Mufti of Istanbul, the empire's highest judicial authority. The office declined in significance from the nineteenth century, and formally came to an end in 1924, shortly after the abolition of the Ottoman Empire. A. Hourani, *Arabic Thought in the Liberal Age*, 234. J.H. Kramers and R.W. Bulliet, "Shaykh al-Islām." in *EI*.

In *Al-Khilāfah aw al-Imāmah al-'Uẓmā*, Riḍā cites the office holder's unwillingness to deliver legal opinions or fatwas on new laws introduced by the Ottoman government as an example of the flawed traditionalist mentality. Riḍā's critique is summarized in A. Hourani, *Arabic Thought in the Liberal Age*, 234–235.

196. In the medieval period, the Isma'ili Shi'ah were known as the Bāṭiniyyah – derived from "*bāṭin*" meaning hidden, and reflecting the Isma'ili emphasis on the esoteric or hidden meaning of the Qur'an and other texts, in contrast to their purely apparent meaning (*ẓāhir*). Riḍā's is not critical of the distinction *per se*, but rather the radical tendency of the Bāṭiniyyah to push it to the extreme of rejecting the *ẓāhir* altogether (for the same reason, Ibn al-'Arabī refused to describe himself as *bāṭinī*, notwithstanding his emphasis on the hidden meanings of texts).

Riḍā's claim that the Fāṭimids (909–1710) were unable to openly endorse the doctrine would be correct if it referred to this radical position rather than Isma'ili Shi'ism. The Fāṭimid rulers designated themselves both caliph and Imam,

So, it is said that religious and civil authority were combined in a party that had a general affiliation with Islam. But then it is known from that stated above that there is no religious authority in Islam. So what is this with which certain Christian writers disfigure Islam? What is this "advice" that those pens direct towards the Islamic ummah, in order to convince it of the need to separate religious and civil authority in Islam? The answer: the intention is that the Muslims relinquish their shari'ah, as will be seen in the forthcoming section.

The Shari'ah and the Religion in Islam

The custom of the European writers and those in the East who follow them, especially the Christian writers, is to apply the word "religion" to that which pertains to belief in God and revelation, and that which revelation promises and communicates concerning matters of the unseen and ordains for worship. They apply the word "shari'ah" to that which pertains to worldly transactions and judicial, civil, and political rulings. Yet, among these writers, every scholar of history [93] perceives that Islam brought a religion *and* a shari'ah. For example, some of them state that Muḥammad, prayer and peace be upon him, founded a nation in twenty years, bringing to it a religion and a shari'ah, while no one in the world but he was destined to combine the three. So these writers perceive that the shari'ah is the religion's partner in Islam, and that that which a Muslim believes of his Lord and that which determines how a Muslim treats the people is all acquired from one light, the light of the revelation that God revealed to Muḥammad, prayer and peace be upon him.

In Islam, there is no distinction between the purely religious and the legal except on one point: that for belief and worship – as they do not dif-

claiming to have inherited the Imamate through Ismā'īl (died 760) and Muḥammad al-Madhī. M.G.S. Hodgson notes that under Fāṭimid rule both *bāṭin* and *ẓāhir* were accepted. Each was deemed to have its sphere of application in ritual and law, and their relationship was understood to be fully symbiotic. M.G.S. Hodgson, "Bāṭiniyya" in *EI*; A. Hourani, *A History of the Arab Peoples*, 40; 489. M. Montgomery Watt, *Islamic Philosophy and Theology* (Edinburgh: Edinburgh University Press, 2nd ed. 1985), 126.

fer as times, places, and nations' conditions differ – reliance on revelation is mandatory concerning the general and particular aspects, the major and the minor. As for worldly transactions, since these differ in accordance with the above-mentioned differences, Islam established general rules and universal principles for them. It authorized in those in authority – who are familiar with Islam's aims, universal principles, and general rules – to derive rulings for particular exigencies that develop. Upon consulting the people about all that affected their welfare, they announced the rulings, deriving them from those principles and rules. The Almighty states, "O ye who believe! Obey Allah, and obey the messenger and those of you who are in authority" [4:59]. Thus, He mentions "those who have authority" in the plural form. And He states, "if they had referred it to the messenger and such of them as are in authority, those among them who are able to think out the matter would have known it" [4:83]. Here also, God mentions "those who have authority" in the plural form, entrusting them with the responsibility of deriving rulings that are needed, or concerning which there is disputation.

Furthermore, legal rulings, textual or derived, require executors, and it is essential that they have a leader, so that matters not become chaotic. After the death of the prophet, the first leader in Islam was called his caliph, and the one following him was called "commander of the faithful," the use of this title continuing thereafter. This leader's role is to protect the religion and its people, and enforce its legal rulings. Thus, he is not a controller over the people in their religion or an independent agent in setting down legal rulings for them. He is only a guardian of order and an executor of rulings. As you observe, this power of his is civil and consultative, not absolute and tyrannical. However, Islam obligates him to act in accordance with the shari'ah, and forbids him from [94] legislating his own [laws]. It obligates obeying him in that which is morally right, as it obligates the ummah to remove his power should he compel it to contravene the law. In view of this consideration, it may be correctly stated that civil authority in Islam derives from the religion, or that civil authority *is* religious authority. But it would be incorrect to compare it to religious authority as it is known to non-Muslims, or to represent its guardian as a combiner of two forms of authority, the one over spirits and minds, the other over bodies and actions.

This is our religion and this is its authority. What, then, does that Christian writer demand of us and what is his advice to us? He demands of us that we make our civil leader a legislator and an executor of the statutes that he legislates for us. He advises us to relinquish our shari'ah, which is based upon the fundamental principles of our religion. He claims that it was building the shari'ah on the foundations of the religion and making rulers the religion's protectors and enforcers which destroyed the 'Abbasid state and sundered the Islamic ummah's unity. It is also his opinion that Muslims will neither succeed nor have a [strong] base so long as their ruler is required to act by and enforce their religious shari'ah!

Were you to gather together all the words in all languages that mean astonishment, and add to that all the signs of astonishment, and indications of it among gestures and signals, bodily and written, and were you able to portray all the emotions and psychological affectations of those who are astonished, and attach all of that to this Christian advice to the Islamic ummah, you would not have sufficed for providing for those who wonder the true explanation of its wondrous, strange, and astonishing nature.

The Doubts of the Instiller of Doubts

(1) This faithful advisor or instiller of doubts about the religion states: the religion's goal on earth contradicts the government's goal on earth. How, then, can Islam combine the two opposites?

We say to him: Islam came to bring reform on earth, and all that opposes reform is corruption whose elimination is enjoined. Hence, it is mandatory that the Islamic government's goal conform to the Islamic religion's goal. Among that upon which there is no disagreement among Islam's jurists is that all of its shari'ah's rulings are erected upon the foundation of "averting evil and enjoining the good." So, which of our rulers could [95] bring us a revealed law superior to this revealed law if, following your advice, we relinquished it and made the ruler the legislator?

(2) The faithful adviser or instiller of doubts about the religion states: among the contradictions between the religion's role and the

government's role is that the religion established foundations and unquestioned conventions for reason, and paths for the pursuance of thought. Thus, it restricted intellectual freedom. The government does not require an individual to follow a designated path in his thought. Rather, it is the guarantor of individual freedom and what follows in the way of money, blood, and honor.

We say: if your religion is thus, the religion of Islam contradicts that without contradicting the governmental role that you have mentioned. That is, intellectual freedom was stipulated in Islam, and a Muslim does not dissent from Islam's ruling in his beliefs (as we explained in the previous part). And it was stipulated that Islam's rulings are derived from five foundations that they call "the five general principles." The author of *'Aqīdat al-Jawharah* combined these principles in his statement:

> The preservation of religion, then, is through [preserving] the individual, property [and] relationships.
> Likewise, [preserving] the mind and honor is enjoined.

(3) The faithful advisor or instiller of doubts about the religion states: it is enjoined that the government treat those it governs equally, even if their religions differ, and also grant them equal protection. In that, the religion contradicts it.

We say: if your religion is thus, our religion contradicts your religion, not in terms of that which is enjoined upon the government. That is, equality is among our religion's fundamental principles. In the previous section of this article, we referred to 'Umar's equal treatment of Imam 'Alī and a Jewish man, and 'Alī's demand that 'Umar be equal in the form of address also. This equality was not attained by a government, nor will be attained by a government, except when it raises Islam to its true form. As for providing protection, among the principles transmitted in our religion is this beautiful statement: "That we protect them with that with which we protect ourselves," and this more excellent statement: "Their rights are our rights, and their obligations are our obligations."

(4) The faithful advisor or instiller of doubts about the religion states: it is not of the nature of religious authority to enter into worldly

affairs, as religions were legislated to prepare the afterlife, not to prepare earthly life.

We say: if your religion is thus, our religion is not, as it was legislated [96] to explain the benefits of both worlds, and provide guidance to the paths of happiness in both. How, then, can you decree for all religions, without exception, that which you believe in your religion? Were you yourself the creator of all religions, such that you would say: indeed I also created the religion of Islam thus. Its people added to it, so I now demand them to return to the original form? Muslims would not accept that from you, because their Imams defined the religion as a divine creation that leads those possessing minds, minds which are sound in the choices they make, to that wherein is their righteousness in the present and their prosperity in the afterlife.

(5) The faithful advisor or instiller of doubts about the religion states: combining the two forms of authority continuously weakens the ummah, as it mandates the suppression of reason and intelligence, exposes the government to the revolution of the ummah through inciting an enemy that agitates the ummah against it, causes religious strife between the groups making up the nation, and exposes the religion to political lies and their chicaneries.

We say: all of this indeed occurred in his religion, and hence we do not deny it. We only contest analogizing about our religion – which differs from his religion – upon that. It suffices us that what befell us was the opposite of what befell them, because the Islamic government – which he calls a combination of the two forms of authority (while you understand its meaning) – gave the ummah a power not matched by any during its time. And the Islamic ummah did not grow weak but through the weakening and non-establishment of the revealed law. This is a matter concerning which there is no dispute. Likewise, reason and intelligence were not suppressed in Islam during the age when the Islamic shariʿah was established. The likeness of such suppression only occurred after the revealed law was weakened and there was laxity in its enforcement. As for the revolutions – of which the advisor is afraid – against Islamic governments if they remain under their shariʿah, these are more liable to occur if governments depart from the shari'ah, because in Islam rebellion against the ruler is not permissible except when he departs from Islam by forsaking the shari'ah. If he errs, it is enjoined for the ummah to turn him away from his error without coercion. The author of *'Aqīdat al-Jawharah* states:

> Enjoined is appointing an Imam just.
> In the revealed law, know that it is not the mind's rule.
> As that is not a pillar believed in the religion.
> Thus, do not deviate from his clear ruling.
> Save unbelief, and then renounce his oath.
> As God alone protects us from his harm.

[97] As for religious schism among sects and religious communities, this was not known in the Islamic lands during the days when the shari'ah was upheld and applied. Rather, the sects were in harmony and peace, because the religion enjoined that, and it was acted upon. That which mandates schism is the rendering of the religion as an interest of particular leaders, each leader and his faction opposing other factions. And that clings more to the two authorities' separation – each being made independent and having leaders for its control – than to their combination, especially the Islamic combination, as defined above. The Christian nation tasted the illness of this form of leadership, and it was it that developed the innovation of warfare between two factions from a single religion's people over a disagreement about religion. Had there not been particular leaders for each faction, nothing of this nature would have occurred. Christianity's contagion infected other religions, and the sparks of this fire afflicted the Muslims. Hence, schism occurred among the adherents of the legal schools, through each faction siding with a special Imam and particular ulama. You learnt that the religious class among the Muslims did not have a superintending role, because Islam's very nature prohibits that. For this reason, factionalism and schism was not great among the masters of the Islamic legal schools, as among the lords of the Christian schools. However, the multiplicity of schools in the religion contradicts the religion's purpose, as it causes division therein. God states, "Establish the

religion and do not be divided therein" [42:13]. He states, "Lo! As for those who sunder their religion and become schismatics, no concern at all hast thou with them" [6:159]. But in this age there comes to us from among the Christian writers one stating about us that factionalism is of the very nature of our religion, and that there is no remedy for this factionalism except our rulers' relinquishment of our shariʿah!

As for the religion being exposed to political lies and their chicaneries if the shariʿah is derived from the religion, this is the opposite of reasonable and contradictory to reality, because, as the writer acknowledges, politics is based upon hypocrisy and deceit. And there is no treatment for hypocrisy except the religion. Indeed, Islam was harsh upon it, to the point of calling it "the lesser association."[197] Hence, when politics is built upon the foundation of religion, it is sound and with it the religion is sound. When politics is separated from religion, it is ruined and it ruins the religion. For this reason, Imam [ʿAbduh], author of the articles entitled *Islam and Christianity*, sought refuge from it with that which he sought refuge, and depicted it with that which he depicted. Verily, the advisor or instiller of doubts inverted the truth, for he made the government's separation from the religion the cause of well-being!

Religious and National Unity

[98] The faithful advisor or instiller of doubts about the religion states: the religious unity sought by Islam is impossible to attain, and striving for it was the greatest cause of the trials that befell Islam and Christianity. He claims that humanity has progressed from seeking religious unity – which had been widespread among them – to national unity. He slipped in his explanation by mentioning France, in which this new unity developed, this new unity that circumscribed human prosperity to such an extent that France eliminated the monastic orders' schools and forbad her leader from mentioning God Almighty's name or the divine care in his speeches. Here, he sensed that through this slipping he was falling into the abyss of falsehood. Hence, he reverted to opposing this "new path" and mentioning

197. Ar. *al-shirk al-aṣghar*. Alternatively, "the lesser polytheism."

its corruptions. Thus is the nature of one who excessively praises that which he does not understand. He infers the impossibility of religious unity from what occurred in Europe in the way of corruptions and trials because of it, the Pope's lack of success with regard to it, and Europe's custom thereafter of erecting a fence between the Pope and legal rulings. Then, he continues in his practice of comparing Islam to Christianity, claiming that that which ruined the 'Abbasids' state was their incapacity to preserve the kingdom through religious unity, and their failure to be rightly guided to national unity! God be praised! How knowledgeable of history is this writer, and how capable of deducing the characteristics of the religious communities from it!

Tell us, O historians and readers of the books of history: which historian states that the cause of the 'Abbasids' downfall was their rule through the Islamic shariʿah, or states that the members of the different religious communities in their countries were rebelling against rule by the shariʿah, and demanding its replacement with other laws set down by rulers or those ruled, and that hence they rebelled against the state until they overthrew it through civil wars, whose stimulant was religious fanaticisms? No one, knowledgeable or ignorant, states that. It is only a claim asserted, fabricated, contrived and invented by the Muslims' faithful advisor, or the one who encourages them to doubt the religion.

Among the causes of the 'Abbasid state's downfall, the two most important are mentioned by the Ottoman state's greatest historian, Jūdat Bāshā Nāẓir al-ʿAdliyyah (God Almighty have mercy upon him). After mentioning [99] al-Ma'mūn's[198] virtue in promoting the sciences and broadening the scope of civilization, he states (in Arabic translation):

> But he made a clear error in a matter pertaining to the kingdom's organization. Namely, he gave the governorship of Khurāsān to a man named Ṭāhir as a reward for killing his brother al-Amīn. Ṭāhir made Nīsābūr its capital and rendered it an inheritance for himself and his descendants

198. Al-Ma'mūn was the seventh 'Abbasid caliph (813–33). He was succeeded by al-Muʿtaṣim (833–42).

> after him. That was the stimulant for the removal of fear of the caliphate from the governors' breasts, and it was the cause of rebellion and the longing for independence. Al-Ma'mūn was succeeded by the caliph al-Mu'taṣim. He gathered together some of the Turkish minors and made them his designated army. And when they grew powerful, they rebelled against him and waged long rebellions, as happened anciently in the armies of the Caesars of Rome.

It is clear that al-Ma'mūn's action contradicts the Islamic shari'ah and is incompatible with religious unity, and that al-Mu'taṣim's action violated the fundamental principles of Islamic rule, such as consultation, the ummah making itself responsible for the Imam, and that care be taken when courtiers are enlisted. The Almighty states, "O ye who believe! Take not for intimates others than your own fold, who would spare no pains to ruin you; they love to hamper you" [3:118]. The exegetes offer two explanations of His statement "others than your own fold." It is said that it refers to the hypocrites, and it is said it refers to the unbelievers. Those minors belonged to one of those two groups, as they were taken as courtiers while faith had not yet entered their hearts, as may be learned from the articles *Islam and Christianity*. Indeed, that which the Almighty stated of them – "who would spare no pains to ruin you; they love to hamper you" [3:118] – came to pass. But our faithful advisor misconstrues the Imam's statement on this issue as relating to political strife. He claims that Imam 'Abduh's intention is to adjudge the Islam of the Turks and Persians unworthy of consideration, and to adjudge the religion as specifically for the Arabs. This is to say that Imam 'Abduh adjudged the Islam of al-Bukhārī, Muslim, Abū Ḥanīfah, and al-Ghazālī unworthy of consideration! We seek refuge in God; we seek refuge in God.

O, what a shame for the Islamic shari'ah's enemies. They sought a defect in it. This tired them and rendered them destitute. So then they sought a defect in the shari'ah's enforcers (such as Abū Bakr and 'Umar). This tired them and rendered them destitute. So then they searched for a defect in those who strayed from the shari'ah's straight path and deviated. And thus, they found a defect and achieved their purpose by attaching it to the shari'ah. They stated that it is the shari'ah which harms people, mandating its relinquishment and the invention of another shari'ah to replace it!

[100] The bond of unity in human society was [originally] limited to houses (families). Thereafter, it widened to tribes. Then, in accordance with the law of development, it widened. Hence, there were peoples and great communities that were united by nationality through language, religion, or place (homeland). Religion was distinctive. Until the appearance of Islam, it did not reach beyond its people, for in the gospels – adopted by the Christians until this day – Christ, prayer and peace be upon him, states, "I was only sent to the lost sheep of the house of Israel" [Mt 15:24]. And he states, "'I did not come to abolish the Law, rather I came to complete it."[199] The "Law" is the law revealed specifically for the Israelites. Its completion is effected through explaining the truth about that which they disputed therein, explaining its secrets, and broadening its spiritual dimension. As for their report about him stating, "Spread the gospel in all of creation," it apparently contradicts that stated above. It is possible that it might be harmonized with it by attaching the definite article to the word "creation" to indicate the well known, that is, "the well-known creation," which is the Israelite nation, wherever it is and where it was.

In accordance with the law of development, humanity was ready after this for a unity wider than all that mentioned above, for a unity into which all peoples, tribes, nations, and nationalities of different places, languages, and religions could enter, for a unity of two bonds. The first bond is corporeal, social, civil, and this-worldly. This is that they rule by a just shari'ah that equalizes their rights, such that there be no advantage for old over young, rich over poor, Arab over non-Arab, or believer in one religion over believer in another. The second bond is spiritual, brotherly, and otherworldly. It distinguishes those united by true belief based on clear demonstration. The Islamic religion brought this unity, and in the early period Muslims acted upon it. Hence, those who differed from them in religion preferred Muslim rule over the rule of those from their own religion, linguistic group, and homeland. And until the present day there has been

199. See Matt 5:17.

no equality or true justice except in Islam. These European countries developing through nationalism do not treat their own citizens and those of their colonies equally in legal rulings. Rather, they compelled weak governments to depart from the principles of justice and equality and privilege [European] citizens over the subjects of every government [101]. Thus, an Egyptian would executed if he killed a foreigner in Egypt, but a foreigner would not be executed for killing an Egyptian. We clearly explained this topic in an article entitled "Nationality and the Islamic Religion" – see *al-Manār* volume two.[200] Numerous investigations in other volumes of *al-Manār* confirm these various matters, and support the numerous theses [advanced] in this article.

Thus, it is clear from the sum of that stated above that the unity brought by Islam is the highest that humanity regards, and the most excellent that it turns toward. But two barriers prevent humanity from benefiting from it. These are spiritual leadership in the Christian religion – which rendered the religion an interest among the interests benefiting the leaders – and the departure of rulers affiliated with Islam from this unity's foundations. Freedom will level these two barriers, and through Islam humanity will combine the two forms of prosperity. (p. 859. vol. 5.)

200. *Al-Manār*, ii, 321–27.

Bibliography

Works in Arabic

'Abduh, Muḥammad. *Al-Islām wa al-Naṣrāniyyah ma'a al-'Ilm wa al-Madaniyyah.* Cairo: Dār al-Manār, 1953.

—— *Risālat al-Tawḥīd*, 2nd ed. Cairo: Maṭba'at al-Manār, 1908.

al-Afghānī, Jamāl al-Dīn. *Al-'Urwah al-Wuthqā.* Beirut: Dār al-Kitāb al-'Arabī, 1970.

Arslān, Shakib. *Al-Sayyid Rashīd Riḍā aw Ikhā' Arba'īn Sanah.* Damascus: Maṭba'at Ibn Zaydūn, 1937.

Ghibrīl, Niqūlā. *Abḥāth al-Mujtahidīn*, 3rd ed. Cairo: Ghibrīl, 1913.

al-Jisr, Shaykh Ḥusayn, *Al-Risālah al-Ḥamīdiyyah.* Tarabulus, Lebanon: Dār al-Īmān, 1998.

Al-Jāmi'ah. ed. Faraḥ Anṭūn Alexandria, 1901–1904; New York City 1906–08; Cairo 1909–1910.

al-Kayrānawī, Raḥmat Allāh ibn Khalīl al-'Uthmānī. *Iẓhār al-Ḥaqq.* Riyāḍ: Dār al-Waṭan, 1992.

Al-Kitāb al-Muqaddas (the Van Dyke Arabic Bible). Dār al-Kitāb al-Muqaddas fī al-'Ālim al-'Arabī, n.d.

Available online at: www.arabicbible.com/bible/doc_bible.htm

Al-Manār 1898–1935. ed. Muḥammad Rashīd Riḍā.

Mubārak, 'Alī Pāshā. *'Alam al-Dīn.* Cairo: Maktabat al-Ādāb, 1993.

Rashīd Riḍā, Muḥammad. *'Aqīdat al-Ṣalb wa al-Fidā'.* Cairo: Maṭba'at al-Manār, 1934.

——*Fatāwā al-Imām Muḥammad Rashīd Riḍā*. Beirut: Dār al-Kitāb al-Jadīd, 1970.

—— *Ḥuqūq al-Nisā' fī al-Islām*. Beirut: Dār al-Aḍwā' li al-Ṭibā'ah wa al-Nashr wa al-Tawzī', 1989.

—— *Al-Khilāfah aw al-Imāmah al-'Uẓmā*. Cairo: Maṭba'at al-Manār, 1922. Serialized in volumes 23 and 24 of *al-Manār*.

—— *Al-Manār wa al-Azhar*. Cairo: Maṭba'at al-Manār, 1934.

—— *Muḥāwarāt al-Muṣliḥ wa al-Muqallid*. Cairo: Maṭba'at al-Manār, 1906.

—— *Al-Muslimūn wa al-Qibṭ*. Cairo: Maṭba'at al-Manār, 1911.

—— *Shubuhāt al-Naṣārā wa Ḥujaj al-Islām*. Cairo: Dār al-Manār, 1905; 2nd ed. Cairo: Dār al-Manār, 1947; 3rd ed. Egypt: Al-Mu'tamar al-Islāmī, 1956.

(Note that in some printings of the second edition the publication date is incorrectly given as 1928.)

—— *Al-Sunnah wa al-Shī'ah aw al-Wahhābiyyah wa al-Rāfiḍah*. Cairo: Maṭba'at al-Manār, 1929.

—— *Tafsīr al-Manār*, 4th ed. 12 vols Cairo: Dār al-Manār, 1953.

—— *Tārīkh al-Ustādh al-Imām Muḥammad 'Abduh*. Cairo: Maṭba'at al-Manār, 1931.

—— *Tarjamat al-Qur'ān wa mā fīhā min Mafāsid wa Munāfāt al-Islām*. Cairo, 1925/6.

—— *Al-Wahhābiyyūn wa al-Ḥijāz*. Cairo: Maṭba'at al-Manār, 1925.

—— *Al-Waḥy al-Muḥammadī*, 3rd ed. Cairo: Dār al-Manār, 1948.

Sa'ādah, Khalīl. trans., *Injīl Barnābā*. Cairo: Maṭba'at al-Manār, 1907. Edited by Rashīd Riḍā.

al-Sharabāsī, Aḥmad. *Rashīd Riḍā Ṣāḥib al-Manār*. Cairo: Maṭābi' al-Ahrām al-Tijāriyyah, 1970.

Works in European Languages

Abrahamian, Ervand. *Khomeinism: Essays on the Islamic Republic*. Berkeley: University of California Press, 1993.

Abu Rabi, Ibrahim M. *Intellectual Origins of Islamic Resurgence in the Modern Arab World*. Albany, NY: State University of New York Press, 1993.

Adams, Charles C. *Islam and Modernism in Egypt: A Study of the Modern Reform Movement Inaugurated by Muhammad 'Abduh*. New York: Routledge, 2000, 1933.

Almond, Gabriel A., Appleby, R. Scott, and Sivan, Emmanuel. *Strong Religion: The Rise of Fundamentalisms around the World.* Chicago: University of Chicago Press, 2003.

al-'Aqqād, 'Abbās Maḥmūd. *The Genius of Christ.* Translated and edited by F. Peter Ford. Binghamton, NY: Institute of Global Cultural Studies, Binghamton University; Provo, Utah: Center for the Preservation of Ancient Religious Texts, Brigham Young University, 2001.

Ayoub, Mahmoud. "Islam and Christianity: A Study of Muhammad 'Abduh's View of the Two Religions." *Humaniora Islamica* 2 (1974): 121–37.

—— "Jesus the Son of God: A Study of the Terms Ibn and Walad in the Qur'an and Tafsir Tradition." In *Christian-Muslim Encounters*, eds Y. Y. Haddad and W. Z. Haddad, Gainesville: University of Florida Press, 1995.

—— "The Miracle of Jesus: Muslim Reflections on the Divine Word." In *Christology in Dialogue*, ed. Robert F. Berkey and Sarah A. Edwards, 221–28. Cleveland: Pilgrim Press, 1993.

—— "Muslim Views of Christianity: Some Modern Examples." *Islamochristiana* 10 (1984): 49–70.

—— "Nearest in Amity: Christians in the Qur'an and contemporary exegetical tradition." *Islam and Christian-Muslim Relations* 8 (1997): 145–167.

—— *The Qur'an and its Interpreters.* Vol. 1. Albany: State University of New York Press, 1984.

—— *The Qur'an and its Interpreters.* Vol. 2. *The House of 'Imran.* Albany: State University of New York Press, 1992.

—— "Roots of Muslim-Christian Conflict." *The Muslim World* 79 (1989): 25–45.

—— "Towards an Islamic Christology: An Image of Jesus in Early Shi'i Muslim Literature." *The Muslim World* 66 (1976): 163–88.

—— "Towards an Islamic Christology, Part 2: The Death of Jesus, Reality or Delusion: A Study of the Death of Jesus in Tafsir Literature." *The Muslim World* 70 (1980): 91–121.

Badawi, M. A. Zaki. *The Reformers of Egypt.* London: Croom Helm Ltd, 1978.

Baljon, J. M. S. Modern *Muslim Koran Interpretation 1880–1960.* Leiden: E. J. Brill, 1961.

Boullata, Issa J. "Fa-stabiqu 'l-khayrat: A Qur'anic Principle of Interfaith Relations." In *Christian-Muslim Encounters*, eds Y. Y. Haddad and W. Z. Haddad, Gainesville: University of Florida Press, 1995.

Busool, A. "Shaykh Muhammad Rashid Rida's Relations with Jamal al-Din al-Afghani and Muhammad 'Abduh." *The Muslim World* 66 (1976): 272–86.

Butterworth, Charles, E. trans., *Averroes: The Book of the Decisive Treatise Determining the Connection between the Law and Wisdom & Epistle Dedicatory.* Provo, UT: Brigham Young University Press, 2001.

Cole, J. R. I. "Muhammad 'Abduh and Rashid Rida: A Dialogue on the Baha'i Faith." *World Order* 15 (1981): 7–16.

—— "Rashid Rida on the Baha'i Faith: A Utilitarian Theory of the Spread of Religions." *Arab Studies Quarterly* 5 (1983): 276–291.

Commins, D. Islamic Reform: *Politics and Social Change in late Ottoman Syria.* New York: Oxford University Press, 1990.

Cragg, Kenneth and Isḥāq Musa'ad. trans., *The Theology of Unity (Risālat al-Tawḥīd).* London: George Allen & Unwin, 1966.

Crollius, Ary A. Roest. "Mission and Morality: *al-Amr bi-l-ma'rūf* as expression of the communitarian and missionary dimensions of qur'ānic ethics." *Studia Missionalia* 27 (1978): 257–283.

Denny, F. *An Introduction to Islam.* Englewood Cliffs, NJ: Macmillan, 1994.

Enayat, Hamid. *Modern Islamic Political Thought.* Austin: University of Texas Press, 1982.

The Encyclopedia of Islam. CD v.1.1. Leiden: Brill, 2001.

Esposito, J. *Islam: The Straight Path.* New York and Oxford: Oxford University Press, 1998.

Faruqi, Isma'il. "On the Nature of Islamic Da'wah." *International Review of Mission* 65 (1976): 391–400.

Gaudeul, Jean-Marie. *Encounters and Clashes: Islam and Christianity in History.* 2 vols. Rome: Pontificio Istituto di Studi Arabi e Islamici, 1990.

Gilliam, R. T. "A Muslim Response to Protestant Missionaries: The Case of Al-Manar." M.A. diss. American University of Beirut, 2000.

Goddard, Hugh. *Christians and Muslims: from double standards to mutual understanding.* Surrey: Curzon Press, 1995.

—— *A History of Christian-Muslim Relations.* Chicago: New Amsterdam Books, 2001.

—— *Muslim Perceptions of Christianity.* London: Grey Seal, 1996.

Gran, Peter. *Islamic Roots of Capitalism: Egypt 1760–1840.* Syracuse: Syracuse University Press, 1998.

Haddad, M. O. "Arab religious nationalism in the colonial era: Rereading Rashid

Rida's ideas on the caliphate." Journal of the American Oriental Society 117 (1997): 253–278.

—— "Rashīd Riḍā and the theory of the caliphate: Medieval themes and modern concerns." Ph.D. diss. Columbia University, 1989.

—— "Syrian Muslims' Attitudes Toward Foreign Missionaries in the late Nineteenth and Twentieth Centuries." Working paper.

Haddad, W. Z. "A Tenth-Century Speculative Theologian's Refutation of the Basic Doctrines of Christianity: al-Baqillani (d. A. D. 1013)." In *Christian-Muslim Encounters*, eds Y. Y. Haddad and W. Z. Haddad, Gainesville: University of Florida Press, 1995.

Hourani, A. H. *Arabic Thought in the Liberal Age: 1798–1939*. London: Oxford University Press, 1962.

—— "Rashid Rida and the Sufi orders: a footnote to Laoust." *BEO* 29 (1977): 231–41.

—— The *Emergence of the Modern Middle East*. Berkeley: University of California Press, 1981.

Hourani, G. F. *Averroes on the harmony of religion and philosophy; a translation, with introduction and notes, of Ibn Rushd's Kitāb faṣl al-maqāl*. London: Luzac, 1961.

Jafar, Iftitah Ujung Pandang. "Modern Qur'anic Exegesis: a Comparative Study of the Methods of Muhammad 'Abduh and Muhammad Rashid Rida." M. A. diss. McGill University, 1998.

Jansen, J. J. G. The *Dual Nature of Islamic Fundamentalism*. London: Hurst, 1997.

—— *The Interpretation of the Koran in Modern Egypt*. Leiden: E. J. Brill, 1974.

Jomier, J. *Le Commentarie Coranique du Manar*. Paris: Adrien-Maisonneuve, 1954.

—— "Quelques positions actuelles de l'exgese coranique en Egypte." *Melanges de l'Institut Dmoninicain d'Etudes Orientales du Caire* (MIDEO) I (1954): 39–72.

Kamali, S. A. trans., *Al-Ghazālī's* Tahāfut al-Falāsifah (*Incoherence of the Philosophers*). Lahore: Pakistan Philosophical Congress, 1958.

Keddie, N. R. and H. Algar. trans., *An Islamic Response to Imperialism, Political and Religious Writings of Sayyid Jamal al-Din al-Afghani*. Berkeley and Los Angeles: University of California Press, 1968.

Kedourie, E. Afghani and 'Abduh: *An Essay on Religious Unbelief and Political Activism in Modern Islam*. London: Frank Cass, 1966.

Kerr, David A. "Islamic Da'wa and Christian Mission: Towards a Comparative Analysis." *International Review of Mission* 89: 150–171.

Kerr, Malcolm, H. *Islamic Reform: The Political and Legal Theories of Muhammad 'Abduh and Rashid Rida.* Berkeley: University of California Press, 1966.

Khadduri, Majid. *Political Trends in the Arab World: The Role of Ideas and Ideals in Politics.* Baltimore: John Hopkins Press, 1970.

Kramer, M. *Islam Assembled.* New York: Columbia University Press, 1986.

Kurzman, C. ed., *Liberal Islam.* Oxford: Oxford University Press, 1998.

Lincoln, Bruce. *Holy Terrors: Thinking about Religion after September 11.* Chicago: University of Chicago Press, 2003.

McAuliffe, Jane Dammen. *Qur'anic Christians: An Analysis of Classical and Modern Exegesis.* Cambridge: Cambridge University Press, 1991.

Marmura, M. E. trans., The *Incoherence of the Philosophers* (Tahāfut al-Falāsifah). Provo, UT: Brigham Young University Press, 1997.

Nispen tot Sevenaer, Christian van. *Activité humaine et Agir de dieu: le concept de "Sunan de Dieu" dans le commentaire coranique du Manar.* Beirut: Dār al-Mashriq, 1996.

Omar, Imady. "Journals, Associations and Political Parties: The Institutions of Islamic Reform (1871–1949) (Egypt, Jamal al-Din al-Aghani, Muhammad 'Abduh, Rashid Rida, Hasan al-Banna)" Ph.D. diss. University of Pennsylvania, 1993.

Peters, Rudolph. "Idjtihād and Taqlīd in 18th and 19th Century Islam." *Die Welt des Islams* 20 (1980): 131–45.

Poston, Larry. *Islamic Da'wah in the West.* New York/Oxford: Oxford University Press, 1992.

Reid, Donald M. *The Odyssey of Faraḥ Anṭūn.* Minneapolis: Bibliotheca Islamica, 1975.

Riḍā, Muḥammad Rashīd. *The Muhammadan Revelation.* Translated by Yusuf T. DeLorenzo. Alexandria, Va.: Al-Saadawi Publications, 1996.

—— *The Revelation to Muhammad.* Translated by Abdus-Samad Sharafuddin. Bhiwandi (Thana) Bombay State, India: Ad-Darul-Qayyimah, 1958.

Ridgeon, Lloyd V. J. *Crescents on the Cross: Islamic Visions of Christianity.* Oxford: Oxford University Press, 2001.

Robinson, Neal. *Christ in Islam and Christianity.* Albany: State University of New York Press, 1991

Ryad, Umar. Islamic Reformism and Christianity: A Critical Reading of the Works of Muhammad Rashid Riḍā and his Associates (1898–1935). Leiden: Brill, 2009.

—— "Rashīd Riḍā and a Danish Missionary: Alfred Nielsen (died 1965) and Three Fatwā-s from Al-Manār." *Islamochristiana* 28 (2002): 87–107.

Safran, Nadav. *Egypt in Search of a Political Community.* Cambridge, MA: Harvard University Press, 1961.

Saliba, Issa A. "The Bible in Arabic: The 19th-Century Protestant Translation." *The Muslim World* 65 (1975): 254–63.

Scholz, Norbert J. "Foreign education and indigenous reaction in late Ottoman Lebanon: Students and teachers at the Syrian Protestant College in Beirut." Ph.D. diss. Georgetown University, 1997.

Seferta, Y. H. R. "The Prophethood of Muhammad in the Writings of Muhammad 'Abduh and Rashid Rida." *Hamdard Islamicus* 8 (1985): 11–29.

—— "Rashid Rida's Quest for an Islamic Government." *Hamdard Islamicus* 8 (1985): 35–50.

Shahin, E. E. "Muhammad Rashid Rida's Perspectives on the West as Reflected in *al-Manar.*" *The Muslim World* 79 (1989): 113–132.

—— *Through Muslim Eyes: M. Rashid Rida's and the West.* Herndon, VA: International Institute of Islamic Thought, 1993.

—— "Muhammad Rashid Rida: Renewal, Renewing, and Renewers," in *Modernist Islam: A Source Book*, ed. Charles Kurzman. New York, Oxford University Press, 2002.

Skovgaard-Petersen, Jakob. *Defining Islam for the Egyptian state: muftis and fatwas of the Dār al-Iftā.* Leiden and New York: Brill, 1997.

—— "Portrait of the intellectual as a young man: Rashid Rida's Muhawarat al-muslih wa'l-muqallid (1906)." *Islam and Christian-Muslim Relations* 12 (2001): 93–104.

Ṣiddīqī, Muḥammad. *Ḥadīth Literature.* Cambridge: Islamic Texts Society, 1993.

Sirriyeh, E. "Rashīd Riḍā's Autobiography of the Syrian Years, 1865–1897." *Arabic & Middle Eastern Literatures* 3 (2000): 179–194.

Smith, Jane. "Christian Missionary Views of Islam in the 19th and 20th Centuries." *Islam and Muslim-Christian Religions* 9 (1998): 357–373.

—— and Yvonne Y. Haddad. "The Virgin Mary in Islamic Tradition." *The Muslim World* 79 (1989): 161–87.

Speight, Marston. "Christians in the Ḥadīth Literature," in *Islamic Interpretations of Christianity*, ed. Lloyd Ridgeon. New York: St Martin's Press, 2001.

Taizir, Aswita. "Muhammad 'Abduh and the Reformation of Islamic Law." M. A. diss. McGill University, 1994.

Tauber, Elizabeth. "Rashid Rida as Pan-Arabist Before World War I." *The Muslim World* 79 (1989): 102–112.

—— "Rashid Rida's political attitudes during World War 1." *The Muslim World* 85 (1995).

Thomas, M. F. trans., *A Muslim Theologian's Response to Christianity: Ibn Taimiyyah's al-Jawāb al-Ṣaḥīḥ*. Delmar, NY: Caravan Books, 1984.

Troll, Christian W. *Sayyid Ahmad Khan: A Reinterpretation of Muslim Theology*. New Delhi: Vikas Publishing House, 1978.

Van Den Bergh, S. trans., *Averroes'* Tahāfut at-Tahāfut (*The Incoherence of the Incoherence*). London: Luzac, 1954.

Voll, J. O. "Fundamentalism in the Sunni Arab World: Egypt and the Sudan." *Fundamentalisms Observed.* eds Martin E. Marty and R. Scott Appleby. Chicago and London: University of Chicago Press, 1991.

Waardenburg, Jacques. ed., *Muslim Perceptions of Other Religions: A Historical Survey*. New York: Oxford University Press, 1999.

Watt, David H. "The Meaning and End of Fundamentalism." *Religious Studies Review* 30 (2004): 271–274.

Watt, W. Montgomery. *Islamic Philosophy and Theology*. Edinburgh: Edinburgh University Press, 1985.

—— *Muslim-Christian Encounters: Perceptions and Misperceptions*. London and New York: Routledge, 1991.

Index

Aaron 111, 112, 123, 130
'Abbasids
downfall of 200, 205–6
'Abd al-Rāziq, 'Alī 20
'Abduh, Muḥammad 18, 28, 35, 49, 50, 56, 57 n15, 100, 107 n71, 146 n131, 153 n145, 156, 172 n169, 204
on Christian scripture 13–14, 16, 43
debate with Anṭūn 153
on the incarnation 16
Islam and Christianity between Science and Civilization 13, 14, 16, 21–2, 174, 177, 178–9, 206
Islamic modernist 20–1, 25, 48, 55
reason over tradition 22
Refutation of the Teachings of the Dahriyyah and Explanation of their Depravity and Proof that Religion is the Foundation of Civilization while Unbelief is the Ruination of Culture 155
Tafsīr al-Manār 13–14, 26–7, 39, 43, 57, 60, 61, 63, 172
The Theology of Unity 21–2, 40, 183, 183–6, 187–8
al-'Urwah al-Wuthqā 24–5
'Abīdiyyūn 197
abode of Islam 33
abode of war 33
Abraham 5, 39, 115 n86, 122, 133, 145, 180
as Muslim 4
sin of 132, 134
Abrahamian, Ervand 50, 52
abrogation of Qur'anic verses (*naskh*) 125 n102
Abū Bakr 136, 137, 148, 206
Abū Dawūd
hadith collection of 6 n10, 7 n12, 148 n139
Abū Hurayrah 7 n12, 152 n143
al-Abū Ṣīrī
Lāmiyyah 121–4
Abū Zahrah, Muḥammad 15, 37, 47
Acts of the Apostles 92
Adam 94, 96, 121, 122, 133, 135 n118, 141, 151 n142
not a messenger 132 n113
sin of 132, 137, 141
al-'Adliyyah, Jūdat Bāshā Nāẓir 205–6
affirmation of religion 84–5
al-Afghānī, Jamāl al-Dīn 20, 21, 22 n10, 25, 28, 36, 49, 53, 154, 155
Refutation of the Teachings of the Dahriyyah and Explanation of their Depravity and Proof that Religion is the Foundation of Civilization while Unbelief is the Ruination of Culture 155
al-'Urwah al-Wuthqā 24–5
afterlife 142–3
Āl Su'ūd 28, 49

alcohol 91, 137
Allah *see* God
allegorical interpretation of scripture 56–8, 60, 99 n55, 111 n80, 112, 171–2, 176–7, 182–3
Almond, Gabriel
  Strong Religion: The Rise of Fundamentalisms around the World 22 n11, 49, 62 n28
Amīn, Qāsim 55, 56, 63
anthropomorphism 53, 111 n80, 112–13, 172
Anṭūn, Faraḥ 20, 25, 63
  Al-Jāmi'ah 30, 153–69
  debate with 'Abduh 153
Appleby, R. Scott 48 n1, 50, 54
  Strong Religion: The Rise of Fundamentalisms around the World 22 n11, 49, 62 n28
'Aqīdat al-Jawharah 201, 203
'aql 39
al-'Aqqād, 'Abbās Maḥmūd 7 n11
  'Abqariyyat al-Masīḥ 15
Arabs 84, 105, 111, 112
  pagan 3, 144, 151
  and unity 206, 207
Ardashir 130
Arjomand, Said Amir 58, 60, 63
Artaxerxes, King 130–1
asānīd 43, 76 n12
Ataturk, Musṭafā Kemāl 19, 20
authority, religious 191–2, 195–8, 200–4
Averoes *see* ibn Rushd
Ayoub, Mahmoud 9, 15, 37
al-Azhar 19, 26, 27, 28, 63, 172, 188

Bacon, Roger
  on God Almighty's Ways 166–9
al-Badawī, Sayyid Aḥmad 80, 81 n17
Bahā Allāh 116 n88
Baha'ism 27–8, 115–16
al-Bannā', Ḥasan 22, 23, 50, 55, 58, 62
Barnabas, Gospel of 43–4, 72 n7
baṣā'ir 170
Bashā'ir al-Salām (*Glad Tidings of Peace, The*) 30, 36, 44
  Ishmael in 114
  on the Israelites 109–10
  on Muḥammad 110, 113–14
  pagan interpretation 111–13
  revelation in 113–14
Bāṭiniyyah 197
al-Bayḍāwī 89 n30
Berque, J. 61
Bible 12–14, 31, 36, 40–4, 47, 53, 72 n7, 74 n10, 75 n11, 136
  "Van Dyke Arabic Bible" 74–5 n11
Blankinship, Khalid 50, 65
Bonaparte, Napoleon 79–80
bonyadegar 52
Braume, W. 81 n17
Britain
  control of Egypt 18
Buddhists 196
  as People of the Book 3 n4
Buhrā (Isma'ilis) 116–17
al-Bukhārī 186, 206
  hadith collection of 6, 7 n12, 43 n13, 76 n13, 104 n64, 113 n83, 145 n130, 186–7 n186
burhān (evidentiary argument) 31
al-Burhān al-Jalīl 'alā Siḥḥat al-Tawrah wa al-Injīl 72 n8
Burrell, D. 159 n152
al-Būṣīrī, Sharaf al-Dīn Abū 'Abd Allāh Muḥammad b. Sa'īd b. Ḥammād al-Ṣandājī 121 n93

caliphate 51, 81 n17, 206
caliphs
  rightly-guided 196
Chalcedon, Council of 3
Chinese people 119
Christ 6–7, 14 n36, 43, 46, 76, 82, 84, 86, 92, 100, 102, 113, 114, 115–16, 119, 122, 132–3, 134, 139, 152
Christianity 185–6
  'Abduh's interpretation of Christian scripture 13–14, 16
  Docetic Christology 3, 12
  abandoned in Europe 96–8
  and European civilization 82, 83–4
  and the incarnation 95–6
  and Islam 154
  and *islam* 4–5
  as libertine 81–2
  Muslim interpretations of: medieval period 6–12
  Muslim interpretation of: modern period 12–16

Muslim interpretation of: Qur'anic period 1–6
as pagan 82
and salvation 141–2
teachings 89–90
Christians 192–3, 200
mistrust of in the hadith 7
Monophysite 3
Nestorians 3
as People of the Book 2
Protestant 43
in the Qur'an 1–6
Cole, Juan 24, 28 n29
colonial policy 25
colonial rule 33
colonialism 12, 17–18, 155 n146, 208
common good 22
Companions of the Prophet Muḥammad 39, 63, 115 n87, 130, 194, 196
consensus of 58, 60–1
and God's blessing 135–8
Confucians
as People of the Book 3 n4
consensus (*ijmā'*)
of the Companions 58, 60–1
corruption 85
Christian 9–10
of texts 10, 13, 14, 16, 40–1, 72 n8, 102, 104, 106, 120, 125 n104
Council of Chalcedon 3
Council of Nicaea 3
creation 94
Creator (God)
human understanding of 173–5
crucifixion 44
of Jesus 72 n7, 82, 125 n104, 137, 141

Dahriyyah, Dahrī School 36, 53, 154–5
dalīl 31
Daniel, Book of 41, 75
Dār al-Da'wah wa al-Irshād 27
al-Dārī, Bakr b. al-Sayyid 'Umar Tamīmī
The Polished Sword in Response to the book The Sublime Proof 72 n8
al-Dārimī
hadith collection of 6 n10, 148 n134, 171 n168
Darius 130
Darwin, Charles 24, 155
David, King of Israel 122
Psalms of 5
Davidson, Lawrence
Islamic Fundamentalism 51, 54
da'wah 32–5, 47, 67, 117 n89
De Lorenzo, Yusuf Talal 25
Demonstration of the Truth 72, 74
Deuteronomy, Book of 41, 42, 43, 77, 90, 91, 127
dīn al-fiṭrah 39–40
dissociation of God (*tanzīh*) 53, 57, 111 n80, 112, 138, 144, 172
diversity
in the Qur'an 2–3
Docetic Christology 12
in the Qur'an 3
du'ā' (prayer of supplication) 150

education 27, 63
religious 188–9
Egypt
under European control 17–18
enclave culture 62–4
Encyclopedia of Islam 52
Ende, W. 28
Enlightenment, the 15, 17, 22, 55, 56
Europe
as Christian 82, 83–4
Christianity abandoned in 96–8
exegesis
Qur'anic 8–9
see also allegorical interpretation, literalism, *taslīm*, *tawfīḍ*, *ta'wīl*
Exodus, Book of 41, 42, 43, 77, 90, 111
Ezekiel, Book of 41, 75, 92–3, 95, 112
Ezra 104
as author of the Torah 128–30

faith
and hadith 139–40
in Moses 145
in Muḥammad 145–6
and the Qur'an 140
and reason 87–8
al-Fārābī 155 n146
Faruqi, Ismā'īl 15, 37
Fāṭimids 197–8
fear
al-Ghazāli on 138
First World War (1914–18) 49
fiṭrah 39

five general principles 90, 201
Ford, Peter 11, 14, 15
France 104
  incursion into Egypt 17–18
fundamentalism 21, 22–3, 48–51
  fundamentals of 54–5
  linguistic interpretation 51–2
  and literalism 56–8
  and resistance to rationalism 55–6
  and *uṣūl al-dīn* 53–4
Fundamentalism Project 49, 50

Galatians, Paul's letter to 92
Gardet, L. 61
Gaudeul, Jean-Marie 72 n7
Genesis, Book of 41, 47, 74, 88, 93, 122 n *i*, 123 n *iv*
al-Ghazālī, Abū Ḥāmid Muḥammad 21, 28, 35, 44, 49, 56, 155, 179
  The Book on Trusting in God (Kitāb al-Tawakkul) 157–61, 166
  on God Almighty's Ways 157–66
  on fear 138
  Iḥyā' 'Ulūm al-Dīn 11, 24, 157
  The Incoherence of the Philosophers 162–6, 173–5
  Al-Radd al-Jamīl li-Ilāhiyyat 'Īsā bi Ṣarīḥ al-Injīl 10–11
Ghibrīl, Niqūlā Afandi 40
  Abḥāth al-Mujtahidīn 30, 42, 44, 78, 99–108, 118
Glad Tidings of Peace, The see *Bashā'ir al-Salām*
God
  and blessings 135–8
  God Almighty's Ways 156–69
  Law 92
  messengers of 114–15 n86
  metaphorical interpretation of 111
  named linked to Muḥammad 148–50
  oneness of 84, 85, 86
  pre-existence of 151 n142
  trust in 157–61
Goddard, Hugh 10, 11 n26, 14
Goldziher, I. 154 n146
Gospel 11, 13–15, 67, 73, 77, 85–6, 91, 95, 115, 134, 149, 152, 207
  accepted by Muslims 103–5
  of Barnabas 43, 72
  integrity of 124–31
  in *Lāmiyyah* (al-Abū Ṣīrī) 121–4
  and Muḥammad 43–4, 102–3
  Muslim view of 76–7
  and the Qur'an 5, 85–6, 103–8, 109, 124–5
  Rashīd Riḍā on 43–5
  "Sermon on the Mount" 77
  and the Torah 99–103
  veracity of 117–21, 124
Great French Encyclopedia 74

Ḥabīb, Muḥammad Efendi
  The Cutting Swords in the Teaching of Christopher Jibārah 125
hadith 6, 43, 58, 73, 76, 129 n109, 136 n122, 139–40, 142–3, 145, 146–7, 151, 158 n147, 159, 171, 174
  and chains of transmission 76 n12, 136 n121
  Christians in 6–8
  collection of Abū Dawūd 6 n10, 7 n12, 148 n139
  collection of Aḥmad ibn Ḥanbal (*Musnad*) 6 n10, 7 n12, 147 n132, 148 n134, 187 n186
  collection of al-Bukhārī 6, 7 n12, 43 n13, 76 n13, 104 n64, 113 n83, 113 n84, 145 n130, 186–7 n186
  collection of al-Dārimī 6 n10, 148 n134, 171 n168
  collection of Ibn Mājah 6 n10, 147 n132
  collection of Mālik 6 n10, 152 n143
  collection of Muslim 6, 7 n12, 140 n124, 145 n130, 147 n132, 186–7 n186, 171 n168
  collection of al-Nasā'ī 6 n10
  collection of al-Tirmidhī 6 n10, 148 n134
  and faith 139–40
  and fundamentalism 59
  Jesus in 6–7
  missionary misinterpretation of 113
  mursal tradition 148 n134, 171 n168
  mutawātir 143 n127, 146 n131
  nine collections of 6, 7 n13, 104 n64, 139–40 n124, 174 n174
  pollinating dates 147
  and the Qur'an 7–8, 53–4, 146–7
  as revealed 147 n133

Riḍā's stance on 27, 54, 143 n126, 146 n131, 147 n132
and the Shiʿah 146
al-Ḥalabī, ʿAlī b. Burhān al-Dīn
Insān al-ʿuyūn fī sīrat al-Amīn al-Maʾmūn 108
al-Ḥamawī, Ṣāḥib al-Saʿādah Salīm Bāshir
al-Falāḥ 78
Ḥanbalism 29, 49, 50, 60
Ḥanbalī doctrine 61, 146 n131
ḥanīf 39
ḥarakat al-iṣlāḥ 20–1
Hidden Imam 28
Hindus 119
as People of the Book 3 n4
Horne, T.H. 13
Hosea the Pious 128
Hourani, Albert 28, 61
ḥujaj 31, 32
Hussein, Adel 54
Huxley, Thomas 74

Ibn Abī Ṭālib, ʿAlī 136, 137, 194, 201
Ibn al-Muqaffaʿ 107
ibn Ḥanbal, Aḥmad 20, 49
hadith collection of (*Musnad*) 6 n10, 7 n12, 147 n132, 148 n134, 187 n186
ibn Ḥazm, ʿAlī ibn Aḥmad 154–5
Kitāb al-Faṣl fī al-Milal wa al-Aḥwāʾ wa al-Niḥal 9–10
Ibn Kathīr 146
Ibn Mājah
hadith collection of 6 n10, 147 n132
ibn Rushd, Abū al-Walīd 39, 57, 60, 155, 167, 183
The Book of the Decisive Treatise Determining the Connection Between the Law and Wisdom 175–7
The Incoherence of the Incoherence 178, 180–1
Ibn Sallām, ʿAbd Allah 104
Ibn Sīnā 155, 179
ibn Taymiyyah, Taqi al-Din 21, 49, 50
al-Jawāb al-Ṣaḥīḥ li-man Baddala Dīn al-Masīḥ 10
Kitāb Iqtiḍāʾ al-Ṣ irāṭ al-Mustaqīm 10
on transcendence 11
idolatry 93
ijmāʿ (consensus)
of the Companions 58, 60–1
ijtihād 21
Al-Imam
Malayan journal 25
Imams
compared to prophets 136
Fāṭimid 197 n196
and religious schism 203
Shiʿite 151 n142
Sunni 175
and the ummah 206
incarnation, divine 5, 10, 11, 53, 137, 141
ʿAbduh on 16
Christian view of 95–6
as paganism 46
instiller of doubts 200–4
intercessor
Muḥammad as 151–3
Isaiah, book of 41, 43, 75, 77, 95
Ishmael
in *Bashāʾir al-Salām* (*Glad Tidings of Peace, The*) 114
Islam
beliefs of 189–90
and Christianity 154
culmination of all religions 186–9
as the religion of reason 169–81
religious authority in 195–8
islam 40
exemplified by Qurʾanic Christianity 4–5
Ismaʿili Shiʿism 28, 197
Buhrā 116–17
Israelites
in *Bashāʾir al-Salām* (*Glad Tidings of Peace, The*) 109–10
Muslim interpretation of 112

Jāhilliyyah (pre-Islamic Arabia)
Islam compared to 144–53
al-Jāḥiẓ, ʿAmr
Al-Radd ʿalā al-Naṣārā 9
Al-Jāmiʿah 30
Jamʿiyyat al-Jāmiʿah al-ʿArabiyyah 27
Jansen, Johannes 49
Encyclopedia of Islam 52
Jesus 80–2
crucifixion of 137, 141
faith in 145
in the hadith 6–7
as messiah 5, 72

Jesus (*cont.*):
as Muslim 4
in the Qur'an 9, 72
and shari'ah 80, 100
as the "Spirit of God" 11
Jews
as People of the Book 2
al-Jīlī 80–1
al-Jisr, Shaykh Ḥusayn 75 n11
Al-Risālah al-Ḥamīdiyyah 24
John (New Testament author)
Gospel of 11 n26
as messenger of God 114–15 n86
Josephus 129
Joshua 126–7
jurisprudence 8 n15, 19, 21, 52, 89 n30, 136 n121

al-Kayrānawī, Raḥmat Allāh ibn Khalīl al-'Uthmānī 12, 13, 72 n7, 76 n12
Iẓhār al-Ḥaqq 40, 43, 44, 72
Khān, Sayyid Aḥmad 12–13, 15, 17, 37, 40, 155
Khān, Wazīr 12–13
Khomeini, Ruhollah 22, 23
Khulāṣat al-Adillah al-Saniyyah 'alā Ṣidq Uṣūl-Diyānah al-Masīḥiyyah (*Summary of the High Proofs for the Veracity of the Fundamentals of the Christian Religion*) 128
Khusraw, Nāṣir 9
Kings, First Book of 123 n*vi*

language 19–20, 63
see also translation
al-Laqānī, Ibrāhīm 56
al-Jawharah 172
Latin alphabet 20
Lawrence, Bruce 50
legal schools 21, 26, 49 n3, 69, 131, 146 n131, 147 n133, 203
Leviticus, Book of 41, 42, 43, 77
Lewis, Bernard 20
Lincoln, Bruce 23 n13, 50
literalism 111 n80, 158 n147, 171–2 n169
and fundamentalism 56–8
Lot (nephew to Abraham) 122
Luke, Gospel of 89
lusts 91
Luṭfi, al-Sayyid, Aḥmad 20, 55, 56, 63
Luther, Martin 66

Ma'ādh ibn Jabal 148
madhhabism 59
Mahdism 28
Makkah
people of 105
Mālik
hadith collection of 6 n10, 152 n143
al-Ma'mūn 205–6
al-Manār 13, 26, 29, 95, 96, 118, 184–6, 193–5
Marmura, Michael E. 162–3, 164 n159–60, 165 n161
Marty, Martin E. 50, 54
The Glory and the Power: The Fundamentalist Challenge to the Modern World 62
Mary, mother of Jesus 3, 7 n12, 46, 81 n18, 95, 122 n97, 158
Matthew, Gospel of 43, 77, 89, 91
Mawdūdī, Mawlānā 15, 22, 23, 49
Mawlawī dervishes 24
maximalism
as response to modernity 23 n13
McAuliffe, Jane 1 n1, 8 n17, 27
Mecca *see* Makkah
messengers
of God, distinguished from prophets 114–15 n86
messiah
Jesus as 5, 72
as title 95
Middle East, Arab 24
miracles 15, 81, 84 n25, 115, 163–4, 178–81, 183, 184
of Jesus 5, 80
missionaries, Christian 53, 73, 115–17
corruption of the Qur'an 149–50
polemic against 68–71
portrayals of Islam 35–8
modernists, Islamic
'Abduh as 20–1, 25, 48, 55
response to modernity 20–2
modernity
Muslim responses to 17–23
Monophysite Christians 3
monotheism 3, 153
see also polytheism
morals 88–90

Moses 79–80, 111
  as author of the Pentateuch 126–7
  faith in 145
  and shari'ah 100, 126, 129–30
  sin of 132
Mubārak, 'Alī Pāshā
  The Standard of Religion 46, 93–6
Muḥammad, the Prophet 82–3
  in *Bashā'ir al-Salām* (*Glad Tidings of Peace, The*) 110, 113–14
  conveyor of the Qur'an 195–6
  faith in 145–6
  and the Gospels 43–4, 102–3
  as intercessor 151–3
  master of Muslims 150–1
  name linked to God 148–50
  pre-existence of 151
  and shari'ah 82
  sinlessness of 131–5
Muḥammad 'Alī 18
Muir, William 126–7
mursal tradition 148 n134, 171 n168
Muslim (d. 875) 206
  hadith collection of 6, 7 n12, 140 n124, 145 n130, 147 n132, 186–7 n186, 171 n168
Muslim
  Abraham as 4
Muslim Brotherhood 48, 50, 54 n12
Muslims
  acceptance of Torah 103–5
  beliefs of 189–90
  interpretation of Christianity: medieval period 6–12
  interpretation of Christianity: modern period 12–16
  interpretation of Christianity: Qur'anic period 1–6
  interpretation of Israelites 112
  Muḥammad as master of 150–1
mutawātir 63, 143, 146, 147 n133, 163 n158
  hadith 143, 146
Mu'tazilah 172
  and Qur'an as uncreated 58
  al-Zamakhsharī's Qur'an commentary 89

naskh (abrogation of Qur'anic verses) 125
Napoleon Bonaparte 79–80
al-Nasā'ī
  hadith collection of 6 n10
natural science 162–3
Necari 155
Nehemiah, Book of 130
Nestorian Christians 3
Newman, A.J.
  Encyclopedia of Islam 52
Nicaea, Council of 3
Noah 94, 115 n86, 122
  sin of 132, 133, 134
Numbers, Book of 41, 42, 43, 77

oneness, divine (*tawḥīd*) 4, 34, 39, 40, 68, 83, 84, 85, 86, 144, 172
original sin 46
Ottoman Empire 19, 197 n195 *see also* Turkey
Ottomans 18, 24, 27, 197 n195, 205 *see also* Turkey

paganism 46, 119, 145–6
  in *Bashā'ir al-Salām* (*Glad Tidings of Peace, The*) 111–13
  Christianity as 82
  incarnation as 46
  pre-Islamic Arabia 3
Palmer, Edward H.
  the Qur'an 97
pan-Arabism 27
Paul, Saint 12, 42, 100, 91–2, 119
  as messenger of God 114–15 n86
Pentateuch 41–2, 47
  as historical 128
  Moses as author of 126–7
People of the Book 2, 14, 101, 104–5
Peter (New Testament author)
  as messenger of God 114–15 n86
Pfander, Karl Gottlieb
  Mizān al-Ḥaqq 42, 72
Pickthall, Mohammed M. 2 n2, 106 n69, 109 n76, 150 n140
pluralism
  religious 1, 8, 47
polytheism 3, 145–6, 149, 150, 153
Pophyry
  Īsāghūjī 107 n70
pre-existence 151
prophecy 4, 114–15
prophetic tradition 59

prophets 132–3
  and salvation 133–5
  Shi'i view of 135
  Sufi view of 135
Protestants 43
Psalms of David 5

Qur'an 190
  commentary of al-Zamakhsharī 89
  diversity in 2–3
  exegesis of 8–9
  and faith 140
  and the Gospel 5, 85–6, 103–8
  and the hadith 7–8, 53–4, 146–8
  Jesus in 9, 72
  Muḥammad conveyor of 195–6
  Mu'tazilī view of 58
  text corrupted by missionaries 149–50
  and the Torah 5, 41–2, 85–6, 93–5, 103–8
  translations of 97
  uncreated 58–9
Quṭb, Sayyid 15, 22, 37, 47

Rashīd Riḍā, Muḥammad
  'Aqīdat al-Ṣalb wa al-Fidā' 44
  early life 23–5
  as fundamentalist 21
  on the Gospel 43
  al-Islām dīn al-fiṭrah al-salīmah wa al-'aql wa al-fikr wa al-ḥikmah wa al-burhān wa al-ḥ ujjah 39–40
  al-Khilāfah aw al-Imāmah al-'Uẓma 61, 197
  al-Manār al Īslāmī 25, 26, 29, 30–1
  Al-Manār wa al-Azhar 24
  Muḥāwarāt al-Muṣliḥ wa al-Muqallid 26, 62–3
  Shubuhāt al-Naṣārā wa Ḥujaj al-Islām 28, 30, 32, 33–5, 36, 49, 50, 51, 56–7, 60, 70–1
  Al-Sunnah wa al-Sh ī'ah aw al-Wahh ābiyyah wa al-R āfiḍah 28
  Tafsīr al-Manār 13–14, 26–7, 39, 43, 57, 60, 61, 63
  The True Gospel 43–4
  universalism 39–40
  Al-Waḥy al-Muḥammadī 25, 59, 126
rasūl 114 n86
rationalism
  and fundamentalism 55–6
Rāyah Ṣahyūn 30
al-Rāzī 56, 60
reason 21
  'Abduh on 22
  and faith 87–8
  Islam religion of 169–81
religion
  affirmation of 84–5
  Islam culmination of all religions 186–9
  pluralism 1, 8, 47
  and shari'ah 66, 67, 189–200
Renan, Ernest 16
resurrection 95–6
Reuben (son to Jacob) 122
revelation 13
  in *Bashā'ir al-Salām* (*Glad Tidings of Peace, The*) 113–14
  hadith as revealed 147
Ridgeon, Lloyd V.J. 13
rightly-guided caliphs 196
Rodwell, J.M.
  translation of the Qur'an 97
Romans, Paul's letter to 91–2
Ross, Alexander
  The Alcoran of Mahomet 96
al-Rumi, Jalal al-Din 11–12
Ruthven, Malise 10, 11

Salafī movement 20–1, 50, 58
salat 150 n141
Sale, G.
  translation of the Qur'an 97
Saliba, Issa 75
salvation
  and Christianity 141–2
  and the prophets 133–5
Samuel, Second Book of 122 n *iii*
Sanad, Muḥammad al-Dīn Zakī
  The Polished Sword in Response to the book The Sublime Proof 72
al-Sāwī, 'Umar B. Sahlān
  al-Baṣā'ir al-Nāsiriyyah 107
Schleiermacher, F. 65–6
science 168
  natural 162–3
scholastic theologians 84 n25, 89 n30, 155, 161, 167, 168
scholastic theology 167, 173
scripturalist fundamentalism 56–8

scripture 53, 190
allegorical interpretation of 56–8, 60, 99 n55, 111 n80, 112, 171–2, 176–7, 182
corruption of 13–14, 16, 40–1, 43, 149–50
secularism 63
as response to modernity 19–20
"Sermon on the Mount" 77
Shahin, Emad Eldin 63
al-Shahrastānī 155
Shalabī, Aḥmad 15, 37
shari'a 11, 26, 32, 61, 114–15 n86, 137, 194–5, 202–3, 204, 206–7
of Jesus 80, 100
of Moses 100, 126, 129–30
and Muḥammad 82
and religion 66, 67, 189–200
rulings of 200
and Torah 92, 100, 127–8
"Shaykh al-Islam" 197
Shi'ah (Shi'ites) 28, 116, 146, 151 n142
Akhbarī and Uṣūlī schools 52
Buhrā 116–17
Isma'ili 28, 116–17, 197 n196
Riḍā's view of 28, 57
view of Jesus 6 n9
view of prophets 135 n118
Shinto
practitioners as People of the Book 3 n4
shir'ah 2
shirk 3
shubuhāt 31, 32
sin
and the Old Testament prophets 132
original 46
sinlessness
of the prophets 67, 131–5
of Muḥammad 131–5
Sīrat al-Ḥalabiyyah 108
Sivan, Emmanuel 50, 62
Strong Religion: The Rise of Fundamentalisms around the World 49
Six-Day War (1967) 48
slander 68 n1
Smith, Eli 74, 75
Smith, Jane 35
Solomon 123
Speight, Marston 7, 8 n14
Spencer, Herbert 16, 74
"Spiritual Authority of the Sheikhdom of the Spiritual Path" 193–5
Standard of Zion, The 71
Stobart, James William Hampson
Islam and Its Founder 125
Sufism 11, 108 n73
and al-Ghazālī 11
and *al-Manār* 26
and Muḥammad's pre-existence 151 n142
and Riḍā's universalism 40
Riḍā's view of 24, 57
and Sufi saints 10, 80–1, 115 n87
and "Shaykh al-Islam" 197 n195
and *tawakkul* 157–8 n147
as traditionalist 19
view of prophets 135 n118
Summary of the High Proofs for the Veracity of the Fundamentals of the Christian Religion (Khuāṣat al-Adillah al-Saniyyah 'alā Ṣidq Uṣūl al-Diyānah al-Masīḥiyyah) 128
sunnah (practice of God) 158–60, 166–8
sunnah (tradition of Muḥammad, hadith) 8 n14, 169
and the Qur'an 26, 53, 59, 146, 148
and Muḥammad as "master" 150
sunnah (practice of the Qur'an) 177
Āl Su'ūd 28, 49

al-Ṭabarī, 'Alī ibn Rabbān 61
Al-Radd 'alā al-Naṣārā 10
tafwīḍ 57, 171–2 n169
taqlīd 19, 21, 26, 34, 35, 40, 68
taslīm 57, 172 n169
tawakkul 157–8
tawātur 44, 143 n127, 146 n131, 163 n157
ta'wīl 57
tawḥīd 68, 158 n147
texts
corruption of 13–14, 16, 40–1, 43, 149–50
al-Thawrī, Sufyān 136
theology *see* scholastic theologians; scholastic theology
al-Tirmidhī
hadith collection of 6 n10, 148 n134
Tolstoy, Leo 16, 74 n9, 98 n48
"The Kingdom of God is Within You" 98

Torah 184
accepted by Muslims 103–5
authenticity of 41–2
Christian attitude towards 42–3
Ezra as author 129–30
and the Gospel 99–103
integrity of 124–31
in *Lāmiyyah* (al-Abū Ṣīrī) 121–4
Muslim view of 73–7
and the Qur'an 5, 41–2, 85–6, 93–5, 103–8
and shari'ah 92, 100, 127–8
veracity of 117–21
worship in 90
tradition
'Abduh on 22
mursal 148 n134, 171
traditionalism
response to modernity 19
transcendence
ibn Taymiyyah on 11
translation 65–6, 96–7
transmission of hadith, chains of 76 n12, 136 n121
Trinity, the 3, 5, 44, 45
Tritheism 44
Turkey as secular state 19–20 *see also* Ottoman Empire; Ottomans

Uḥud, battle of 194
ulama 107, 149, 194
al-Azhar 188
comprehension of Creator (God) 173
and consensus 61
failure to engage modernity 34–5
leaders' enticement of 189
and prayer 150
and prophets 133, 147
and religious schism 203
Riḍā's position towards 34–5, 61, 63, 98
and "Shaykh al-Islam" 197 n195
traditionalist mentality 32, 69
uncreated
Qur'an as 58–9
unity, religious and national 204–8
al-'Urwah al-Wuthqā 21
uṣūl al-dīn 51, 52
and fundamentalism 53–4
uṣūl al-fiqh 52
uṣūlī 51–2

Van den Bergh, Simon 178 n178, 181 n181
Van Dyke, Cornelius van Alen 74–5 n11, 181
"Van Dyke Arabic Bible" 74–5 n11
Venuti, Lawrence 65
Voll, John 49, 50, 55, 63

Wahhābism 28, 49, 50, 51
al-Wahhābiyyūn wa al-Ḥijāz 28
war
First World War 49
Six Day War 48
Watt, David 50
Watt, W. Montgomery
"Akida" 111
"without how", expression 110–11 n80
worship
in the Torah 90

al-Zamakhsharī 89
Zarathushtra 94, 130
Zebiri, Kate 3
Zoroastrians
as People of the Book 2 n4
Zwemer, Samuel 35